Over Under Sideways Down

Over Under Sideways Down

by

Mark Rye

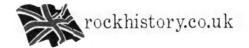
rockhistory.co.uk

Over Under Sideways Down
A RockHistory Book
www.RockHistory.co.uk

1

Published and printed in the United Kingdom and the United States of America by RockHistory Ltd.

RockHistory Ltd
PO Box 509A, Surrey KT7 0WQ

Cover: Raven Design
Book Design: Velin@Perseus-Design.com

PAPERBACK ISBN   978-0-9576881-1-7
EBOOK ISBN   978-0-9576881-2-4

For the Professor, the kids and music, the four loves of my life.

Dedicated to my father, Geoff Rye F.L.A. who I feel honoured to resemble more and more as each day passes.

Many thanks to Kate Highfield, Roger Dopson, Steve Water & Willie Williams.
A huge thanks to all the interviewees in this never ending RockHistory project, some of whom appear within these pages. For their time, their memories and for the music.

The spread of Rock and Roll across Europe was all Adolf Hitler's fault you know

Oh yes it was!

I don't mean Adolf had slicked back black hair, a dubious moustache and a worrying liking for early Rockabilly, no sir! But because of him and his doubtful plans for world domination, the Nazis had constructed massive radio transmitters to broadcast right across Europe, which enabled them to communicate with their troops throughout WW2 as well as bombarding all who could not avoid it with the propaganda of Joseph Goebbels and Lord Haw-Haw. And so after D-Day, as the allied troops fought their way back across Europe, they captured them and used them themselves. Then with the end of the war, the Americans used these very transmitters to broadcast to all their troops still stationed in Europe, entertaining their boys by playing them some good ol' music from back home: Western Swing, Blues and Country, all the very ingredients that later merged into the Rock and Roll musical menu. Thus the good residents of Europe, who wanted anything more than just the standard fare from their own state broadcasters, used to spin that radio dial and listen to all this alien music, and they grew to love it. So Ladies and Gentlemen, the spread of Rock and Roll was all Adolf's doing. I bet he never saw that one coming either.

We love a good theory, that one was suggested by Ted Carroll and is a beaut. Another credible theory from ex-Sound man, Willie Williams is that we will, one day, have a hugely successful group formed around the children of ex-road crew. These gentlemen, having amassed considerable quantities of 'surplus' equipment over the years feel that with their contacts and insight into the business, they are destined to guide their offspring to huge international success. Apparently you can always spot these kids at school concerts because they are playing genuine Gibson and Fender guitars.

In your hands is a book recounting some of the stories of pet projects and fond remembrances by a whole variety of British music insiders, from the Fifties pioneers, the Sixties survivors, the Seventies excesses and even some young Eighties popsters. After this first forty years I must admit the interest wanes a bit and to be fair, one could argue that music was no longer as central to the British cultural changes that had so nurtured it before. So maybe we should commence with WW2 and some causes for the subsequent worldwide British music explosion.

In fact, in so many, many ways the events of WW2 caused a massive lurch in the subsequent direction of popular music in our nations. Post war, the downtrodden, battered and bombed inhabitants of Great Britain needed cheering up. So as well as getting our fill of the 'Bluebirds Over The White Cliffs Of Dover' we also got a baby boom and a heady mix of all sorts of different music everywhere we went: Dance Bands, Folk, Jazz, R'n'R and Skiffle. The young Baby Boomers acclaimed Lonnie Donegan as he headed along the Rock Island Line, grabbing Skiffle to their hearts. Along with washboards from the kitchen and their mum's thimbles, they fashioned a makeshift tea chest bass from the very packing boxes that had brought the nation's drink in from around the empire. In our schools and youth clubs, acne ridden Skiffle groups sprouted up like the proverbial buds in May making a fine old racket wherever they were allowed. Every group obviously needed to have this thing called a guitar, so packs of pale-faced young men descended on music shops for this latest craze and those three chords spurted and spluttered into life. The girls screamed and there was no looking back. You learnt the chords, got on a stage in your village hall which was probably still made out of old beer crates and showed off furiously to anyone who would watch and listen – all in black and white of course.

And music always starts with that special song you know, as it always has; it is a timeless human reaction. There is always a popular tune that people can hum in the bath or whistle while they work. When some genius writes a really catchy song, it just sticks in the brain, it just keeps repeating and repeating it until eventually another one manages to replace it. If you were that sort of a music obsessive, you would just leave the arm on your Dansette record player up and the auto-changer would play the song again and again and again. Utter bliss!

For centuries, thousands of people in Britain would have stood in church and sung all the best loved psalms and hymns; the ones they were all most familiar with. The ones with all the best tunes were always the most popular because people could remember them and would then join in with gusto on the bits they knew best – which, probably, was the chorus. Of course it was the same thing in the other temple of religion too, the Public House; standing round the old Joanna as the pianist banged out the tunes of the day and, glass-in-hand, the drinkers would sing-along in fine voice when it got to the bit they too knew and just hum along with the rest.

Good catchy songs are like that, utterly addictive. The performer would never give enough credit to the songwriter, because for them the singer was the star of the show after all. Well unless they wrote it themselves, which in the early days was rather rare. Did Elvis write his own songs? Did Cliff write his own songs? Nah – and neither did Vera Lynn before them. But then The Beatles did, and when they came along, they blew the whole Tin Pan Alley music publishing era wide open. Finding a song you thought was a H.I.T. was what it was all about, that was what turned a Harry Webb into a Cliff Richard after all. Hit records got you on television and on the radio and that then got you in the newspapers and thus you become a Pop star. In ye olde record companies it used to be the job of the Recording Manager (later called an Artists and Repertoire man) to try and match the song to the artist and then to pick the best arranger for the recording of the song. After all you can have the same artist, the same studio, same arranger, same orchestra, same A&R man and this very same artist would probably go on to sell much the same number of records as the one they had out before. But change the song and it sometimes becomes the career changer.

Nowadays after the songwriter's craft comes a whole explosion of musicians, performers, programmers, session musicians, managers, roadies, record companies, music publishers, record shops, producers and promoters, disc jockeys, pluggers, secretaries and groupies. In fact every living thing it seems can now revel in the joys of music and the pleasures of this particular youth culture.

This book lets the people who worked in and around the British music scene in their own glory years tell their own stories, in their own words and in their own way. Be they musicians or the back room boys and girls. Their tales are relayed here not in any chronological sequence, I have given myself licence to dart around all over the place, changing decades at will. Otherwise you could be stuck in the Fifties for the first part of the book and that might not be your thing. Or worse we could have just started with drummers' stories, perish the thought. Many of the names mentioned you may not recognise or know at all, well I have no idea who some of them are either, so you are in good company. But that does not matter, if they are name-checked, they stay in and good for them and their fifteen minutes of fame-in-print. You see, all these stories are first hand as told by the person who was really, actually there, themselves. We are not interested in collecting apocryphal stories that happened to a mate-of-a-mate. Well we are, but you won't see them included here. So no salacious stories about Status Quo and a kangaroo or Led Zeppelin and a red snapper. These are the stories of the people who were there and can actually remember it in person, plus they have managed to survive long enough to tell their tale – so maybe not too many from the Sixties then.….

Where you lived in those distant dank days in Britain in the Fifties there was no central heating, no ring main electricity, no fitted carpets. Your house was often cold in winter, the countryside wet, your radio choice was the Home Service or the Light Programme; there was little TV, and you went out dancing to meet the opposite sex. It was under twenty years after WW2 had ended and everyone seemed so young and happy to still be alive. You created your own entertainment, played sport, read, smoked, drank, danced and sang those popular songs.

In Britain 'Before Elvis', the British Dance Bands used to play all the popular tunes of the day to an adoring crowd and these bands often featured a glamorous young singer out front. How do you think

Frank Sinatra started in America after all? Well, here in Britain we had all these Dance Bands and big orchestras but we also had two further popular styles of music – Jazz and Folk. Jazz imported from the Americas with syncopated rhythms that swung like Daddy-O, and our own Folk music as still taught in school, that had travelled across the pond and came winging straight back on the rebound. Post WW2, the young communist party activists decided to put their weight behind Folk – the music of the people – and it all went up a gear, coffee bars flourished and the music poured out onto the streets.

Then something happened that was utterly unique and completely British in evolution. For a short period Lonnie Donegan set off an explosion with his Americana tasting 'Rock Island Line' that changed not only this British musical backwater but went on to have an enormous effect right around the world of popular music. Without Lonnie the British musical scene might still be as inferior in its development as in most other European countries are to this day. Lonnie was a mid-show break for Ken Colyer's Jazz band and he played some souped up versions of old American Jazz and Blues songs. Skiffle was born with a huge hit in 1956 all just one year after Bill Haley had managed to 'Rock Around The Clock'.

The craze did not last long – just a few years if truth is told, but the effects were seismic. By the end of the Fifties it is reckoned there were between 30,000 and 50,000 Skiffle groups in Britain pounding it out in church halls and cafes. Learning to play their instruments as they went, some of these young men also discovered R&B and the Blues too. They mashed and mixed up all of these musical influences as best they could. Then these Beat Groups proceeded to get louder and louder thanks to the work of British equipment entrepreneurs such as Jim Marshall, Tom Jennings and Charlie Watkins. Not slow to react to the massive pent-up demand for equipment and instruments, these would-be's and engineers created amplifiers and instruments that Britain's teenagers could now afford. Cheap instruments fanned this musical revolution albeit often on the never-never. After all, nobody had credit cards or bank overdrafts, so your parents signed the papers and you bought them on the knock, paying for them in weekly instalments.

Pop music was a young man's game; George Harrison was just seventeen when he first went to Hamburg with The Beatles, and in this book you will find that Paul MacCallum was just fifteen when his group supported them on one of those eternal Larry Parnes Pop package tours across post war teenage Britain; Lulu was all of 'sweet sixteen' but then of course she was not a young man, but a wee Scots tornado. Nevertheless it still used to take The Beatles' Neil Aspinal ten hours to drive the group to London from Liverpool to record their latest batch of tunes; transport was very rudimentary compared to today.

Beat Groups flourished – and the girls loved them. Competition was fierce but largely friendly, and you would meet so many of the other groups at the Blue Boar Transport Cafe on the way back to London in the early hours. As they flourished, so more and more groups bought more equipment and they all got gradually louder as they endlessly criss-crossed Britain, hitting all of the places big enough to have a town or village hall. Heading up to Scotland then down to Cornwall or Wales before driving maybe to Norfolk. Groups 'gigged' and agents did not actually need to bother with an atlas of the British Isles for years and years: nobody 'toured', that came later because that involved your actual forward planning.

In the glory days before Sat Nav, or indeed for many a touring group, proper road maps, those pioneer Beat Groups only had the musicians and a few Vox AC30 amps plus a drum kit all jammed into the back of an old van or ex-ambulance. On stage everyone, the vocalist and the guitarists, all plugged into these amps leaving the drummer to sort himself out as well as hump his own kit up and down endless stairs. Your group played as loud as your drummer did. Then came the early PA systems, a couple of WEM loudspeakers at the side of the stage to try and make yourself heard above the screaming girls if you were so lucky.

In the Sixties, a local mate became your gofer, and, as the scene grew and grew, they got named Roadies. By now the groups had covered all of Britain and lots of Europe so they used to say 'tell the Roadie' if you wanted to get your gear to, say, Gelsenkirchen for a gig. It was still a bit like in WW2 where their fathers had done much the same thing only twenty years before, but that time it was probably behind a British tank. Now it was taken for granted, roadies could find a hall in some obscure town unaided, setting the gear up before having the first drink, and were to be found waiting fag in hand for the group to turn up ready for their fans. This was progress and it was FUN as British groups swarmed all over the UK and Europe playing to enthusiastic young fans who could not get enough of this musical euphoria. As for the musicians, well I mean let's face it, why would you not want to play a gig in sunny St Tropez for Brigitte Bardot AND get paid for it as well. They had never had it so good.

From Beat Groups there was a gradual evolution into Rock bands as this music business became more serious, and so we found groups leaving the UK and going on endlessly long tours trying to 'break' America. After all, compared to the UK it is a ridiculously big, big country; so from rent-a-car, to rent-a-truck, to rent-a-plane and the number of people employed behind the scenes of this business just kept on growing, and for some, so did the suitcases full of dollars.

The funny thing is that in the twenty-first century we have a business full of people working in 'the music biz' who have never even been on a stage. There are hundreds of people who work behind the scenes to make the show happen – some are Pop stars manqué, some are more modest, most were in love with the music at some stage, some just in love with the idea. Now when you hear some drunken seventeen year old slur 'Rock'n'Rawl' you realise that it has all become an ideal, a concept that apparently allows for a different type of behaviour where the boundaries are changed – Ian Dury was spot on, God bless him.

Over the years I have been a musician, a song plugger, record company employee, producer, band manager, music publisher, expert witness and fan, but never, I am sad to say, a songwriter. So I give thanks to these special people with that gift, I wish I had it, but I don't. But spending so much time hanging around with lots of talented people always led me into swapping stories of the bizarre things we had done and the great places we had been. The extra-ordinary people you had met and the absurd situations you found yourself in. To me these insider music stories were always wonderful and so I started to collect them, filming people talking about what they used to do. Nowadays I will even tell you about Paul McCartney, a hernia and my border collie Bob, if you buy me just one more drink. Let us take a pause and give thanks to Keith Richards who managed to record the riff to 'Satisfaction' onto a tape machine while still out of it, which was apparently followed by hours of snoring. After all it does not matter how you capture that germ of a million selling song, so long as you do it. You have their word for it.

Mark Rye

BOB MERCER,
MD EMI Records

I think it was 1974 here in Los Angeles, and John Lennon was finishing the album 'Walls And Bridges'. John was living over here, working over here, because he couldn't move, because he couldn't get a green card. Tricky Dicky wanted him to leave the country so they wouldn't let him back in. He was on J Edgar's list. I ran EMI in London, which was where The Beatles' contract was, so I had to deal with John Lennon and I knew him reasonably well, particularly when he was finishing the record.

I would come over to LA, to help the Capitol Records people get all the parts and bits and pieces and bring them back to London. This was the period of the 'Lost Weekend'; this was the period while Lennon was hanging out here, he was staying at the Beverly Wilshire Hotel in a suite on the top floor, and so I was staying in the same hotel. We just misbehaved ourselves for three days; I don't think we went to bed. We drank vodka, we took a lot of cocaine, we were in terrible shape. Keith Moon was just along the corridor, so he joined in, Keith Moon, Harry Nilsson, me.

So it was mid-afternoon and I got this Uher tape recorder because I have to do a mock interview with John where I ask this list of questions, then you leave a five second pause so they can edit in anybody else they want; we were doing this for EMI International. I'd finished that, and now I was asking John to say something for all the people at EMI in London, and all the people at the factory in Hayes, because he couldn't come back to London, and to explain about his situation.

We were doing that and the curtains were mainly drawn, and outside the window was a space and then a balustrade, and I'm trying to do this bit for EMI and I look up and this figure goes across the balustrade in a raincoat. I go to John, is that Moony? He looked around, said: Take no notice of him, so I take no notice.

Obviously what had happened was that Moony, whilst we were doing these interviews, had called a couple of times wanting to come in and John told him he was working and he couldn't come in. Moon obviously thought we'd got a new batch of drugs and were holding

1

them from him. He knocked on the door a couple of times and Tony King was there and told him to go away.

So Moony had gotten frustrated with this, obviously, he climbed out of his window in a raincoat; but he'd gone on to the balustrade the wrong way round and he couldn't turn around because it was too dangerous, even for him. So he'd gone crab-like, with his back to us, over to the corner where he could grab hold of something and turn himself around. Then he came back and flashed us.

At that very moment the sirens went off, because someone had seen him from the street, thinking maybe a suicide; they didn't know it was Keith Moon, you couldn't tell from that far. Well, there's police cars, there's fire engines, there's all kinds of shit, and we're ignoring all of this, we've got work to do, trying to get this little bit of bollocks done.

The phone rings; Tony King takes the call and I hear him saying: How does he know Mr Lennon is in this suite, you're supposed to keep things like that quiet. He listens a bit more, puts his hand over the phone, looks at John and says: This is the hotel manager and he says that the fellow in the suite underneath us, because of all the fire engines and the sirens and so forth, called him to say what was going on, and he had said it was something to do with the rock stars living on the top floor. The fellow had said: What rock stars? and he said: Well John Lennon, Keith Moon, and the fellow had said John Lennon? I'd love to meet John Lennon. It was Fred Astaire.

So Tony King puts his hand over the mouthpiece and goes to John: Do you want to go down and have afternoon tea with Fred Astaire? John looks at me and I look at John and John goes: Fred fucking Astaire? Fucking right. You on Bob? Right. So now we have to dash around sober up, see if we've got any cocaine that can keep us awake, and we go downstairs to the suite immediately below and knock on the door, and there's this little old fellow in a smoking jacket, opens the door and leads us back into his suite.

I tell you, for John Lennon and me it was just a magical moment. We're walking behind him, Fred Astaire's feet don't touch the ground when he walks, and John and I are desperately trying to do this walk behind him.

Then we sit down and talk about music for an hour. So it goes from John Lennon to Keith Moon to Fred Astaire, all in an afternoon.

NICKY HORNE, Capital Radio Disc Jockey

It was just an amazing time to be part of that revolution. No-one had ever done a radio programme like *Your Mother Wouldn't Like It* before me; I had rivals, my main rival I suppose was John Peel, but John's was much more eclectic and out there than my show. But to be able to play two or three tracks on the trot, to play Soft Rock and Hard Rock, and album tracks, and just sort of let the music breathe, it was a wonderful experience. They gave me carte blanche. Michael Bukht said: you've got a programme; it's called *Your Mother Wouldn't Like It*; you can go as far left as Mott the Hoople. But Michael, God bless him, didn't know much about music so we went a long way left of Mott the Hoople.

There were a few promotion people who really knew what they were doing, who loved being in it for the music. Then there was another lot who were just in it because it was a gig and they were maybe good at schmooze. But the ones that really loved the music, they were incredibly helpful, because they would ring up and they'd say: Look Nick, I've got a white label of Bruce Springsteen, or Elvis Costello, or whoever. Can we bring the white label to you, and if you like it you can have first play. Because of this rivalry with Peel particularly, I would seek out exclusives, and Peel got very upset; Peel and his producer got really pissed off. One time when I got an exclusive of Elvis Costello, I think it was the first album, Peel said to the promotion people who were doing it, if you give Horne another exclusive we will never play your records again, ever. So that kind of strong-arm stuff went on.

I was doing the Pink Floyd story at Capital Radio, where we negotiated to do six one-hour programmes on the history of Pink Floyd, culminating with the very first play of 'Animals'. We had this tortuous negotiation with Steve O'Rourke, their manager, but I'd become friendly with Nick Mason. Nick and I had met at a gig that I was compering, and he was backstage and he was really nice and came up and said: I know you play a lot of our music and I'm really grateful to you, can I buy you a drink? Sure, great. We got quite friendly and I went to his house in Highgate, I remember he had a miniature Bugatti, because he collects these vintage cars. But he had a miniature Bugatti in a huge garden in Highgate, and this miniature Bugatti had a proper engine in it and it could seat one person in it. So I remember driving round in this little Bugatti with this petrol engine, driving up and down Nick Mason's garden in this wonderful little car. Anyway, so Nick kind of smoothed the path and I spent months with them while they were recording 'Animals', and it was incredible to watch how they recorded and how they actually interacted together as people, because there were a lot of tensions within the band at that time, and they didn't tend to crossover.

Roger would do his bits and then he'd leave the studio, and probably at that point once he'd left and was ten minutes down the road, David would get a call to say: It's alright to come in now because Roger's left. Gilmour would come in and do his part.

Because I was interviewing all the people that had been involved with them, I needed really to get Syd Barrett. So Gilmour said: Look, I know where Syd is, he's staying at the Playboy Apartments in London, in Park Lane. Because they always made sure that they knew where he was so he could get his royalty cheques. They really took care of him, particularly Gilmour was always looking after Syd's interests.

So I went to the Playboy Apartments and they said: He's not here, he's at the Hilton Hotel where he's been living for the last month. So I find out from David Gilmour what room he's in and I go up to the room and knock on the door and the door is opened by this huge man, huge man, with no hair, no facial hair at all, no eyebrows, and no hair, and he's big. I thought, oh, this has got to be the roadie; so I said: Hello, I'm Nicky Horne and I've been sent here by Dave Gilmour to talk to Syd. He looked down at me and with all the energy that he could muster, he said: Syd...can't...talk. And closed the door. So I went downstairs, it was in the days before anyone had a mobile phone, and I rang Gilmour from the lobby of the Hilton, and I said look, I've just seen the roadie and he said Syd couldn't talk, but he was really weird. He said: Well what did he look like? I told him what he looked like, and he said: What did he say? Syd can't talk. He said: Well, that was Syd, and Syd was telling the truth. I never got my interview with Syd, but I did meet him and I did shake his hand.

4

BRYAN MORRISON,
Music Publisher

Syd Barrett left his managers Peter Jenner and Andrew King at some point, I can't remember now, I suppose '71 or something like that. He came to me and asked me to manage him. So one way or the other I seem to remember becoming his legal guardian, because he was in and out of asylums for periods of time. Well he came out and I remember he went and stayed in the Hilton Hotel and he had three televisions and about fifteen guitars, and sat there all day and all night long, playing his guitar, with the three channels, BBC1, ITV and whatever the other one was; maybe it was just two channels, I don't know; I think there was three. Anyway amongst other things, I looked after his money coming in from EMI and from his publishing that I didn't have at the time.

One day he rang me up and said he needed some money, could I lend him some money. So I said: Yeah, come in and Cora, who's been with me since before those days, said: He must sign for everything. I said: Alright, do a bit of paper. He came in for £300, or whatever it was, and I gave him the money. I said: Sign this, and he signed for it. This process went on for a couple of months; once, twice a week he'd come in, £100, £200, £300, £400; sign for it and go. Two or three months went by and I got a big cheque in from Essex Music for him, about £20,000 I seem to remember it was. I rung him up and said: Come in, I've got a cheque for you. So he came in, and I had the cheque in my hand and I said, Syd, this is a cheque, but I want the money I've loaned you back first. Give me a cheque for it. He said: What money? I said Syd, I've been giving you money for the last three months. He said: Well, a little bit. I said: Whatever it is Syd, and as it happened it was £2,500. Really? Cora, gave me the invoices. There you are Syd, and I showed him the pile of papers. So he goes in the corner over there, stands there for about fifteen minutes, comes over to me and says: These are forgeries! I said: What do you mean they're forgeries? He said, I've never signed anything in red ink in my life. I said: Syd, you obviously did because they're in red ink, and I didn't forge them.

No they are forgeries! I said: Syd, the cheque from Essex Music is paid to me, right, I'm just giving you a cheque for £20,000, and you say these two are forgeries, I think they were £350 between them. I said: I wouldn't nick your money. I'd nick £15,000 out of your £20,000, not £300, don't be ridiculous. So he did write me a cheque and he left.

That evening, Cora and I are sitting there, about 7 o'clock, just about to go to the pub and have a drink and I heard this banging coming up the stairs and then this bashing on the door. I opened the door and as I opened it Syd looks at me and goes smack, and hits me straight in the face. I put my hands up to grab him and he caught my finger in his mouth and he started to bite through the finger; I mean right to the bone. I screamed: Stop it, or I'll hit you. But he didn't, so I just whacked him straight in the head and he collapsed on the floor. I jumped on him, all my East End came out now, right, because I'm not a fighter but, you know, I did have ten years in the East End. I'm just about to fucking kill him and he looked at me and he started laughing, and foam started coming out of his mouth, and convulsions. Well, I had a complete fit, I jumped up: Call an ambulance. So we picked him up and put him on a chair, he sat in a corner. We're standing there looking at him, don't know what to do next, and I turned to phone someone and he jumped up and ran straight out the door. The ambulance came but he'd gone. The next day I wrote to him and said: I can't be your guardian, here's all your stuff back. Thanks very much but this is not my game. He came and he stood on the corner of Bruton Place in Berkeley Square, three or four days a week for hours on end, just staring at my office for months, and then he disappeared.

KEVIN AYERS,
Musician

The one important factor of The Sixties was, there was kind of a feeling of unification of people coming together of that generation, people questioning their supposed betters, saying why do we have to have this set of rules? The bands were kind of the glue if you like, the reason you could get together. We had light shows and stuff like that, but for me it was just totally normal, I can't really make any comparison. I think it was a counter to the fact that the world had just been changed terribly by the War. What was great was for the first time in history you had a younger generation fighting back and saying we don't really want wars, and we don't want all that shit. The first time ever in the history of man that a young generation has got up and stood and complained, and questioned even. The music at that time, the bands like Soft Machine and Pink Floyd, they were like the marching bands: they provided the rhythm and social reason, and asking the same questions, saying we don't really want to do what our parents did.

Because we were groups on tour together we were often in the same hotels; normally you have your support group's hotel then you have the stars' hotel. Sometimes we stayed in the same hotel and occasionally I saw Jimi Hendrix in the early morning before he started to become 'Jimi Hendrix'; and he was just a real sweet little kid, really innocent, once the groupies had gone, and very shy. Then he'd have to go through this whole process of various things to get to being that 'other', the one that was expected. The difference was staggering, between seeing the guy who wakes up in the morning and the guy who's onstage burning his guitar and humping amps and stuff, and playing brilliantly. That alone is a massive challenge for anybody to have to keep repeating. I think it was written into his contract after a while, that he had to go through those motions of like humping the guitar, setting fire to it, humping the amps and all that stuff, and he was really pissed with that. He said: It's something I did spontaneously, and now

I have to do it. I was a real fan; I used to watch the supporting act and used to see him, he used to grimace, oh no, I've got to do this again. That's the thing about the business isn't it? It gets you, takes away things you do that are original, that are spontaneous; suddenly you're obliged to do it and you have to 'get there' every fucking night.

Fortunately both people involved are dead now, Mike Jeffries and Chas Chandler. They were just feeding him enough money so he could indulge in what he wanted, and maybe a car here or this, that and the other. But the real money went offshore and Hendrix never saw it. I think a lot of people worked on that assumption in those days, basically keep your artist stoned and supplied with girls and whatever, and they won't actually ask you how much they earned. I saw that happening. It happened to Soft Machine. All the money that we earned from our first album in the States was nicked by Chas Chandler.

LSD, I mean, you can't play on acid, as Syd Barrett found out. But yes, it does make your mind work in a way that you're not taught at school. I went to his flat, that flat you see on 'The Madcap Laughs', where he's sitting on the floor, because I was thinking of joining up with him to play something. But he wasn't 'In', he was definitely losing it somewhere.

ROBBIE WILSON, Roadie

I got started with groups in Glasgow because I was a failed drummer at a very early age. But my father owned a mini-bus company, which made me popular because we had vans and mini-buses. When I got sacked as the drummer, I became the roadie supporting Deep Purple, Blodwyn Pig, Fleetwood Mac, Slade in Glasgow, in Edinburgh. When they were doing town halls in those days, which were big gigs, I mean, 2,000, 3,000 seaters, they had Deep Purple, Number One band, who would play those type of venues. I was with a £25 a night, £10 a night, opening act. I did a lot of work with Slade, when they were getting £50 and we were getting a tenner, and I became good friends with Noddy Holder. I was nineteen or twenty years-old so when they came to Glasgow, if I wasn't working I would go hang out with Slade, work with them, and then eventually when they got a hit record Noddy kindly offered me a job and I spent six years, from early Seventies till '76 with Slade. I started off drum roadie, stage manager, did a bit of sound, did a bit of everything. I worked for Chas Chandler, who taught me the music business; he was my second father. He taught me everything about the music industry, live music, how you deal with missing drummers; how to steal an extra ten minutes before you put the band on so the lights get better use because it gets darker outdoors.

Slade at their height would do shows with a seven-and-a-half-ton truck, where we had two lighting towers, no backdrop, one spotlight for Noddy, because three were more expensive. Promoters such as Mel Bush thought one was enough, which I guess it was in those days; nobody knew any different. No big set design, no big champagne riders, six bottles of coke, bottle of wine, some grubby old ham sandwiches if you were lucky. No catering, no twenty-four local crew; it was seven floors up at Blackburn St George's Hall and me and two other guys. Then we progressed to buying a PA system from the legendary and lovely Charlie Watkins at WEM. Sound systems were being developed and WEM at that time supplied everybody, Slade, Status Quo, Rod Stewart. We would all meet at the factory in Brixton; cups of tea and people sold them things; it was marvellous. It was a music business in London where everybody knew everybody from the days of driving down the motorway to Watford Gap. Driving in there and seeing Pink Floyd, all the groups, in there at 3 or 4 o'clock in the morning; Status Quo especially, they were always around. Bob Young driving their Bentley. They were actually at one time a £15 support act for Slade, after having been one of the biggest groups in Britain, and then ultimately resuming their correct title in that genre.

There's so many memories, every first country I ever visited, Japan with Slade, Australia, playing to 75,000 people and carrying suitcases of money back to the hotel because we didn't have security, and I get entrusted with a suitcase full of money. It was the days when that's what happened. You built the stage, you did a show, you sat with the promoter at the end of the day with buckets full of money, counted it all out and you walk away with a suitcase. When I toured with Slade they were the biggest band in Europe, the biggest band in Australia, very big in Japan, very big in Germany, France. There was just a few of us; there was a tour manager, who drove the band, that was his function, collected the money at the end of the show; there was me, there was the stage manager, the drum roadie, the monitor mixer, the other guy did the lights on and off, and the sound engineer who mixed the monitors from out front. I was with the biggest band in Great Britain and Europe and I was getting £15 a week but if they'd have said you're not getting paid I'd still have done it.

I was on practically every Slade record, as was the rest of the crew, because Chas Chandler would put us out in the corridor at Olympic Studios with our platform boots which we all wore, and we would stomp along, and I'm on 'Merry Christmas' singing the chorus. Chas, God rest his very, very good soul, paid us royalties from his production company, and the crew would get a split of everything we sang on, from Chas, it was from Chas's share, so he allocated us. So for many years we'd get a little cheque every few months, which was nice.

KEITH ALTHAM,
Journalist

One of my closest friends was a chap called Chas Chandler from The Animals days, and Chas had always said to me that when he left the Animals he was going to go into management and he was going to find a huge star and when he did find a huge star he would take me to America with him. I thought, oh yeah, great Chas. But Chas was always a man of his word, and he told me all about this guitarist he found in New York. He said: He's just brilliant Keith, you won't believe it; he's better than Clapton, better than Page, better than Beck. I went, oh yeah. He said: He's black, but he's just wonderful; I'm going to bring him over, you've got to do something on him. I said: Well, if he's as good as you say he is Chas, I will. I was still a journo, still on the *New Musical Express*.

He brought over this guy and I saw him the second night he was in London, playing at the Scotch of St James; he wasn't singing, just jamming with Brian Auger of the Brian Auger Trinity, and a few other guys. I listened to him for two or three numbers and he was a brilliant guitarist. Chas came over and said: What do you think Keith? I said: He's great Chas but he's a Jazz guitarist. He's going to go straight over the heads of the kids; they're not going to understand that. He's brilliant but he's a Jazz guitarist. Chas replied in his thick Geordie accent: Not if I can help it, he won't. The next time I saw him he'd got Noel Redding with him and Mitch Mitchell; it was the Jimi Hendrix Experience of course, and they were playing at The Speakeasy I think on this occasion. Much more interesting; much more interesting. I don't think he was singing even then, mainly instrumental; maybe he did one or two. I thought, this is beginning to get interesting now, and I started dropping the odd one-liner in the NME's Alley Cat column for him, 'amazing new guitarist', you know. Then they did a gig, I think a preview gig for the press prior to the release of the first single, 'Hey Joe'. I went to that and he blew my socks off, he was just extraordinary and he did a version of 'Wild Thing' that The Troggs had previously got to Number One. It was just amazing; I'd never heard anything like it. I said: Okay Chas, I'm in; you've got me sold.

Then there came one of my infamous claims to fame, which is that I invented the guitar flambé for Jimi Hendrix. I suppose I was now moving towards PR, but I was still giving Chas unofficial PR advice, although I was still a journalist. We were at the Finsbury Park Astoria and Chas and Jimi were involved on this tour with Englebert Humperdink, The Walker Brothers and Cat Stevens, at the Finsbury Park Astoria which later became The Rainbow. I was sitting backstage in Jimi's dressing room, and Chas is saying: You're a journalist Keith, what can we do to steal all the headlines? I said: I don't know Chas, it's a pity you can't set fire to the guitar. There was this silence in the room for a minute and Chas says, to the roadie: Gerry, go out and buy some lighter fuel. Gerry went out and bought some lighter fuel, and of course that's what they did. They spread it over the face of the guitar, and Jimi lit it with matches on this particular night, and couldn't get it to light. Eventually it went whoosh and nearly took his head off. He took it on stage and waved it around like a torch around his head. It drove the security guy on the side of the stage absolutely apoplectic. The compere rushed on with a fire extinguisher and sprayed the security guard by mistake which was quite good fun. The whole thing caused chaos, which was exactly what he wanted of course.

We went backstage and the producer was a guy who rejoiced in the name of Tito Burns, the promoter of the tour. He was in on it, but he had to pretend he wasn't. So he came backstage and he had to pretend to be ticking him off, poking his head round the dressing room door: You'll never work on this circuit again Hendrix! Chas is looking at me, and off they went. I think Jimi only ever did it four times in his life, but every time he did it, he caused a sensation. The net result of that was that Jimi was then cited for the Monterey Festival, and Chas kept his word to me and said: You're coming with us. So my first trip to America was with Jimi Hendrix for the Monterey Festival. The Who paid the return leg, and coming back Townshend took acid and conceived the idea for 'Tommy', so it was some trip. I also saw, for the first time on that festival, Otis Redding, Janis Joplin, Simon and Garfunkel, Mamas and Papas and Eric Burdon with his new band. I went to Janis Joplin after she finished her set. I walked up to her and I said: You're the best female Rock singer I've ever heard in my life. She looked me up and down and said: Do you get out much honey?

DAVE AMBROSE, Musician

I came from the suburbs of Reigate, deep, deep suburbia, and we used to play at tennis club dances, me and Clive Pickford, and that's where it all began really, doing Eddie Cochran songs. Great fan of Eddie Cochran, 'Summertime Blues' and all those great tracks, and Rick Nelson. I used to be a guitarist and help Clive singing and we started from there.

My father decided to throw in his suburban umbrella and we moved to Kensington, he decided we were going to live there because he worked at the University of London, Kensington. So we all moved to this small house in Callcott Street, Notting Hill Gate, behind the old Coronet Cinema. Very small. It was pretty weird moving into London, pretty strange. So he suggested I join a youth club; I joined the Holy Trinity Youth Club, Old Brompton Road, and they were all Mods and Rockers in those days and they had the beehive hairdo's, and the Rockers really had the big do's, and golden bicycle chains, gold plated, all that sort of stuff. It was great. I was a young chap out of the suburbs, pretty lonely, and there was a Rock and Roll band playing there doing Shadows songs with all the steps, and then the bass player hurt his hand and the Vicar said: Can anyone play, and I just took a chance and put my hand up. Because I could play the guitar I suddenly found myself playing with extraordinary people like Hamilton King and Ray Davies, Peter Green, and all these people, Mick Fleetwood and Peter Bardens, while I was still at Art School.

It was a bit of an accident going into this music thing, and then there was a great moment when I finished Art School and I worked at a design group as a graphic artist. Peter Bardens was a bit of a star at Art School because he joined Them and he was rushing around in a Cadillac, and he was only eighteen, so he was very important, and Mick Fleetwood was rushing around learning to play the drums anywhere; he just wanted to be part of the scene. So they rang up and Pete said: I've left Them and formed a band, I'm signed to EMI, join the band. So he offered me lots of money to join and I left the advertising world and then we got Rod Stewart in as a singer and we were signed to

EMI, and off we went. It was quite an extraordinary time we had. Rod Stewart had to carry the equipment too, may I add, which was very painful for him even then. We were managed by the infamous Johnny Gunnell, the Gunnell Brothers, who ran the Flamingo Club. We were a sort of house band; we were paid this retainer. The retainer was quite good actually; Johnny was very generous to us, but in the end he made us work for that money. We ended up playing at the Flamingo afternoon sessions, evening sessions and all night sessions, and it was tough, it was Georgie Fame and Zoot Money and all those people playing, but it was a great time; we all really learnt to play.

IVAN CHANDLER, Musician

I got all my O-levels but the two subjects I was top at, Music and French, well when you came to A-levels you had to start reading lots of books, so I did those at evening class. I got a job in the BBC in the Equipment Department at Chiswick, typing out the invoices that went out with the resistors and capacitors, mainly because in the stores the swearing was so bad that no women would work there. So my dad bought me a book: 'Learn To Type', and I'm pleased about that now because I'm a pretty good typist, and I can certainly type British Broadcasting Corporation faster than anyone else. I kept on applying for internal jobs, and finally got into the BBC Music Library, which was in Aeolean Hall in Bond Street at the time. It was dealing with all the song copies and providing the scores and parts for all the orchestras. We used to go up to the studios and see people like Georgie Fame recording, poke our heads round and say hello.

This guitarist, Stuart, who was in the library, said: Are you interested in music, do you play piano? And I said: Yes but I've only done Classical, I quite like Pop and I quite like the John Barry strings on Adam Faith's records. He then introduced me to Blues like Muddy

Waters, Howlin' Wolf, and I remember also he once played me an album by Julian Cannonball Adderley Live with Joe Zawinul on piano playing 'Work Song'. I've even got the tingles now thinking about it. I thought, I want to do this.

So we formed a band and we got very matey with Georgie Fame's agent, Ruby Barb. By then we had a seven-piece band with Stan Saltzman, a top sax player now, who was seventeen at the time, and I was only eighteen. We got the support act at the famous Flamingo Club, supporting Georgie Fame, Zoot Money, Bluesology. I used to get off the Hammond organ and Reg Dwight, pre Elton, would swap, we used to think he looked like Billy Bunter. We would get £25 between seven of us; we had to pay £5 to some guy with the van to take all the equipment there, and then of that £25 we had to give 10% to Rik and John Gunnell as their commission for booking us into their own gig.

I was getting a bit fed up and I put an ad in the *Melody Maker* saying 'Pianist Available'. Dusty Springfield's secretary, Pat Barnett rang me up and said: Would you come do an audition? So I went to this little rehearsal room somewhere in London, met Dusty. The piece was 'Shake' by Sam Cooke. I remember she said: You play hard. It was £60 a week. What they don't tell you, in those days you don't think about contracts or guarantees, but you only got £60 a week when you worked. So we did this wonderful tour with Dusty; my big first professional night was at The Rainbow, and the opening song was 'You Don't Have to Say You Love Me', so it was quite a big piece. On the tour were The Alan Price Set, there was Boz Burrell, bless him, Boz who recently died, Episode Six, which spawned Ian Gillan. We played all over the country. But then Dusty was taking a break so we went off and played with Lulu, did some gigs with Lulu. We played with Cat Stevens on his seventh gig on Morecambe Pier; yes we went all the way up to Morecambe Pier. We packed up our gear, we left the Pier, and Cat's walking along or Steve as he was called then, I think he had a driver or something, and there was a couple of rowdy people walking along with drinks. So Stuart says to Steve and me: Come on, let's go and sort them out; come on. Steve was like: Oh no! But we were just winding him up of course.

15

MIKE HURST,
Musician

Dusty Springfield was the most professional, but then conversely, the most outrageously rude person you could imagine. You could say that's in her private life, this is in a pub, that's fine. But no, no, no, she was the same in her professional life. My favourite story of her was we were doing a concert in Blackpool at the Winter Gardens and we were rehearsing, getting a sound check together. We had gone electric. You know when everyone went crazy when Dylan went electric in '65 or '66, I can't remember which. Well, we got amplifiers, so we were going to be amplified, because I loved playing guitar, more than Tom Springfield, so I wanted to make some noise.

So we're doing this run through and this voice out in the auditorium says: What are those boxes? So Dusty says: They're amplifiers. The voice says: Well, they'll have to go, they ruin the look of the act. Now, this was Harold Fielding; he was one of the biggest promoters in Britain at that time, and he said: They'll have to go.

Dusty said: They're not going, they're part of the act; they're staying. A female voice from the auditorium then pipes up: Don't let her talk to you like that Harold. And Dusty just says: You can tell that stupid bitch to shut her mouth. It was Harold Fielding's wife. At which point Harold Fielding said: That's it, you'll never work in one of my theatres again – and we didn't.

CHARLIE WATKINS,
Inventor of the PA

Lonnie Donegan happened: 'Rock Island Line'. Typically music industry, conflagration: a massive surge of this new, exciting music, with guitars or banjos, whatever you wanted to call them; they were guitars. I had a music shop then and a record shop. In a week I'd finish selling accordions, which was the instrument I had dealt with along with trumpets and things, and I wanted to sell guitars, because they were queuing out the door for guitars. The Maccaferri guitar made instantly famous by Django Reinhardt was adopted because of the cutaway; you could get a few more notes on your left hand.

The situation was such that I got on an aeroplane, propeller aeroplane then by the way, at London airport and went to Germany and found a German guitar wholesaler with stock of cheap, flat guitars. They used them in Germany for learners, and I bought them all; I bought his warehouse. I always remember the occasion because his name was Voss, Muller Voss, in Dortmund, and he was a proper old German war man. He probably had an Iron Cross; he was a pilot of a bomber and I was a British seaman. I was on the receiving end of the likes of him, so he was treading on dodgy ground when he said: You should haf lost the vor, you should haf lost the vor. I said: Here, hang on, and I had a bit of a dingdong with him. I go red around my neck when I get upset, which isn't very often but I mean I can't handle that, but when he saw his order going through the front door, we called it a deal, because he was going to lose and I was going to lose and all we were going to get was our opinions in somebody else's memory.

I brought them back, and my new shop was in Balham. I hung them up like joints of meat in a butcher's warehouse, all along the ceiling. The power of Skiffle was such that they'd come from Glasgow to Balham to buy a £7 guitar off me and take it back up there. They'd bring the whole Skiffle group down and do everything in my shop. I thought, well, this is the way to go, and I was obviously right because in about the time it took me to get to Germany and have a dingdong with the German bomber pilot, which he lost, come back, have my dinner, in about the same time I sold the bloody lot; they'd all gone. Hundreds, and literally thousands of young guys picked up a guitar.

Beside the Skiffle they found, they used to have this thing called the three-chord trick, which would be the tonic chord, the dominant chord, and the sub tonic; it's all you needed. You could do any song you wanted on that, even though it varied a little bit, but you could do it. You could do all those lovely things, and they found they could do a little riff like King Django could do.

A lot of them, like Pete Townshend for instance, and Alvin Lee, found they could get a sound, but you could never hear them, so I decided that the next step would be to make an amplifier. I made an amplifier called a Watkins Westminster at 10 watts. I made a box, I put a speaker in it; I went up to Tottenham Court Road into Lasky's or Premium, one of the many electronic component shops who were selling small, pound modules. He started asking me what I was going to do with it, so I said: I want to make it play a guitar loud. He said: Oh, be careful, won't you. I asked, why? He said: Well, you can kill someone with that. It was a DC amplifier you see. So I said: If you think of anything that's going to help me, here's my phone number. I'd hardly got back to the shop, it's him. He said: Here, bejasus, I'd like to work for you. I said: What can you give me? He said: Well, I can make this amplifier for you. Which he could, which he did. So I stayed up and worked that night until I built a prototype, and I made a new Westminster, red on the front, cream band round the middle, and red on the back; put the handle on the top, put the controls on the top with a celluloid control panel, sent the first one up to a dealer called Jimmy Reno, and he came back like a lunatic. That's what I want, he said: and I'll have a dozen. That was my Watkins Westminster.

MO FOSTER, Musician

We slowly worked our way up through Hofner's and Selmer guitars and things that were dreadful. Joe Brown once described Bert Weedon as playing a yard and a half of German plywood, which I quite liked. You couldn't get Fenders. I know why now, as until 1960 there was an American trade embargo with this country, so nobody could buy anything American, which was why there were no Fenders in the country until 1960. The whole English Rock and Roll scene sounded different because it was played on German and Swedish guitars. That's why it was really naff. Or the ones you built at home, everybody built something; all the amplifiers were home-built. It wasn't until I was twenty-three I played through an amplifier I hadn't built. It's amazing.

To illustrate the difference, there were two sets of magazines I used to enjoy: one was *Practical Wireless*, which had all these circuits in of things you could build, guitar amps and tremolos and stuff; and one set of magazines I'd seen around but I actually bought a bit later called *Practical Householder*. I've got these magazines from the mid-Fifties, and it really shows you that Britain was going through an austerity period, because everybody built something; it was all DIY. You couldn't buy anything you couldn't afford. The articles are fantastic. One was 'Building A Fridge'; you actually built a fridge from nothing. A whole article on chromium plating at home, and there's this guy all excited at his kitchen table with lots of wires and beakers and God knows what. How on earth would Health and Safety cope with that now? The stink and the lethal things coming off, the vapours. In the photograph there was always a man dismantling a gearbox on his kitchen table. He always had a pipe, and in the background his wife's looking admiringly; she loved him opening his gearbox on the table.

Because we hadn't got any money at school we couldn't afford the amplifiers, which were the big stars of the day; well, it became the Vox 30, which The Shadows used. Forget it, the price was astronomic. But we saw this advert for a thing called the Watkins' Dominator, which Charlie Watkins had built. It was triangular, blue and white;

it had four inputs, and it was rated at 17 watts power, which is more than the 5 watts we'd been used to, like little radios really. There was an argument in our band, because one half of the band thought it might be too powerful and would frighten the audience and empty the room, 17 watts. But we bought it, and of course with four inputs, wham, the whole band is suddenly, two guitars, bass and vocals, all in the same amp. The professionals used to have their amplifiers on chrome or steel stands, which we couldn't get, but in this Practical Household I'd seen an advert for Brianco Legs, they were like screw-in wooden legs, and the advert said: Convert your spare wood into elegant furniture. So we had elegant wobbling amplifiers, wobbling on their spindly legs.

After university some ex-university friends, we formed a band called Affinity, which was kind of Jazz-Rock Hammond organ based thing, with a girl singer called Linda Hoyle, and through a sequence of events we ended up being managed by Ronnie Scott of the Jazz Club. We were resident there for about two-and-a-half years, played there, met a lot of people, it was fantastic. Then that folded and through this sequence of events I discovered the session scene, something I'd never heard of, didn't know it existed. But I slotted in to it; it was just what I wanted. I liked the people, the humour. It was fantastic turning up, playing something brand new in those three hours, doing it as well as possible and having a good laugh as well, and being paid for those three hours what I used to earn in a week. It was fantastic.

BIG JIM SULLIVAN, Musician

When I was about fifteen or sixteen I joined a group called The Soho Group, and we used to play out of a bistro, a restaurant bar, which was very Folky, called The Troubadour at Earls Court. This must have been '56, '57. From The Troubadour we used to go up to The 2i's coffee bar and go in and sit in and play at The 2i's. It was there that Marty Wilde heard me play and asked these guys, the bass player and the drummer, Tex Makins and Bobby Woodman, asked them to ask me if I'd like to join The Wildcats as it were. I said: Yeah, but you've got to get your hair dyed blond. So we had the hair dyed blond and sure enough we went on tour with Marty for the first couple of months' tour, and then Marty sacked them, kept me and a guy called Tony Belcher, who was a rhythm guitarist, and got in Brian Bennett and Licorice Locking, who later both joined The Shadows, if you recall that. So they were the original Wildcats and they're the ones who did all the major hits that Marty had.

My mother had died when I was two so I lived with my grandparents, and when I was fourteen, I moved in with my aunty and uncle over the other side of Hounslow by the airport, and I always remember coming home with my first wage packet from Marty Wilde, which was £30. My uncle, who was a milkman, who probably earned about £4.10.0d a week, saying to me: Son, when are you going to get a proper job. I went out to Cecil G and got a complete new outfit; it was winter, big coat, jacket and trousers and shoes, and the whole thing; and I still had about £8 left or something with all this lot.

We went out on tour that week and I came out of the theatre that night and got torn apart by teenagers, teenyboppers; torn apart, coat was ripped off me, everything, hair pulled out. Christ knows what they'd have done if they'd have got hold of Marty Wilde.

Oh Boy! was my introduction to sessions really, because Jack Good who was the producer of *Oh Boy!* and he used to use me on all his session work. He never used me on *Oh Boy!* at all, not once. I don't think I had the looks for TV. But he used me on all his recordings he did, all the early PJ Proby, Lulu, Jimmy Powell; he produced all of those for the major labels.

I had started off in sessions in '58 with Marty Wilde, 'Teenager in Love', and 'Bad Boy', all that stuff. All from that day onwards, when you had three hours to do four tracks. The bands couldn't do that; they used to come in and because of nerves or inability to play, most of them, they couldn't play the songs. Although they could play them live, it was a totally different thing when you get in the studio, because everything is recorded and you can hear everything, if you make a little glitch. So studio musicians played on most of the group records during the Sixties. Vic Flick and Eric Ford were the main guitarists when I started. Eric and I used to play with Reg Guest and the Nashville Five, doing all the BBC recordings. We did quite a lot of them actually. Every Friday night we did a live broadcast; and then of course there was the *Saturday Club*, I did loads of *Saturday Clubs* with various people. That's what's they used to call us guitarists, Big Jim Sullivan and Little Jimmy Page.

In the real early days I was the first one to bring in solid. I had my Gibson that I used with Marty; a Gibson Les Paul 1955 that had belonged to Sister Rosetta Tharpe. It was quite a beasty that was. In '59 I got a Gibson 345 from Ivor Mairants; I bought that and Marty went guarantor for me. I used a little Watkins for the heavy sound. If I wanted a real grunty sound the little Watkins was great for that. I think Hank Marvin had the first Watkins Copicat and I had the second. I got my Copicat nicked, we went for a tour of Ireland with Marty and it got nicked off the train, so that was that.

I did all these sessions but I even get some of the guitarists from the groups phoning me up and telling me I didn't play on their record, which really pisses me off; I really get angry with that. There's one of them especially who phoned me up, we had a good old chat. By the way, he said: I'm claiming for the guitar on PPL because I played on it. I said: No you didn't. He said: Yeah. I said, don't you remember, I lived in Woodside Park, you came over to my house in Woodside Park and I taught you the solo that I played on that record. What can you say!

CHAS McDEVITT, Musician

My Chas McDevitt Skiffle Group did a Radio Luxemburg talent contest at the Chelsea Palace and we won three weeks running. We'd paper the audience with all our mates because the voting was done on audience applause; so we won three weeks running. The last one was given to a piano player, because they wouldn't have had to pay so much to get him into the final. It was a bit of a fix, but we got the exposure.

We sang three songs, one a week and the last song we sang, believe it or not, was 'Freight Train', and that's when we lost. But I was singing 'Freight Train' at half the tempo we eventually recorded it at. Record companies nearly all had Skiffle groups on their books and we were one of the last to be signed. I was furious with my manager for not getting us signed and he said: you've got to get something different. We'd done the same talent show in Chelsea that Nancy Whiskey had been in, and she didn't get anywhere in the talent show, and he said: why don't you get her into the group. We'd seen her around the Folk clubs, and we asked her to join the group. She was reluctant, because she didn't want to play Skiffle, but eventually she did and we re-recorded 'Freight Train' for Oriole Records, and it took off eventually.

At one stage there were supposedly 30,000 Skiffle groups in the country; that's not hard to understand. The number of guitars they were selling a week was stupendous. Anybody could learn the three chords and they'd persuade their bass to get a guitar and they'd have a group. Every barrack room had a couple of Skiffle groups playing; military call-up was still around in those days. All the youth clubs had a Skiffle group. So it just spread like wildfire. As they got better they progressed into earthier music, Blues or Rock and Roll.

The Rolling Stones used to come and hear us when we played in Kingston-on-Thames, and I believe Mick Jagger first started playing a washboard at one time. People like Albert Lee told me they started playing in Skiffle groups, and Brian May of Queen was influenced by Lonnie to play the guitar. Van Morrison had a Skiffle collection that really got him going. The Shadows were The Railroaders in Newcastle, a Skiffle group. They came to hear us the last week Nancy Whiskey played with the group in August '57; they came to hear us in Newcastle, and invited us to a gig they were playing at a wedding. I thought they were pretty good and advised them to go to London.

Recently, I've seen on television a clip of a Skiffle group being interviewed; I think it was by Hugh Weldon or somebody like that, and it turns out that Jimmy Page is playing guitar in this Skiffle group, and one of the songs they play is 'Cotton Fields', or 'Cotton Song' as we called it, and the version he sings, although most of the words are Leadbelly's, the version he sings is from our record; I can recognise it. So it's nice to know we influenced people of that calibre.

MIKI DALLON,
Producer

I was at the Tottenham Royal with a bunch of my pals one night; we used to go down there for a fight every Saturday night with the Bethnal Green lot, or whatever. There used to be a pub opposite called The Eagle, and a copper station next to that, so, you know, we were so stupid, to go in a pub and get tanked up and then go to The Royal and it would all kick off, and then of course the cops used to be waiting outside and they used to put us straight in the nick next door! We didn't have the brains to figure it out. It was so funny.

I can remember being in there one night and the disc jockey said: Oh, we've got a new record here by a guy called Jerry Lee Lewis, 'A Whole Lot of Shakin' and he just dropped the arm and it just echoed all around the hall, 'Come Along My Baby', and the echo and the drum sound and everything, it was just like everybody stopped and said: just not heard a sound like that. Being a piano player, when I heard that piano, well. We played it eight times straight off; we kept going up there, whole crowd of us, play it again, play it again.

I wasn't into Elvis Presley too much because we didn't know much about the Sun Recordings in those days. We only really knew about Presley when 'Heartbreak Hotel' came out. He was always a little bit of a pretty boy; I appreciate him now of course. But Jerry Lee Lewis, and Little Richard, whoever before that has sung like that? Frank Sinatra, Bing Crosby, or Dickie Valentine; you know what I mean? It sort of just changed the way that we thought and the way we started singing and playing.

I left school in January '55; we went to the movies to see *Blackboard Jungle* and 'Rock Around the Clock' came on, and, you know, thinking about the Lewis thing and the Little Richard thing, that was the first big shock that we got, because no-one had heard music like that before. They just smashed two or three front rows of the seats right out, pulling them out, and started dancing and going in the aisle, you know; and all the lights went on and the movie stopped and bouncers came round. Then we all got in again to see the second show, did the same thing, and then we get in the next day. We used to get in around the back, that was at the Edmonton Granada, and then we were barred. So then it went to The Regal, Tottenham; we all went up there for three nights until we got barred there too. We'd never heard anything like it, for the first time it was our music; it wasn't our dad's, or our grandpa's, it was aimed at us.

We were wearing flat caps then, at fifteen; you'd go out on a building site, or your father used to say you've got to get a job, I don't care where it is, down the River Lee loading barges or whatever, you have to bring in a bit of money. I used to go to work as a miniature of my father, and so did all the other kids. In '55 that all stopped because the shops then started stocking the bumpers and the thick-soled, and the Sloppy Joes, and the Rock and Roll stuff like Gene Vincent got to wear. Everything was aimed at this massive teenage audience throughout the world.

NEIL CHRISTIAN,
Musician

We got a group of our own together called Red E. Lewis and the Red Caps, and I was looking for a good lead guitarist. A pal of mine that was doing gigs all around town at the time, from The 2i's said: get yourself out to Epsom because there's a boy playing with a hometown group out there and he's absolutely dynamite. He's only a kid but he's dynamite. So off I go this Friday night to Epsom Hall, and on comes the local band, and this kid blew me away; I couldn't believe it, he was like fourteen or fifteen. So I made myself known to him; I said: who are you? what are you? what are you doing? He said: I'm still at school, but I'm leaving in a couple of weeks and then I'm going on to college. So I said: how would you like to play with us for a couple of gigs before you leave? So he said: Yeah, okay; what, round here? I said: No, in London. I'll come out and pick you up and take you home at night. So we did the four gigs we had lined up and we used him, and the kid was dynamite. His name was Jimmy Page.

I don't know how I could explain to you how good he was but he just got better and better. Anyhow, Jimmy became the guitarist with that group and then he turned round to me one day because the singer that we'd got was rubbish and says: Why don't you sing?. I'd never sang before but I said: okay; I got up and we had one night's rehearsal. The thing is we could not get a record contract as we were. Anyhow in the meantime, time rolls on, and after about three years Jimmy had had enough. He said: I just can't take it anymore, just got to have a break. He brought another kid he was working with, in for an audition as his replacement. I thought he was rubbish and gave him ten shillings to go home, his name was Jeff Beck, and Jimmy went back to his studies.

Somebody that used to come along to watch us told me that there was a good guitarist up Blackheath way called Albert Lee. He was playing local groups in local halls, and he was quite a dab hand; so off I went. So I said to Albert: do you want to start travelling and moving around England? and he said: Yeah, okay. So I got hold of Albert.

He wasn't too keen, because he was a bit of a London bird; anything as long as it was around London, but if you started moving away he didn't like the idea so much. So I brought down Mick Abrahams from Luton; he was quite good, Mick.

Then I got hold of Ritchie Blackmore, and Ritchie said: Yeah, okay, come on let's go for it. He was with me for a quite a few years. Ritchie had been doing tours with Gene Vincent and everything; he'd been doing a lot for Don Arden. I became friends with Ritchie before he started to play with us. Then I took Ritchie to Germany, and it's funny seeing that all happen. He gets married after a few months we were out there, marries a German girl. That went on for a while, then he got a divorce. Then we go out to Germany again and he meets another one and gets married again.

JOHN CRAIG,
Music Publisher

I started work on Saturday, 29th of August 1960 at Mills Music, which was one of the hot publishing companies at the time. There was an advert in the *Evening Standard* believe it or not, for working in the sheet music department. We used to be called 'Trade Boys', which doesn't sound too good these days, does it, which was basically schlepping sheet music. But it was in Denmark Street and we had the top writers at the time: Johnny Worth who wrote all the Adam Faith stuff and John Barry was a writer for us. So it was a buzzy sort of place. And of course I was there at the birth of The Beatles and all the rest of it; so it went from being a music publishing world where we were a backwater of America and suddenly we were the epicentre of the world. It was a fantastic time to be in Denmark Street.

Our boss, believe it or not, used to wear a bowler hat to work; can you imagine someone running a music publisher now going to work in a bowler hat anyway? Cyril Gee his name was; he came down one day with this pile of sheet music and put his bowler hat on top and said: Send that to the New York office. So the whole bloody lot went, bowler hat and all. I mean, nobody would think of going to work in anything other than a suit. If you were one of the bosses you went to work in a suit, even me, moving a wheelbarrow around full of sheet music, I was wearing a sports jacket and a tie.

Eric Hall was the office boy and Reg Dwight was a trade boy too. We always had great Christmas parties because Reg/Elton always played the piano. Everybody started playing guitar because of Lonnie Donegan and Skiffle, The Quarrymen were a Skiffle group. That's probably what made John Lennon pick a guitar up. But Denmark Street was absolutely fantastic; apart from Elton being there, Roger Cook and Roger Greenaway were our writers. There was one Christmas I remember there was this crowd of kids downstairs selling knocked off whiskey. Probably shouldn't be saying this but the band was called Them, and you probably know Van Morrison was in Them, and they were making their Christmas money selling off cheap whiskey; God knows where they got it from. It was an interesting time.

Then at the end of the Sixties we started getting those album selling bands like Zeppelin and Floyd, Deep Purple and people like that. I left and got offered a job working in New York. In 1970 working class kids like me didn't go to New York. BOAC. So I was the very first representative for ASCAP, which I did for three or four years. The high spot of that job was signing Rod Stewart to ASCAP when he was Number One with 'Maggie May', I pulled him away from BMI. Several years ago I saw him at Rob Dickins's fiftieth birthday party, and Rod went: Hello mate. I said: You can't possibly remember me. He said: I'll never forget anybody that gave me twenty grand.

I was on the road with Rainbow where they had this Danish promoter, and we'd arrived in Paris. I was with the group because we were working with the local record company, and Ritchie Blackmore had gone to this promoter: Can I have a word with you? And he kept him talking in the lobby. When the promoter goes back up to his room, there is not a stick of furniture in it. This is Rock and Roll. So the Danish guy goes back downstairs and says: There's no furniture in my room. And the hotel went: Oh, I'm terribly sorry sir, here's another key. But by the time he got up to that room of course there's no furniture in that one either. There were roadies with wardrobes and double beds going up and down in the lifts and dumping them on the service landings and things. So yeah I've seen some funny ones. But you know, quite often at the hotels, as long as you don't do too much damage they think it's funny too. It breaks up their day. There was one hotel in Preston somewhere where the night manager actually used to join in. But it's all got far more serious than that now, hasn't it?

I mean, these tours, you see things at the O2; you can't mess about, that's 20,000 people beautifully presented. I've yet to see anything that's not actually been perfect in there, as far as the sound and lighting and whatever. In the Seventies it was a happy band of amateurs really. It's moved on miles since then.

Ritchie Blackmore's not an easy man to deal with, he wouldn't go on a label called Purple; so we started a new label, Oyster, which was a bit like a copy of the Apple label because one side was a shell and the other side was the opened oyster. The first album that had an Oyster label was the first Ritchie Blackmore and Rainbow. It was a big time really for us; and it was interesting because of the demise of the super groups at the end of the Seventies. Rainbow had this lighting rainbow that was absolutely huge, that went across the stage, and now it'd probably be run by an App. But at the time it worked off punch cards; you used to put punch cards through this machine, and it would change the colours of the rainbow going over. But this rainbow cost $300,000, in 1976, to cross the Atlantic. That wasn't the cost of the rainbow, that was just the shipping costs. Those bands, when punk came along they became like dinosaurs; it was a time when you really couldn't tour because there wasn't enough money in touring and the cost of all these four bloody great articulated lorries, or whatever, just didn't justify it. So these groups had a tough time then.

MALCOLM FORRESTER,
Music Publisher

I was in a brass band, Wimbledon Army Cadet Brass Band, flugelhorn, and this woman came round the school and I promise you, she was a School Board Officer' and I wasn't in Borstal; I know she was called a School Board Officer. She said: what do you want to do? I said: I want to go into the music business. That's all I said: that was my introduction to the music industry. She got me an interview, go with your mother, and I did to Campbell Connelly sheet music and that was 'Goodnight Sweetheart' and 'Showboat' and all that stuff.

Anyway George Seymour, who was my boss, fantastic man; I never said a word, my mum did all the talking, and she said: will he get Luncheon Vouchers Mr Seymour? And he went No, but I'll make sure he eats. Which became a pain, because all the other boys would be up the pub and things; I had to go round the corner and have spam and chips or something.

It was great; offices were all round, the arrangement, the copyist. So that was proper music publishing; a piano in every room. Great days, we had Dickie Valentine, and those people were coming in, sat down at the keys. I'm old, but not that old, because I caught the tail end of that industry, of the music industry where they used to sit at the end of the pier and sell sheet music, I caught a bit of that. The Aberbachs was run by a man called Franklin Boyd, who was a singer. So then I had to go and plug the band leaders, and people like Lionel Conway and Don Black they were all there; we used to queue up with an acetate and the top line.

So then Franklin Boyd calls me upstairs, because I was based in the basement, and they said: Okay, would you like to be a plugger? I hadn't got a clue what he was talking about, but then they kind of explained it, so I said great, brilliant. My first meeting, they were dishing out songs and this is the strange thing, they never played the records. They never actually played the product, because Aberbachs was the biggest publishing house in the world at the time and they had everything.

Jeff, I forget his name now would just sling you a record, and he went, 'Runaway', Del Shannon. Here you are Malc; and that was it. It was Number One in America as well so then I had to phone London Records here. Funnily enough if I had known what I knew three or four years later I would have gone in the studio and covered 'Runaway'. No question I would have done it. But then I was just a kid and didn't know what was going on anyway. It was the beginning, that was the beginning of Rock and Roll, because they had 'Blue Suede Shoes' and stuff like that; but we never realised it was happening. We never realised it was happening. 'Rock Around the Clock' just meant nothing to me. In fact I was almost disgusted that people were tearing cinemas up. We never realised it was happening.

Then I met my hero, who is a man called Bobby Pratt who was the lead trumpet player with the Ted Heath Band, and he said: what do you want to be a trumpet player for? Carry on doing that plugging business. You had to go round to Aeolian Hall at the BBC and we had to kind of bung the doorman, give him half-a-crown, because you weren't supposed to go in, were you, pluggers!

DAVID KASSNER,
Music Publisher

Because things were quite tough in England after the war, the land of opportunity was America for sure; all the exciting music was coming from there.

England had also been influenced by the American GI's and so forth, so there was real interest in American music and my father saw that as the opportunity. England was very flat and pretty exhausted by the war effort and first opportunity he got he took a boat out to America; by 1950 he had had I think seven hits. He would take English songs to America, and American songs back to England. He said look, what have you got, I could take it back, let me work on it for you; and he started to do the cross Transatlantic trade, opening an office in New York in around 1952 or '53.

In 1953 a guy called Jimmy Myers came into his office with this song; he was a big American, I don't know if he was a Marine but he was what they call a grunt. In more modern parlance he was an American GI; big guy, smoking a cigar. He said look, you've got to take this song, 'Rock Around The Clock', it's the greatest song, it's going to be a huge hit. My father heard it and everything was ballads in those days, it was a different era, and the guy was very persistent and my father, as he told it, just to get rid of him said: I'll give you $250 and just get out of here. So he took this song from him for the world outside of the US. A year later it was in that film *Blackboard Jungle*, and changed the whole face of everything.

Jimmy Myers was quite a character. He wasn't a great songwriter by any means but he was a hustler; he was a very determined guy and he believed in the power of PR. Subsequently you hear of different stories; apparently it was the son of the film's producer that loved this song and wanted it in the film. The story goes that they had a recording session booked; I think the guys arrived late. They spent only a two hour session I think; they lost the first hour because of a late arrival I think, and they worked the whole session on the 'A' side, which was 'Thirteen Women', and Jimmy said well what about my song, what about my song? Then in the last single take they put down 'Rock Around the Clock', and they didn't have time to get the balance quite right, so it had a little bit of distortion, and it just had magic.

CLEM CATTINI, Musician

I suppose the first Rock and Roll record was 'All Shook Up' by Elvis Presley, because basically I'm a Rock and Roll freak if you know what I mean. I like Rock and Roll; it showed me a good living. How did I become a drummer? The real honest truth is, I went there with some friends of mine who played guitar, a guy called Terry Kennedy, who eventually produced Donovan, he was a guitar player, and another mate of mine was a guitar player, and after we went to see *Blackboard Jungle*, and 'Rock Around the Clock', they decided let's form a Rock and Roll group. I said all right then; what do I play? They said: well you play drums; I went, okay then. So that was it; the start of it.

I played washboard and stuff like that in those days, and it started from there. I bought myself a drum kit for £20, all bits and pieces people had slung out, a snare drum, which was worth about a fiver or something. That's how it all started. I never ever really thought I'd make a career of playing. Then I suddenly thought, I like this, this is nice, so I started practising a lot. I was very lucky because I was only young, and most of the guys my age then went in the army. I didn't go in because I was Grade 4B. The first band, the first group was Terry Kennedy's Rock and Rollers, was a guy on tea chest bass, originally, then we had the two guitars and I played washboard and drums. Skiffle started I think because people couldn't afford instruments, so it was a cheap way of making music, tea chest bass, broomstick handle and string and all that;

it's quite effective. Lonnie was one of the starters of it all wasn't he, although they called it Skiffle. I think really I was looking at it as towards Country Rock rather than Skiffle. But it was just called Skiffle; they have to have boxes don't they, oh, that's Skiffle, that's Rock, that's Jazz, that's this, you know. They like to put you in boxes for some reason.

I was playing in The 2i's as well; we all were, Terry Kennedy and all of us went down there. We were like one of the groups who played in The 2i's itself. By this time I'd got a drum kit, although only a cheap one. That was it; it was where myself, Brian Bennett, all the guys in The Shadows, Bruce Welch, Hank Marvin, and all that lot, and Tony Meehan, that's where we all virtually met, in The 2i's. Then, the guy that owned The 2i's opened another club in Gerrard Street, called The New 2i's. He had both of them going; it was like a club. We were playing in there and this agent called Hyman Zahl, I never forget his name, right my boy, going to make you stars, and all this and he said: would we do a tour with Max Wall, believe it or not. Max was doing a skit of Bill Haley, he had the jacket on and the kiss curl and all that, so we went out on tour with him, and we did our own spot. We didn't realise then the potential we had, if we'd have known, because the place was packed and all they came to see was the Rock and Roll group. I felt sorry for Max because he used to get booed; it was a shame because he was a great artist.

It sort of went on from there. We finished the tour, nine-months tour of all the theatres, because in those days you could play a theatre every week; we did for nine months and we never played the same theatre twice. You weren't allowed to play the same theatre within the nine-month period.

MICK GROVES,
Musician

I went to the Teacher Training College when I was eighteen; I'd failed my army medical because they said I was going deaf, strange then that I then went into music. They had a Jazz band and I was mad about Jazz then; I used to listen to The Saints in Manchester. They said there was a Jazz band at College, and when I got there it had been disbanded but they put me onto the guy who used to run it and it was Tony Davies. He was then 6'7, with a big red beard, and he said: No, I'm not doing that any more, but my fiancé and I are doing weekends at the Mersey City Jazz Club in Liverpool and we do Ken Colyer-type Skiffle stuff, not Lonnie Donegan stuff. I said: do you need anybody to help out? He said: Well, we badly need a washboard player. So I got a washboard and started playing and the Skiffle thing happened, we were called the Gin Mill Skiffle Group. We were joined by a bass player and we did all the Skiffle stuff round the Liverpool area and became quite famous. We actually did the Empire Theatre and the Palace Theatre Manchester with The Squadronaires. We were playing the interval, sort of the little interlude band, because we were quite famous in the northwest then. By then I was playing guitar and singing Lonnie Donegan stuff, but when we first started doing gigs and I was on washboard, Tony said: You have to join the Union, so I joined the Musicians' Union, and I still have, amongst this pile of stuff that I've got, a letter from Hardy Amies, who was boss of the Musicians' Union, welcoming me into the Union and saying they didn't think they'd find a lot of work for us and there really was a good washboard player in London called Bill Brighton. So I quickly gave up the washboard and Tony taught me a few chords and started playing and singing Skiffle stuff mainly. I did all the popular Pop stuff, and Tony did all the hard, Bluesy stuff, the Ken Colyer. Tony had a guitar and I bought one; there was a lovely fellow in Liverpool who used to take in guitars from the ships, a lot of Liverpool lads going to America were bringing good guitars back. His main work was doing violins for kids at schools and that.

The first real guitar I bought was a Gretsch dance band guitar, and that didn't last long. As Skiffle went on I then started playing better instruments in that I managed to save some money; I'd started teaching by then, and I bought myself a Gibson guitar. I bought it in 1962 in Rushworth & Dreaper in Liverpool, sadly they're demised now as a music shop, they had imported two into Liverpool; one was this one I've bought and the other one was a similar guitar, a Gibson, with a pick-up, and that was bought by John Lennon. I see now that Gibson are calling it the John Lennon Gibson guitar.

I started Skiffling in 1956, it was '57 I moved to Liverpool to start teaching, and I had my 21st birthday at the Cavern Club, which was then like a Jazz club really, it wasn't a Beat club, it was a Jazz club set up by Alan Sytner. It was quite funny because my family came down from Salford in a double-decker Salford bus, down Matthew Street, and I don't know if you've been there but it's a very narrow street, and they came tottering off this Salford bus down into the depths of this cellar, thinking they were going to some kind of drug or drink den, and found they couldn't even get a drink. Well, they could, because Alan allowed a little leeway for my birthday and if they went up to the counter and said: can I have a coke and, wink, I'm with Mick wink, and then they'd either get a whisky, gin or whatever they wanted in the cup; that was good.

What happened then of course, a lot of people came into the Jazz clubs in those days and one of them was a visiting Blues guy called Redd Sullivan, who was well-known on the London scene singing London songs and stuff. He was a stoker on the Elder Dempster line I think. Redd said to us: what are you guys doing singing all these American songs when you're English and you've got all your own stuff here? We said: what do you mean all our own stuff? Well he started talking to us about shanties and sea songs, and of course we all knew Maggie May because that was still current in Liverpool as a song that was sung in the pubs and that. So we just went from there, and in 1964 we actually bit the bullet and went full time professional as The Spinners. We had six months wages in the bank that would pay us actually a bit more than I was getting as a teacher then, which when I started it was £56 a month; I think it must have been about £80 or £90 a month and we had enough in the bank to give us £100 a month, each of us, for six months, and we'd have to take it from there.

SHIRLEY COLLINS,
Singer

There was the Folk Cellar, the Skiffle Cellar, where you could go and hear, what to me was fairly ghastly Skiffle. There was the Folk And Blues club, and there was The Cranbourne. I cannot remember honestly the names of them all; they've all blurred into one really. I remember my mum being very worried because I was going into coffee houses, you know, dangerous places then! I don't know what she thinks when she walks past Starbucks nowadays.

But I can remember one night, because I always wanted to go and hear Folk song, I wasn't interested in Skiffle. I didn't want to go and watch people rubbing away at washboards, and I didn't like their music. I didn't like Lonnie Donegan, because I knew by then that he didn't write those songs. The songs he was singing came from Leadbelly, and he was claiming copyright on them and I knew that was wrong, and I just thought it was appalling. Then the way he sang it was all so fast, and it was exciting and everybody loved it but I didn't, and I felt quite outside the whole thing. To such an extent that one night when I went to one club, it might have been at the Hungry Eye, where Martin Winsor and Redd Sullivan used to sing, and it had a poster outside saying Folk, Blues and Skiffle, and I went in for an evening and there wasn't any Folk, or Blues either; it was all Skiffle, and I got my lipstick out and crossed out 'Folk' on the poster. Martin Winsor caught me and said: if you do that again you'll get knifed and he got his knife out, dangerous bloke. So perhaps my mum was right about not going into Skiffle Cellars or coffee bars.

That's where you heard people like Bob Dylan who came over for the first time and sang there; he was allowed to play a couple of songs and didn't go down very well because we all loved Ramblin' Jack Elliot from the States, a cowboy singer complete with cowboy hat, laconic speech, really attractive. We liked his music and we thought Bob Dylan was just a lesser Ramblin' Jack, you know, so he wasn't too successful.

I also sang on a concert with Paul Simon when he came over in his early days, when he was bottom of the bill at the De La Warr

Pavilion in Bexhill-on-Sea. I was called 'Shirley Collins, Britain's versatile young instrumentalist'; I could play three or four chords on a banjo and guitar, but Paul Simon was bottom of the bill. I didn't think much of him, and I didn't reckon he'd do very well.

I did go to Muddy Waters concerts, and I saw Memphis Slim and Sonny Terry and Brownie McGhee; just wonderful performers, and good music as well. Of course they were all very big in Paris as well. There was a huge Blues movement over there and so all those musicians were doing awfully well. The thing about being a Folk artist is that you never make any money unless you're Joan Baez or Julie Felix.

BILL LEADER,
Engineer / Producer

There's always been a gramophone in the house, one of those that made Britain what it was at the time, fit and healthy. Because every three minutes you walked across the room and you wound up, and you walked back three minutes later and did the same thing again. It was better than the gym really. That's why we won the Second World War, because we had wind-up gramophones, I'm sure. That's why the nation's gone to pot, because you put on a record and you slump on the sofa. Anyway, I had a splendid HMV cabinet-style wind-up gramophone with my mum's record collection. My mum was deeply into light music, so I was brought up on Gilbert & Sullivan and that sort of thing. I had a bit of a geekish, that's not a word we used at that time, interest in records as artefacts I suppose, and music as a product of the artefacts. I don't know how that somehow transpired into this fantasy of being a sound man in a studio.

Then I left school, mother and father were both working-class background, father was a factory worker, and my mother was too during the War; and at this time we were living in the outskirts of Bradford, so when I came to leave school I said: I want to do something in sound recording. There wasn't very much happening in Shipley at that time in sound recording, and there still isn't actually, but I thought, I'd really like to get into this. I'm not technical, I'm useless with a soldering iron, I'm not particularly technical, but I do have this sort of warmth towards music in its creation. I mean, I don't play an instrument for instance. There's nothing justifies what I've been doing for the last sixty years at all. I've been doing it, muddling my way through as best I can. But this was '55 when I arrived in London, and for me the Sixties started at that point; it started for me in '55. The big thing in the section that I was involved in was Ewan MacColl, the A.L. Lloyd led thing, it was left-wing; it was the people's music. MacColl and the WMA had published industrial songs; A.L. Lloyd had brought out a book about coal mining songs and things like that that he'd collected, without leaving Greenwich as far as I can work out, but that's the time-honoured way of doing it. It was a time when Peter Kennedy at Cecil Sharp House was playing down that there was any sort of input from industrial workers, in fact denying it as far as we could understand.

In 1955, things were happening; Skiffle was happening, Elvis Presley was happening. Records were beginning to happen, long-playing records and the 45rpm were alive. When they started making records again in the Fifties they'd had to face the problem of purchase tax, which was at that time, it varied a little from budget to budget, but there were times when purchase tax was 70% of the retail price, on the retail price of the record. Records were very expensive items, deliberately so; purchase tax was a reflection of how much the government considered the thing was a luxury, and records were quite obviously entirely a luxury thing.

JACKIE LYNTON,
Singer

I think Billy Fury was as straight as a die, and I'm going to say that to anybody that asks me. I knew Billy for a couple of years, I loved him to death. Not a very well man; he was never very well, but what an act he was; he was fantastic. I used to stand there every night and I was absolutely amazed. I used to share a dressing room with him because Billy Fury was the only one that had a hotel room. But we all used to sleep in the coach, there was me, Shane Fenton, we all slept in the coach. We'd take the seats out and all sleep in the back; save the money, because we were getting £40 a week, and I was married at time, so I had to send some home. It never cost us.

Billy Fury had read one day that Marlon Brando used to have an egg in his turn-up, for no reason at all, Brando. You can imagine him, out of his head; you know, completely stoned. Billy read that and he went out one night with one too, it's funny now when you think about it. I told Larry Parnes, who said: What's he doing? I said: I dunno Larry; he's doing something, and we were all stunned. It wasn't funny; we just thought, what a wonderful thing, so stupid. He had an egg in his turn-up, an egg. He read that Marlon Brando did, so he thought that he'll do it. He's gone on stage and of course the egg fell out and the punters, well no-one laughed; no-one sort of said: oh dear, oh dear, look at that. They all thought, uh, oh. That was it, that was it. No-one bothered, no-one bothered and we were all sort of feeling for him, rather than going what an arse.

But the funniest thing I ever saw was Eden Kane. He's come on stage, he tried to do something different, so what he's done was, he's come on one of the big stages in those Granada Theatres. He said: What I'm going to do is I'm going to stand underneath the stage, on the platform that you wind up, and I'll come up like that. What a fantastic thing in those days; the kids, they go mental. We all had the make-up on, you all had to wear the make-up. If you didn't wear the make-up you couldn't see our face you know, because of those big massive lights. So we all had Max 21, or 28, or something. I loved it I did; that's that little gay thing coming out. I'm not gay but that's the thing, I loved it, loved looking at myself like that with the lipstick and all the business. He was an incredible looking man, Eden Kane. He said: you wind me up, and as it starts, I'm going to appear out of the centre of the stage, going up, going up, going up. Fantastic; we're all looking forward to this.

So it's come the night, Eden would close one act and Billy Fury would close the night, but he would close the first half. He'd have Joe Brown and Shane Fenton and all this. His act started with 'Be My Girl' I think it was called, Eden Kane. They got a bit of smoke, some geezer's winding it up; they've got dry ice and who knows what they've got blowing about, and the band's playing. Up he's come, the punters are going mental; he's come half way up and it stopped, it got clogged. The bloke downstairs is underneath the stage going spare. Now, you've got half of Eden Kane on the stage going mad! He's had to climb out, talk about an anti-climax, he's had to climb out of the hole in the middle of the stage. I couldn't believe it; he's scuffling about. He always used to wear a white suit; he looked fantastic, an amazing looking geezer. Of course we were all stunned. It's funny now but it wasn't then. It was horrible, and I felt for him; I thought you poor bastard. He had to scramble out, and stand there.

But Billy was gorgeous. We used to be making up in the mirror and he'd come behind you in the dressing room, he'd open the door and he brought a bow and arrow; he was a big child. I absolutely loved Billy Fury; he was a big kid, and he bought an arrow with a sucker, and he'd fire that at you and all that and you'd be trying to make yourself up and he'd go whap on your neck, and you couldn't turn around and be nasty. You'd turn around and go, 'alright Billy boy?'. He'd go: ha-ha-ha, and run off.

Screaming Lord Sutch pulled a wonderful stunt one day. He got me down by that lake in London, where they jump in, ice cold and all that, the Serpentine; he's got me down there for a stunt. I said: what are we going to do then? He said: get down here, this is going to get you off, we'll get the papers. Because the papers absolutely loved Screaming Lord Sutch, didn't they, they absolutely loved him. He was always up to something.

He said: what we're going to do, because we were both managed by Tom Little, he said: you jump in the river; I said: yeah, he said: you jump in, make out you're falling, I'll jump in and save you. Screaming Lord Sutch saves Jackie Lynton. We both got the thing, you're Jackie Lynton, you've got a record out at the moment; I'll get a photographer down there and we'll get the thing set up, there'll be no problem at all. I said: yeah but the only thing is, what I don't think you've thought about, I can't swim, which I can't to this day. He went: I never thought of that, nor can I. To my mind that was one of the amazing little sort of things really. It's not very important but it is to me. We packed all the gear up and went back home!

DEKE ARLON,
Singer

So we formed the group, The Tremors. I get a phone call one day from a guy; the first gig, Angmering Village Hall on Friday night, a shilling to get in, The Tremors. So a guy phones me up and he says, You can't be called The Tremors, you've got to be 'Something and The Tremors'; you can't be The Tremors. I said: what are you talking about?. He said: No, we've got to advertise it. There was a poster on the oak tree outside, a big crayon poster. Alright then. He said: You've got to come up with a name. I'd just seen Elvis's movie, *Loving You*, so I thought Deke Rivers, there's a great name. Deke Rivers. So I got the telephone directory out and being a lazy bastard I only got to the A's. That's it, Deke Arlon, fine, that's the name. So I phone up the village hall, I said right, it's 'Deke Arlon and The Tremors'. I tell you, I cycled by that oak tree fifty times to see my name in lights; there it was on this big poster in crayon, Deke Arlon and The Tremors, one shilling, Friday night, and off we went. But we became one of those top three groups down there, and we did great.

One day I'm on stage at the Top Hat, Littlehampton, shaking my legs and doing my Elvis, and in walks Lionel Bart, who has a penchant for pretty young men, and I was quite pretty. We got a chance to play in London at the Scala Theatre in a review with Flanders & Swann, and Charlie Drake. I go on stage and I think at the time I'm doing 'All Of Me', 'all of me, why don't you take all of me...', so I'm shaking the hips, I'm doing the wiggle, and a voice comes from the side of the stage, from prompt corner: Take one step back! So I take one step back, kids are screaming, and they dropped the safety curtain. Dropped the safety curtain on me while I'm doing it! We Don't Have That in our theatre, he said, this nice theatrical man.

Then I went to Holloway Road through Lionel Bart, who introduced me to the great Joe Meek, and Joe had a group there called The Off-Beats, and their lead singer was a guy called Ricky Wayne I think. Anyway he was a body builder, a black guy; I don't know how well he sang, I was never really told that but he did body things on stage, pumped his muscles. Anyway, Joe decided he couldn't make a record with this guy, but The Off-Beats were a fabulous group, and indeed they were; so it became Deke Arlon and The Off-Beats.

Joe Meek was wonderful; dear oh dear, the rhythm section was in the front room, I was in the bathroom and the string section, conducted by Charlie, was on the staircase. Charlie used to stand in the street, on the pavement in Holloway Road with his baton; they opened the front door and there were the string players. Never saw Joe of course; Joe was in his little room at the back with his two-track, his four-track; you never heard what he was doing. He never played it back to you, he just used to make you sing it again and again; you'd sing the song forty times and you didn't know why, but of course he knew what he was doing because he was a genius, and great to work with. You'd work there for ten hours non-stop, sing, sing. He'd come in with a box of ice creams: would anybody like a nice vanilla ice cream? We were living on ice creams and cups of tea!

MICHAEL COX,
Singer

The first thing I ever did was television. My sisters wrote in to *Oh Boy!* saying I could sing. I'd never sung professionally before, and I didn't know they'd written in. Well they had written in and said 'my brother', or 'our brother' can sing as good as any of those on the show. I didn't know this had happened and I got a letter from ABC Television addressed to me. My mum said: what's this? I said: I don't know; I don't know anyone at ABC Television. I opened this, and it said: Sir, you're requested to come down to London for an audition. Then the girls said: we wrote in. I said: well you can un-write; I don't want to be on TV. But if you've got four sisters after you it's very hard.

So anyway I did; I took the weekend off work and I came down to London. But I didn't even know what an audition was, I was green, completely green. It was Finsbury Park where we auditioned, and I went along in my best suit; didn't have a clue. There were singers with their own pianists, and groups and everything, and they're all doing the business. Jack Good called my name out, so I walked up. He said: What are you going to sing? I said, I don't know; what do you want me to sing? I said: I don't know many all the way through. Well anyway I knew a Pat Boone song, so I said I'll do that. He said: have you got any music? I said: No. He said: well no-one can play for you. I said: that's alright, I don't mind. Like an idiot; standing at the mic, no backing, nothing. I started to sing, and people were sort of looking, who's this idiot?

Anyway I finished it, and Jack Good said: Do you know any more? I said a few; he said: Sing some more. I didn't know it but he went round the back and put on a tape, because after one or two numbers he'd said to everyone: thank you very much, we'll let you know. He kept saying: sing some more, sing some more. I'm singing with no backing at all, and everyone is looking at me. I must have looked like an idiot. Anyway he said: wait around. So after the audition finished he said: get up and sing some more. So I sang some more and I'm thinking, I've got to get back to work; I've got to get the train back to work for Monday. So he said: Right, you're on Oh Boy! in a month's time. I went, you're mad. He replied: We'll be in touch. That was it.

MIKE HURST,
Musician

I wanted to be a Rock and Roll star; that's what you did. I turned up for the *Oh Boy!* audition with an acoustic guitar and I sang 'Blue Suede Shoes', and I think one other. That was that, and Jack Good just said, Jolly good, jolly good, come back when your voice has broken and developed properly. I thought, Oh God, I'm sixteen years old. But I met Eddie Cochran on the way up, which was incredible. It was Eddie Cochran. Yeah.

Wonderful innocence, because I also did a couple of the Shepherd's Bush Empire amateur Rock and Roll shows on Saturday afternoons, that tells you what it was like, afternoon, not evenings. You'd turn up for this at the Shepherd's Bush Empire and whichever band, Tom, Dick or Harry, they would be the backing band. Now, you turned up, but how do you know the backing band is going to play what you want to do in the first place? So you get there: Do you know this song? No. Do you know this one? Yes. Okay fine, let's do that one then! You're on the stage and the teenagers in the audience are going mad, just for the noise, because the noise value was just incredible. When you did a show like that you couldn't hear yourself think. There were no monitors, so everything was screaming out of the amplifiers behind you, you could hear nothing but yelling, screaming, and this cacophony of noise. So you staggered through it. The only yardstick you had, I was always told by the people there, was it all depends what they throw at you! I said: That's good. Sure enough they threw coins. Now, was that a sign of appreciation? I'm not sure, but when a halfpenny hits you on the side of the head it actually hurt; so I'm not sure it was appreciation. And the joke was, every singer that turned up to do this looked the same, me included. You wore what passed for a white jacket, because you knew Elvis wore them; but no-one in England could buy a white jacket in 1958, '59, so you had an oatmeal-y type tweedy jacket, with as dark a shirt as you could find, and some sort of medallion. Everyone looked the same, they all turned up like that; it was very funny.

£££

DAVID ARDEN,
Manager

For Rock and Roll, it definitely was Wee Willie Harris: because my dad Don Arden's first tour and my entree into Rock and Roll was Gene Vincent, and Wee Willie was one of the supporting acts. My mum came and picked me and my sister up from school, which was in Brixton Hill. I always remember it because it was, October, November, and it was a real London pea-souper that they used to have in those days, get on the bus, onto the tube at the Oval, up to Walthamstow. We get there, obviously for the first house, and it was half-empty because the weather was so bad and half the people couldn't get there. We walked in and there was Wee Willie in his leopard-skin leotard, bright red hair and boots and these white, skinny legs, running round the stage. I was used to the Met, Edgeware Road and all the dancing girls, and I saw that and I'm, mouth open, and he was one of my heroes. I don't like listening to his music to be honest but he was just such a character. So yes he was my first and then of course Gene Vincent, we went to meet Gene and for me he was the first of the great moody, nutty, Rock and Roll characters. I don't know if you know but Granada Theatres, they all had the same dressing rooms; they all had this emulsion cream paint, with green borders, and it was so stark. He was there, the old man's knocked on the door: Gene, I'd like you to meet my wife and son and daughter; and he was there chin in hand, and he's trying to raise a smile and he's all very moody. So I thought oh, I don't know what he's all about. But he came out and did his bit and it was like, Ooh! I wasn't sure what to make of him to be honest. But after that he became such a part of our lives. He taught me to swim – he did.

There are stories, you hear about things that were going on in the Seventies with Led Zeppelin, different people, Black Sabbath, you name it, but Gene was one of the first. I mean, I was used to all those stories, anything that anybody did in the Seventies I was like, Yeah? One night on Christmas Eve or Christmas Day, there's a phone call, because Gene had got an apartment up in Streatham, Leigham Court Road. Maggie, his English wife said: You've got to come, Gene is playing up, he's been rude to my mother and he's doing this, that and the other. So the old man gets up there and Gene's gone into one and he's insulting the mother-in-law, this one, that one, calling them a fucking whore and the like and it's all on Christmas Day. My dad had taken my older half-brother with him, Rickie, and Gene had one of these Chinese dressing gowns on apparently, I wasn't there, with the big sleeves, and he's gone up behind Rickie, my brother and he's got the carving knife, and he whispered: Don't move Rickie, don't move 'cos I'll stick you.

This is all on Christmas Day. Of course the old man has quietened everything down and he's come back down to join us for Christmas lunch, he says: Gene's all right now. The old man's peeing himself with laughter, so is my mum, it was all kind of part and parcel of the normal run of things. The next thing is the phone call comes through, the police have come, and they've arrested Gene because he knocked Maggie out with his crutch; he had a dodgy leg. He's knocked her out and he's thrown the poodle out the window of their second floor apartment. Fortunately it was snowing, so the dog survived, a little toy poodle. So that was the end of Christmas Day.

CHAS HODGES,
Musician

We went to Butlins Filey as Billy Gray and The Stormers, that summer season, in 1960. At the end of 1960 the band had virtually split up, and a couple of them got married. I got a knock at me front door round about November time, and there was this chap I had met, he was a manager of Danny Rivers, and he said: I've got another singer, called Mike Berry. I've just auditioned with him up at Joe Meek's, and he loves Mike Berry but he's not mad on his band. If I could get your band back together, he said, would you audition with Mike Berry? I didn't know who Joe Meek was then but I said yeah, I'm up for it. Of course he went around everybody's house, I don't think anybody was on the phone in those days, he actually knocked on all the doors and got them all together. We auditioned up at Joe Meek's and passed the audition and we became Joe Meek's house band from then on. The Outlaws; he named the band The Outlaws, and from 1961 till about 1965, different versions of The Outlaws became his house band.

I'd heard about tape editing but I didn't know really what it was. But I remember we did our very first single by The Outlaws, it was called 'Swinging Low', which was like the rocked-up version of 'Swing Low Sweet Chariot', and in amongst it, it had three breaks, one bass break, a drum break and a rhythm guitar break. Of course each 'take' we did, I'd do a real good bass bit that I was happy with, the drummer would mess his one up and the rhythm guitar was half and half; then the next 'take' would be a great drum break and my bass break weren't as good as the first one. Eventually we did about six 'takes' I think, and Joe Meek said: Okay, we've got it. I said: What take are you going to use, because my bass is... and the drummer was going; can you use take Two, and I'm saying; use take One. Joe went: Don't worry, you're all going to be happy, you're all going to have your favourite bits. I really thought, what's he talking about? I didn't know any better then. Joe, in the meantime, cut out my poor bass break and put in the best bass break and then cut out the worst drum break, cut out the worst rhythm guitar break, put it all together into the main 'take' and there it was. When we went back and heard the playback I was: How did you do it? and he showed me how. He said: you just put the tape over the heads, make a mark, cut the tape. So I started doing it with my old Elizabethan tape recorder at home, messing about. But yeah, that's a great memory of Joe; he taught me editing and it stayed with me.

DEREK LAWRENCE, Record Producer

There was always music on the radio as a kid. I remember my best mate Dave running down a hill, it was about 11 o'clock at night saying: Turn on the radio, turn on the radio, Luxembourg, which we used to call Radio Crackle, turn on Radio Crackle. I turned it on and I went, It's Mr and Mrs Smith's five little boys. He was: No, there was a bloke on called Elvis Presley, he's bloody brilliant.

Very soon I was into Rock and Roll big time; fifteen years old going into the local drill halls where there was all these horrible bands doing Rock and Roll, but that led me into R&B. My mate Dave was two years older than me so he got called up; I missed it by three months, thank you Lord. He was a toe rag so he ended up getting put in army prison, and he was there with some black American servicemen. So when he came home he was telling me about all these great records. You've got to get these records these blokes were telling me about, Boyd Bennett and his Rockets, Little Willie John, Big Mama Thornton, all those. So we would try and find these records. Somehow later I ended up in Harrow, I don't know whether I was working or chasing a woman, probably chasing a woman, but I met this group of boys, who were a group called Laurie Black and the Men of Mystery. Because I knew so much about music they were very impressed, so I ended up their manager: how or why or what a manager did I had no idea.

But it so happened two weeks later at Harrow Town Hall there was a talent competition, and Joe Meek was the judge, and Laurie Black and the Men of Mystery won the competition. So we end up going up Holloway Road; the funny thing is, I got to the address and I walked past it about eight times, because there was Shenton's the leather shop, and it was this little door on the side and I kept missing this little door.

Joe, I came to find out quickly, was not impressed with the group, and I asked, What do you want them to do? He replied: Well, you know more than they do, get rid of them and if you feel like coming back, come back. So for a while I started going back to Joe's, who I happen to believe made probably five or six of the best pop records ever made. Despite the abusive letters and phone calls I got, I still believe he also made some of the worst records ever made. But the great thing is I met Big Jim Sullivan, Ritchie Blackmore and Chas Hodges, who became the basis of my career.

Every now and again whilst working with Joe, you'd turn up, and he wouldn't answer his phone or open his door, so you went home. You got fed up with this after a while. I'd met Harold Shampan, so I called him in and he said: Well come up to the office, I'll pay you £8 a week, and I think the fares into Bond Street were like, £4 a week, whatever. But using his phone I got in touch with an American record producer called Jerry Ragovoy, who had produced Garnet Mimms and the Enchanters, 'Cry Baby', which was one of my favourite records. Well by this time I'm all into unknown American R&B records. He came over to London, I went round with him and Jerry said: Look, Garnet Mimms is coming over; will you be a friendly face for him? So for some other reason or another I went to EMI and said: Look, can I do a live album with Garnet Mimms? He was being backed by a Scottish band called The Senate and we end up doing this live album. I did it with Dave Paramor, Norrie Paramor's son. It was live; we did it in Sussex University and a club in Newcastle with the PYE Outside Recording truck. We did that, it came out and sold nothing.

I had met a guy called Tony Wilson who was with Errol Brown in Hot Chocolate. I did five demos with them, which became copied, and became the first five singles on RAK records. But before that, they'd come to me and said: 'Give Peace a Chance'. I said: Yeah? Well, they said: We've done a new version of it; would you come in the studio with us? So I went in the studio with Tony and we kind of co-produced it, but they changed all the lyrics. I went: You can't do that. I'm sorry, you can't do that. Change Beatles lyrics? What are you on?

I'd met this guy in the pub, Tony Bramwell, who worked for The Beatles, so I said: I've got this Reggae version of 'Give Peace a Chance' and the lyrics have been changed. He said: Come over. So I go over to Savile Row and he takes me in to meet John Lennon. John and Yoko are sitting there, anti-animal whatever, sitting there in black leather cowboy hats and boots. So we play it, and he went: No, we can't have that, well unless it's on Apple Records. So that's how it came out on Apple Records. Then I get a call from Tony Bramwell who says Terry Doran wants to meet you. I said: Who's Terry Doran? So I go up and meet Terry, he's a really nice guy. He said: I've got this band, Grapefruit, would you produce that for Apple Productions? We've had a hit with 'Elevator' produced by Terry Melcher, Doris Day's son, but he's too busy doing whatever. So I ended up doing 'Come On Marianne', which was the next single, which just got in the top 20, and about five tracks on the album, for Apple.

MARTIN LEWIS, Press Officer

My first foray and how I got to know some of the publicists was that in 1968 or 1969, wanting a short cut to getting free records and seeing movies, so I invented a student magazine that didn't exist. The magazine was called *Fall Out*, nuclear, radio-active, I thought it would be a cute name, and I was Paul Klein, I thought it all sounded plausible. Paul Klein and the *Fall Out* magazine were soon on the main list for every record company, and I got sent free records. I found an easy way to get through because you'd phone them up and you'd bore them endlessly on the phone and say: Did you read my review of the Moody Blues? – rather than just ask for free records. They would say: Oh, yeah, yeah, when of course they just want to get you off the line as fast as possible. So I was doing really well until Vernon Brewer, who was the Press Officer at Track Records, phoned me up one day and said: We've got a very exciting project, we want you to come into the office to talk about it. I went in there and he said: You're not Paul Klein, you are Martin Lewis. We know who you are. I was exposed. I said: Oh my God, am I going to be arrested? He said: We're not going to say a thing because we don't want people to know how stupid we were that we were taken in by a fifteen year old kid.

Later on the people at Warner Brothers, WEA, Annie Idle, Moira Bellas invited me to become the press office writer, and they wanted people, as they explained it to me, to write press releases and write biographies of artists. Well since I was obviously capable with words that would be a proper job unlike my freelance jobs where it was £5 here, £5 there. This would be a paying job, I would be in the music business. Plus Derek Taylor was working there. He was a legend. I'd been to the Apple offices in late '68, '69; I'd gone into those offices. So to me this was the hallowed person, because he wrote so eloquently, he was erudite, he was sophisticated, he was witty. His writing when he wrote for Disc magazine was beautiful. I just knew who he was and I wanted to be near him. As a consequence of which, once I'd worked there and his office was very close to the press office, I spent all my time there. I was sat at his feet listening to his stories whenever I could. I managed to get my work done but I wasn't interested in the press office, I wanted to be around Derek Taylor.

He introduced me to Nat Joseph, the head of Transatlantic Records. Derek Taylor was a mentor to me and wonderful, warm, generous, and stayed a friend until he passed away in '97. So I was introduced to Nathan Joseph: Transatlantic Records, it was a small indie label. Now, that means nothing today when indie labels are everywhere, but in 1973 there weren't independent labels. There were a couple of Folk labels like Topic, but there weren't independent record companies. Transatlantic Records was an idiosyncratic maverick company. It was formed in 1961 by this guy, Nat Joseph, who was a Cambridge graduate, went to America and saw Folk music and Jazz and Blues, and was fascinated. These days of course we call it Roots, but they hadn't even used the word then, but it was the roots of the music, it was Folk, Jazz, Blues. He saw that there were all these great artists and he came back to England and realised he couldn't get any of these here. He'd bought a load of records while he was there and he suddenly thought, this music is fascinating, and there was the beginning of a Folk boom here in England. Between 1961 and the time I met him, he'd set up what was an amazing company, because it wasn't just easily the best Folk company in Britain. He signed Bert Jansch, John Renbourn, Pentangle, Ralph McTell, and many other artists. It wasn't just that, but he also went for the unusual. He signed the Sallyangie, which was Mike Oldfield and his sister Sally, he signed Gerry Rafferty and Billy Connolly when they were in a Folk group called The Humblebums. He had an eye and an ear for talent and he didn't care if they were going to have hit singles. Of course he wanted hit singles but he didn't care if he didn't get them. That wasn't the raison d'être.

It was around the beginning of the 'albums' time so he knew that there were albums to be sold, so most of all he was interested in the music that he liked and he was passionate about. If it wasn't something he was passionate about but somebody else in the company was, he'd be open to that too, but he was interested in passion. He figured if some people were passionate about it, then there'll be others passionate about it. But he'd rather have something that people believe in rather than just sign twenty Pop singers and just record them and try and hope for a hit single.

I didn't want to be a press officer; I wanted to do what Derek Taylor had done. I wanted to see the whole picture of an artist, only have three or four artists to work on at a time instead of working on a roster of twenty. I didn't like the idea of that. I liked the idea of picking just those artists and then being involved in everything. Nat Joseph was savvy enough to realise that controversial things would also grab attention. He signed The Fugs and released The Fugs in England. He signed Mick Farren and The Deviants, who were I guess the British equivalent of Iggy Pop, they were proto Punk. We put out the 'Uncle Meat' album by Mothers of Invention, Frank Zappa. Warner Brothers didn't want to put that out in England; it was considered too risqué. Nat Joseph did the deal to put out Lenny Bruce, nobody wanted to handle the Lenny Bruce stuff. So we were doing some amazing recordings. Transatlantic was an independent record company; it had its own distribution, own pressing and its own distribution.

The later record labels modelled themselves on Transatlantic. Chris Blackwell claims Island Records was around from 1959 or '61 or '62. Island Records was a production company doing a few little Reggae records, or Blue Beat records, until '67 when it was a proper record label. Before then it was a production company. All the Spencer Davis stuff, Millie, were licensed to Fontana, they were not released on Island Records.

On one occasion I remember that one van rep had no less than three vans broken into and emptied out, and we couldn't figure out at first but we finally twigged it, because records were being taken that nobody wanted to buy even if they were on budget. We realised that this guy just simply couldn't sell records and it was easier for him to get a friend to break into his van, and report it as stolen, so then he could clear out his inventory and not have to try and flog this dreadful stuff that he couldn't sell.

£££

MICK McDONAGH, Manager

My sister's a fashion designer in Toronto and I'd go to stay in Canada quite a lot, or America; I'd been all round America. So this was 1969 and my idea was to take some of these bands on the Underground scene, to take bands and Folk singers and people like Ralph McTell and set them up in America, and do tours of the coffee circuit in America. I'd worked in America through summer and I'd done things like roadying for Sonny Terry and Brownie McGhee; well the only thing I really knew was to do PR. So I started to do PR for Ralph and for Christy Moore. I started doing that from the flat in Camden Town, just trying to do a bit of PR, and in the process I'd heard of The Humblebums, which was Billy Connolly and Gerry Rafferty. We put on the first ever Humblebums concert in London, because Transatlantic had The Humblebums and that was December 19th, 1969 and it snowed like hell and there was probably more people at the end of the gig on the stage in the band than there were in the audience; but that started the first bit of The Humblebums' notoriety in London. Out of that Nat Joseph, who owned Transatlantic, saw the job that I'd done and then approached me, and so in the January I was given the gig of 'managing' for £8 a week The Humblebums, while they got £11 a week each and moved to London. Then we started a couple of years of really trying to build them.

Billy Connolly has told the story of why I got the gig. I'd like to have thought I got it because I'd done a really good job of promoting them. But seemingly it was because I was late. Well if you come from Manchester you don't really know London, so you look at that graphic tube map and you think, where's closest. I was trying to go to be interviewed in Marylebone Lane, and I got the wrong tube and I went to Bond Street and it was a much further walk than I thought. So I was running up Marylebone Lane and Nat Joseph had picked Billy and Gerry up from the station at Euston, they'd come down from Scotland, and they went past me in a taxi. Nat pointed out of the window and said: There's Mick, he's one of the guys we're interviewing. Apparently Billy Connolly said: He's the man for me; he's keen. So I got the gig, and I had a fantastic time with Billy and Gerry. But it gets kind of lobotomised and re-written because now Billy is so huge as a comedian and Gerry became Stealer's Wheel and Gerry Rafferty, but that period of The Humblebums at Transatlantic was actually quite fun and they were getting really good press. Ed Bicknell booked them into Eton; we did a gig at Eton, which is very funny, and that's when Billy first was showing signs of his fantastic comedic ability and I just wonder what leaders of our nation were in that audience watching Billy Connolly and Gerry Rafferty.

So Nat brought me in as Head of Press and Promotion, and that was a good period, we were still working on The Humblebums but we were doing press and promo, I then had a proper job. I don't think I got that much more than £8 a week; I've still got the contract somewhere, but I got some money. I got stitched by Nat I suppose, because the idea was that when they got big and famous and it all happened, I would have a piece of the management contract. That's one of the reasons I think, and I was so stupid now with hindsight, that I think he gave me the full time job, because when they look like they're about to break, and Nat still owned their managing contract. He kind of gave me the full time job and then ripped up our management deal. Then of course later when Gerry was solo, and we did this Gerry Rafferty solo album 'Can I Have My Money Back' when that all happened, and Gerry went on, I think Nat sold the runt to his management contract to Robert Wace. He probably made some money out of that and I didn't participate in this. But that was par for the course; I've always been absolutely useless at making money but just had a lot of fun in the process.

You've got to give it to Nat Joseph, he was a fantastic discoverer of talent. He had Mike and Sally Oldfield who were the Sallyangie, he had all Bert Jansch, he had John Renbourn, he had all these people. He was really good at finding them but then there was always that kind of thing where it just stopped short, I always felt. I lived in a little flat in Camden Town where Billy Connolly and Gerry used to come and sleep on the floor, and the flat just diagonally across into Camden Square was where Bill Leader recorded all those albums on a Revox, which some of them are still selling now, you know the Bert

Jansch albums, the John Renbourn albums. I think for the first Bert Jansch album, the total package budget was about £108 including the sleeve. God knows how many albums it sold over the years because it influenced Eric Clapton, it influenced Jimmy Page, it influenced so many people.

JOHN COOPER, Transatlantic Records Salesman

I started my working life in the first couple of years as a butcher; I couldn't figure anything else to do in the days before real university and all the rest of it. But I was working as a DJ at the time, in the early days of DJ, mostly with a single deck and a speaker; I worked the scene and the scene clubs, and various other things. I was doing that at night and mixing music at night, working on a Saturday in a record shop in Hampstead, and indeed that turned out to be a Sunday too, illegally as well.

At the same time I was paying my way by doing a job. I then decided this was nonsense; I didn't want to do this, and the shop was owned by a guy called Nat Joseph who had a little record company in the basement. I decided that he was useless at doing most things anyway, so I decided I'd just go out one day and sell some records for him. I sold a whole bunch of records; I can't remember how many he was up to then, he was probably up to maybe ten releases. The biggest seller was a series called 'Live With Love', which was how to make love. Actually I never listened to it at the time and I'd love to listen to it now. But it got him going, and I went out and sold lots more records by just going round some record shops in my spare time than he'd sold himself up to date. I went in with these orders and bartered with him to give me a job as a salesman. He had a sales manager as it happened; they'd newly moved from Hampstead down into Marylebone and were beginning to make some waves with Folk. They had Alex

Campbell and The Campbells and some other bits and pieces. So I wouldn't give him the orders until he gave me a job; so he gave me a commission-only job, the bastard.

I had no idea what I was doing. I had an old van, I drove around the country; I didn't know about claiming for petrol or anything else, and until I built up enough orders there,I probably had more on him than he had on me. So I then withheld the orders until I got some proper money and began to establish myself, and understand a little bit how businesses are run.

Part of the secret with Nat Joseph was he came in to the business at the point where we all knew bugger all. The music industry as we know it today was relatively new, none of us knew anything; we were just very pleased to be in the music business, we would have done it for nothing and he quite well knew that. Of course right until the end he gave no-one anything, paid minimum wages and basked in the glory of everyone else working twenty-four hours a day, which was fine. Everybody understood it until you've got to move on and you realise that you've lined his pockets and done very well for the man over the years.

Then he began to change distribution to Selecta, but by that time I was on board so was doing more of the sales directly; I would actually go out on a Monday morning, and by that time I'd got an old company van, I'd fill it up with albums and I would actually go out round the country and come back on a Friday having sold whatever I could sell. My sales were fairly soon outselling whatever could be done through a distributor, and in fairness to him we actually went to self-distribution fairly quickly there because it was clear we were outselling any of the smaller players. Then we went to van sale; by that time we'd built up a sales force of probably ten people in vans around the country. It was a very draconian way of doing things as well because I used to have them all into the office at the end of every month from wherever the hell they were living for a sales meeting. They stayed overnight in the cheapest hotel that we could possibly find. Which turned out, as I found out much later, to be a knocking shop for Transatlantic reps; but hey, it was hippie times really. But by that time we'd built up a very strong self-distribution. I can remember with some pride him saying well we've just passed the million mark.

You walked into a record shop, if you wanted to get your stock into a record shop, you had to invent a way of getting it in there, otherwise the dealer would heave you out the door. My worse battles as a rep for Transatlantic were with the major record companies. I was standing in a record shop in Bristol, presenting in the normal way. I was dressed in jeans and had long hair; it was modern day rep, for all intents and purposes. I get a tap on the shoulder and behind me is a man in a suit and trilby hat and a big case who said: You, out. I looked at this person and said: What do you mean, me out? and he said: I'm the Decca rep, I'm in here. I said: You, fuck off. He tried to manhandle me outside to deck me. I mean, they were driving Ford Cortina's and we were still going round in Mini vans.

LLOYD BEINY, B&C Records Promotion Man

It was the early Seventies and I'm still at Booze and Corruption Records and I'd risen to the lofty heights of Promotion Man. The record business was really in its infancy even though it was early Seventies; the kind of obvious marketing that was done later on and today, wasn't obvious in those days, we were making it up as we went along.

We really didn't know what to do; well B&C didn't, but part of my job was to go on ahead of tours. Normally if a tour was playing on a Tuesday night in Blackpool, I'd get there Tuesday morning, go round the shops, put posters up, make sure they had stock of the product, and blah, blah, blah. So this particular tour was Genesis with Peter Gabriel, Lindisfarne, and Van der Graaf Generator all on Charisma Records, and they were doing mainly colleges I think at that time. It had a name, the Six Bob tour; it was one of Tony Stratton-Smith's lines; you saw three top acts for threepence or something. The tour was going round the country and then it hit London; they were playing at the Lyceum.

I'd done what I had to do during the day, been round all the shops and made sure the posters were up, and then headed over to the gig. As the record company paid me so little, I thought there's going to be thousands of people here who are interested in Genesis, Lindisfarne and Van Der Graaf Generator; this is before merchandising became a massive business. Well in the back of my car I've got hundreds and hundreds of posters saying 'Genesis', 'Lindisfarne' and 'Van Der Graaf Generator', and I thought surely someone might want to buy one for a shilling each or something. So at each gig I'd set up a stall in the foyer with the three posters for the three bands and I was making decent money, ripping the posters off from the record company as you do.

Actually the record company would probably be quite pleased about it because those posters were going up in student dorms etc, and at the end of the night I'd walk away with a tenner, or however much it was. We were doing the Lyceum, and the man who was head of B&C Records, a chap called Lee Gopthall, who's now unfortunately passed away, decides to come along to the gig with his young son, who was ten or something. Now the arrangement between Charisma Records and B&C was that B&C did all the sales and marketing, therefore B&C had paid for all of the posters.

So I'm standing there in the foyer of the Lyceum with the posters of the three bands that had been paid for by B&C Records. The Managing Director of B&C Records now walks in with his son, and he comes over to me, and I thought, Oh my God, this is it, I get the sack, I'm out of the music business forever, it's been fun but bye, bye.

He strolls up to me and he goes: Lloyd, how much are these posters? I said: well you know Lee, they're going for a shilling each. He said: give me two Lindisfarne's, a Van Der Graaf and four Genesis. Is that okay young Johnny? So he's buying from me the posters that he'd paid for, which I thought was A-OK

TONY McGROGAN,
Pye Records Salesman

They said: It's Pye Records in Mitcham, and I used to live just round the corner in Mitcham. They're looking for van salesmen; you just take all the records round in the van and you go to shops and sell them. So I took the job and did that for Pye for three or four years. That record company then, was amazing, unbelievable, they had all The Searchers stuff to come out, and they were all Number Ones: Petula Clark; Frank Sinatra's 'My Way'; Lovin' Spoonful; Status Quo. When you talk about records then, to get it to Number One you had to sell literally 100,000 a day. Well we used to drive these sales vans, if you've ever seen in the back of them, they were racked and all slotted with albums, and then you had the singles. What you did was, you put all the boxes of twenty-five singles in the middle of the gangway. We got so successful that we used to drive those vans out and you couldn't see the wing mirror on the near side because you had boxes inside your cab. It was massive. Of course, in those days there was no computers; so stock checks, you had to write everything by hand. Well you can imagine, can't you; it didn't take too long before people sussed out...

I mean, the stock checks were ridiculous because if you had a van and I had a van, I'd say to you; you help me do my stock check and I'll help you do yours. Well we were mates, and if you didn't know what you were doing, you just put down wrong numbers. In the end it was just a competition, sell, sell, sell. Each week there was top salesmen. You did things like swapping boxes of records with the record shop guys. The guys said: Look, I bought a hundred of those last week, I've got twenty-five over, would you change them for something else? You did it because you knew you were going to get a good order out of it next time. If you said, No, then you were not going to get on so well. But at 3 o'clock in the afternoon you had to ring your order for the next day. If you didn't, obviously you didn't get your records picked; so then you had to guess how much you were going to need for the next day. As I say, it was just madness, absolute madness. You just couldn't get the stock on and off the vans quick enough.

JOHN PEARSON,
Island Record Sales

Clive hired a guy called Graham Mabbutt to run production who used to be at Magnet Records, and was a bit of a train spotter type. He came from Northampton, and when Clive hired him, he didn't want to give him a flash car. Happenstance, I spotted him on the M1 in a Metro so I said to Clive: Offer him a Metro. So he did and he went, Oh yes, can I have a Metro, can I have an MG Metro? So he got this MG Metro and he'd started, and it was just about the days when computers were arriving, and I spotted in a meeting, he was writing down his production figures in a little logbook, so many sleeves, so many labels, so many vinyl. Then I spotted 62mpg. So from Northampton and back he's writing down his miles per gallon. Well I got his petrol cap key off the service manager, and a jerry can, and we started filling him up every day, topping up Graham Mabbutt. About six of us at the back of the office would watch him leave every day and he'd get into his Metro and tap the dashboard, he couldn't believe it.

After about a week-and-a-half, maybe two weeks, we're in a meeting and Graham's looking at me. What's wrong Graham? He says: My Metro. Well, what is it? He says: It's doing 200 to the gallon. I said: Don't be an arse, you've lost it. So we got it up to 300 to the gallon the following week, and he rang British Leyland and said with absolute certainty that he had a Metro doing 300 miles to the gallon. By this time there was six of us out the back every night trying to hold our stomachs as he left for Northampton. Then after four weeks we drained everything out, bar half-a-gallon and he ran out at Milton Keynes on the way home. To this day he still doesn't know why that Metro was doing 300 miles to the gallon. But these sort of things were quite the norm then. It was such a fun environment that you'd find people would do whatever necessary to get the job done but at the same time have fun. I hope he never sees this because he still doesn't know what happened.

JOHN KNOWLES, Island Records Salesman

I was working in America, in San Francisco; I was selling Life Insurance and I met a guy from EMI, called Fred Cantrell, who'd won a trip there. He was the label manager for Tamla Motown, and we went on the piss for two weeks, got absolutely hammered. He said to me, if ever I'm back in England and I wanted a job, he was going to Island Records as a sales manager. He said if I came to see him he'd give me a job.

So about eighteen months later I came back to England, I went and called on this guy Fred Cantrell; he remembered me and he gave me a job. The job was West Indian Sales Van Rep with a Ford Cortina. It was all pre-releases from Jamaica, and I had to go to Brixton Market, terrified, and sell them the pre-releases from Jamaica. I had to go to Wolverhampton, I had to go to Derby, and my job was all cash, none of them had accounts. It was all Chris Blackwell's favourite records from Jamaica that he wanted to promote here.

I'd go to the hairdressers in Brixton market where they sold pre-releases, and a guy would be there with his foot in the back of someone's head, trying to straighten it out, and then he'd go: Yeah, man. I'd have the records and he'd give me the cash, and I'd give him the records. Then I'd go to Wolverhampton; it was a shop called Sir Christopher, and if I got there after the geezer with the ganja arrived, he say: No John, can't buy no record. If I got there before, he'd buy the records off me. But sometimes I used to go there and the door would be open and there'd be nobody there but this guy would be asleep on the floor. The ganja man had been there and he'd be totally out of it. So my job was West Indian Sales Van Rep, and I did that for about eighteen months. It was fantastic; just a wonderful experience.

All the Dub records, all the early Marley records, anything that was hot in Jamaica, Chris Blackwell would want to bring on pre-release, test it out in the stores as to whether to release them. Then those that were popular, Chris would manufacture: 'My Boy Lollipop' etc, and it was fantastic. But I didn't get robbed, thank God. They stole some stuff off the van, and invariably the shops were in debt, but I had to beat the ganja man. If I got there before the ganja man, business was good; if not I was fucked. But it was just fantastic, it was just brilliant days.

NICK MOBBS,
EMI Records
Label Manager

My next step was to be a record producer because that was really interesting me. I wrote around all the record companies, and eventually got various replies saying No Vacancies for that. EMI came back saying, no vacancy for that but we do have a vacancy for a label manager, which I hadn't got a clue what they were talking about but I thought, this is a record company job, I'm going to go in for this. They explained what it was and I genuinely thought at the time it was that you'd stick the labels on the record. I thought that's what a label manager was, I really did. Roy Featherstone and Ron White were the main guys there at the time and they'd just taken on the MGM/Verve label, which I think had been independent 'till that point, they had their own offices, but now they'd been taken over by EMI. They asked: Do you feel you could do it? and I said: Well, I'd really like to give it a go. I was conning them, I had not a clue really what was involved in the job, I just had no idea. I was literally just thrown into an office with piles and piles of tapes and records, some of which had been released, some hadn't. In hindsight all these phenomenal artists, obviously the Jazz catalogue of Verve was just the ultimate and there was Wes Montgomery and Kenny Burrell, Desafinado, all the Bossa Nova stuff and then there was Laura Nyro on the Folk side, there was Tim Hardin, and then you had the really avant-garde, Velvet Underground who had already had a couple of albums. Looking back on it, it was absolutely criminal because they put this guy in who had not a clue what the job involved, just saying, well go in there and sort that out. It was like, sort what out? What do you mean? What they were getting at was some of these records we've got to release, or re-release, so just get a feel of what's there and see what we should be doing with this label we've now got, because they didn't seem to have a clue what to do with it.

Richie Havens was one of the artists who within my first couple of weeks came over to the UK and was doing the Albert Hall at that point; he was the very first artist I had to 'liaise' with. I was so nervous because I didn't really know what was involved in this, but I figured, I've got to take him out to dinner. He had come in to EMI to meet a few of us in the daytime and I took him aside and said: What are you doing tonight after the gig, would you like to go out for a meal? Oh sure, that'd be great. I asked: Do you like Indian food? Oh sure, sure, that'd be great. So I said: What should I do, come round after the gig, back stage? Yeah, yeah, sure, just come round. Well I sat through the gig and went backstage and I said: I've come to meet Richie Havens and take him out to dinner. Oh, he's left! Okay. It was a completely deflating exercise, and I never did get to take Richie Havens out to dinner. So I really shrank away from that again, thinking, I'm not going to enjoy this artist liaison stuff, it's going to be hard, I won't know what to do. But luckily that was a very unusual experience. It didn't tend to recur after that, if I offered people dinner, they tended to accept.

JOHN MAIR,
Record Salesman

I lived in Wigan in those days, on the outskirts of Wigan, and we went to see the Tamla Motown Roadshow in Manchester, and we were out as salesmen selling in the new Tamla records on their own label. The people in the shops were enthusiastic, we sold shiploads of the stuff. Of course the actual tour was an absolute disaster. I remember going to see the one in Wigan, because I lived locally, and I went to the club there, which later became the big Northern Soul club in Wigan, and they were in this theatre and I was standing as it opened. I remember to this day, it still thrills me, the sound of the build-up in music, the Tamla beat, great stuff, and I was standing next to Martha Reeves, The Vandellas are on the other side of the stage, the curtains are still down, and the voiceover said: Welcome to the Tamla Motown Roadshow, and will you give a big warm welcome to Martha and The Vandellas. They came on the other side singing 'Dancing in the Street'. I looked out over the lights and there were two people sitting down there. I doubt there were fifty or sixty people in the theatre. Then suddenly from nowhere about three or four months later, they just popped, and it had its time.

I go back to the Pye Records days, the beginning of '59 and that was Emile Ford. I was selling box quantities and this thing was rolling out, and then suddenly it began to spread round the country. So, hey, we've got a hit; because we'd nothing else. Everybody was going around being quite chuffed about it. How they got him was that Pye Records, to start their business, were doing a lot of talent shows and various things in dance halls and so on. They did a talent contest somewhere in South London, Emile Ford won, and his prize was to cut a record. They got him in the studio; he came in, and nobody's very interested because there's some black guy come in to record so they said: There's this thing being done in America, this might suit you. It was a minor hit in the States, so they put that on the A side, and then they thought, what will we put on the B-side? So they put 'What Do You Want To Make Those Eyes At Me For'. Well it began to take off and it was roaring up the charts, and somebody somewhere in Pye Head Office remembered they didn't have this guy under contract. So we had to rush around like lunatics. I don't think he had any management; he should not have signed the deal, I mean, he really could have had them over the coals.

My brother-in-law Frank, took me to the NEMS shop, it was before the new one opened, and it was in Great Tower Street. I stand in line like the butler, but Frank said: Go and get Mr. Brian Epstein out. So I had to open the back door and stand like the butler. Brian came out and looked me up and down like something the cat had dragged in and said: Yes, very well Mr. Wallis, but you will still call us from Manchester every morning will you? Frank said: Well if you want me to Mr. Brian, but John will be round here and he can come and see you. No, I'm much happier with your service from Manchester. So, I thought, alright, and he just turned on his heel, he didn't speak to me at all. So for the next several weeks I went in and out of there twice a week, and got nothing. I went in one day and he said: No, I have nothing. Oh, he said: Have you got any of the Chris Barber EP, Petite Fleur? and I said: Yes, and he said: Well your depot doesn't have any. I said: Well, I've got some. So he ordered some and then suggested, perhaps you ought to call. So I started calling on him.

Then I left of course, and I went to Thomson Diamonds, that was van selling, and they gave me two labels; I had Capitol and Fontana. I used to go in and see Mr. Brian twice a week. One Saturday morning, I went in to see if there was anything he needed, and he gave me some stuff to order, he said: Oh, have you got any of the Charlie Drake 'Please Mr Custer' single?, and I said: Yeah. He said: How many have you got? I replied: I don't know, 120 or something, certainly four or five boxes. He said: I'll have them. I said: What? You can't, I've got other customers to go and see. He said: John, have you sold them? and I said: No. He said: Well you can only sell them once. I thought: Well, I'll have to give them to him. So all the rest of the customers that day, it was the first thing they asked me for as I went through the door, and I had to tell them, No. When Mr. Brian had got them and signed for them, he said: Now I'll tell you, EMI are out of stock of this and so are Selecta. I've been onto your company in London and they haven't got any stock, so if anybody in Liverpool wants to buy this single today, they're going to have to come to me.

PAUL MacCALLUM, Musician

Kevin Drake, I don't know if he was the leader of the band, but anyway, he had this gig to do three numbers for six weeks in the old Pop package shows that used to happen in cinemas, ABC Finsbury Park and the Odeons. All these things where they used to take the screen up and they'd have several Rock and Roll bands for the night. It was 1963, so I was fifteen, going on sixteen and I could read music, play bass and I was tall.

Kevin spoke to his mother, his mother spoke to my mother; they all had to go to Bow Street Court and I had to be signed for, and all this stuff because I was under age. We did a couple of numbers with the Terry Young Six opening the show, which had The Beatles and The Everly Brothers and Roy Orbison on the same bill. It was quite incredible for me. I mean, how to grow up very, very quickly. We went all over the country. I think it was for the summer season, for want of a better word. The Summer of 1963; must have done twenty odd shows; maybe more. I really can't remember; it was a bit of this wonderful blur.

We travelled in the coach, well Roy Orbison didn't and The Everly Brothers didn't after two or three days, I think they couldn't quite get into the British humour. There was this sort of big Pickford's-type removal van that carried the equipment. You're talking about minimal equipment in those days; you're not talking 40,000 watt PA systems and everything else, you're talking Vox and Marshall columns at either side of the stage. I don't remember there being such a thing as a stage monitor in those days, and I don't remember anything being mic'd up except the vocal microphones. In those days the vocal microphones were Reslo ribbon microphones, or the Shure, the big Shure silver jobby that saxophone players used to use, but you'd see Elvis Presley using one for vocals and things.

You're talking 2,000 people listening to a band that couldn't have been pumping out more than 1,000 watts between the lot of them, including the vocals really. As most of them shouted and screamed all the way through, they couldn't have heard bugger all really. Bands had to play to the volume of the drummer, who wasn't mic'd up. Shea Stadium I think was the first time where The Beatles did their thirty minute set that things were actually mic'd up. What do you mean you want to mic up the bass drum? Don't be stupid. We've only got a column with four by ten-inch speakers on either side. That's how it was.

So you played to the level of the drummer. Particularly like Jim McCarthy out of the Yardbirds, a serious drummer, and he still is today bless him, still pounding the old skins. So if you had your 50 watt, 30 watt, AC30 flat out, which let's face it, they did, or your treble and bass hundred Selmer or Vox bass, that is all you had. That's what you got on with if you know what I mean. The technology changed so much in ten years, from, say, 1963/4 to 1973/4, how it all changed. Bands didn't change, but their sound and the speakers and everything else did change.

DEREK NICOL,
Scottish Promoter

When The Beatles came along everybody wanted to watch the stars, someone that they were watching on TV, on Ready Steady Go and these sort of programmes, and that were having hit records. The record industry had really taken off then, the 45 records. That changed it in Scotland; it changed it from people coming along to listen to the group playing effectively background music for them to jive to, as that's really how it was back in the early days. There would be a break and there would be the smoochy dance as well; there was always the slow one. Everybody knew the last song was time to pull the bird and go home. It was always Sid Phillips' version of 'Stardust', the Hoagy Carmichael written 'Stardust' and that was it; it was a nice slow, smoochy one.

Then later, the groups had the double gigs, doubling from one venue to another on the same night. You would be doing from 9pm to 1am, or 9pm till 2am on a Friday night or whatever, so you would do an early show at one, then travel ten, fifteen, twenty miles to the next one. I remember a situation with The Spencer Davis Group in the Bridge of Allan Museum Hall. I used to use all the village halls basically, up and down the A9 Perth, Auchterarder, Dunblane, Bridge of Allan, Stirling, that type of thing, and the hall was crammed. I can't remember which record it was but it was huge.

I seemed to have a knack in those days of being able to pick a hit record prior to it actually going to the furthest point up the charts, and I think part of what it was: it is almost like the hub is London, and everybody in the London area was so focused on their thing they almost couldn't see what's happening outside. This is my theory. It's almost like I'm looking down on all these things that happen, and I would hear something on radio, that was such-and-such from wherever, and when you hear something on radio at that time and it sounded good. Then I would check out with a record company or whatever, and eventually try and track down who was representing the artist.

Then I would speak to the agent and say, I'm trying to fill this ten-day period in Scotland and I'd always try and choose about eight weeks further on from when I first heard the record. I wasn't calling saying I want to book say Peter Sarstedt, because I just heard him on the radio, it's going to be massive. I'd say I'm looking for an artist to fill this date, what have you got? They would say, in this case it would be: Well there's Spencer Davis, they're available at that time. Oh really, what do they do? A bit of negotiating, it was an entrepreneurial spirit and I would negotiate the deal that would make sense. Generally in those days there were chart clauses; you'd pay a fixed amount, but if it went into the Top 20 by the time of the gigs, then there was a bonus fee. I always tried to negotiate that out, by the way. But the number of times we had bands when their record was Number One, or at the highest point it was going to achieve. We did that with David Bowie with 'Space Odyssey'. I think the highest it went at that time was Number Ten and he was actually touring in Scotland for me when that was there. Peter Sarstedt was Number One in the charts the day he arrived in Scotland for a ten-day tour that we had already sold out completely.

TONY McGROGAN, RCA Records Artist Relations

After Marc Bolan died I got David Bowie back, he'd gone to Switzerland the night Marc crashed and we'd seen him that night, out of his trolly at Morton's with Gloria Jones. They'd just come in from America, and of course David is Marc's son's godfather. We didn't know he'd had the crash because it happened the early hours of that morning. I had taken David to the airport and he'd flown to Switzerland and then it came on all the news that Marc Bolan had crashed, so immediately he came back but the press had gone mad looking for Bowie. So I got him to come in to Gatwick, and he came in a suit and tie and all that; but I didn't put him in a hotel, because if they don't stay in a hotel, I usually find safe houses for them in London. Well I couldn't do it that quickly as it is a twenty-four hour turn-around, so I took him home to my house in Purley and he stayed with me for four days in my house, locked up so the press never got near him.

David was getting too cooped up so we went out and we went into London, and we ended up at Tramp, and when we went downstairs, who was downstairs in Tramp sitting at a table but Keith Moon, well pissed. I've come down with David and David's got his suit on and everything, and he's got a little goatee beard as well. He's got these sunglasses on, and he'd seen Keith and he's gone up to him because they are mates and said: 'Scuse me, are you that pop star? Could I have your autograph? Keith Moon just looked at him and just grabbed him, pulled his glasses off, put them on the table, jumped up on the table and smashed his glasses. I thought, oh shit, he ain't recognised who he is. Now Keith's got his driver with him, big guy, and I thought, this is all going to go off here. So I thought, what I'll do is tip the table over and just run, and take him with me. As I was just about sweating on it, he looked at me, laughed his head off, and David put his glasses back, there was no glass left in them, they had all the frame busted, and had a great big laugh. So then, him, Lionel Bart ended up back at the Kensington Palace Hotel. It was three days later I got out of there.

The three of them got together and apparently they were talking about doing, the Hunchback of Notre Dame musical, and they were going to have Keith to play the Hunchback, Dave was going to write the words and Lionel was going to do the music, or other way round. They were playing that and it never came through, it never come to ruin.

MARTIN NELSON, EMI Records Regional Promotions

Marc Bolan was a great character. EMI Records at one point sent me up to open an office in Manchester, and the deal was I'd go up and get it running and then come back down to London again. I ended up staying in Manchester for eighteen months, which was great because it got me into the housing market, which was very hard to crack in those days, it was hard then. Marc used to think there was a force field around EMI Records in Manchester Square, so when I was up in Manchester he'd ring up and say, can I come and do some interviews. So I'd meet him and Gloria Jones, his partner, at Piccadilly Station in Manchester, and we'd go off and do interviews around the north of England and Scotland, and the Isle of Man.

One day we were booked for an interview with Billy Butler and Radio Merseyside in Liverpool, but Billy was off sick. Normally when that happened you'd be turned away but he'd arranged a deputy, somebody to step in and do the interview on his behalf so he could still use it. When this young girl came out to meet us, it was pretty obvious she didn't have a clue who Marc was. Marc realised this, and he was a fantastic character, brilliant sense of humour. So he turned round and winked at Gloria and myself and went off into the studio. Gloria said: there's trouble. He was there for about twenty minutes doing his interview, and he came out and he was killing himself laughing. We managed to get him into the car and said: what happened, what went wrong? He said: Nothing went wrong, you realise she didn't know who I was? Yeah. He said: So I did the interview as if I was David. David Bowie was his best friend, so he answered all the questions as if he was David Bowie. Typical Marc Bolan, great trickster, very funny bloke and wonderful sense of humour. Twenty years later, at the Brit Awards when David Bowie gets the Outstanding Achievement Award and he plays '20th Century Boy' as a tribute to 'my friend Marc Bolan', I'm standing next to Alan Edwards who looks after David Bowie and I tell him the story, and he said: you've got to get a copy of that tape. David adored Marc; he would love to hear that. Unfortunately, long gone and long forgotten.

£££

PETER JENNER, Manager, Blackhill Enterprises

Because we were groovy, and we gave the Pink Floyd's publishing to David Platz, we were the bright young things; we were the hip happening people on the block. We understood this Underground stuff, we got on with John Peel and we knew who John Peel was and we promoted Underground shows. David Platz had this Underground act, which was Tyrannosaurus Rex. Denny Cordell, whom I hadn't known before then and Toni Visconti were producing it, and David said: maybe you should manage this band, because he had the label; he was doing the label and he wanted someone to take care of them. That's how we became involved with Tyrannosaurus Rex, and that of course also made us kings of the Underground.

Why we then lost Tyrannosaurus Rex was because Marc started going out with June Child, who was our assistant, Andrew and my assistant/secretary, and we didn't really like the fact that he would be coming in and sitting on her lap. We're saying no, come on, you can't do this; it's really uncool, we're trying to run a business here. I know we can have the odd joint, but, you know.

In the end we said to June: Look June, you've got two choices; we're pretty easy on this but you can either go off and live with Marc and be cuddlesome, or you can stay working here and work for Marc. In other words be Marc's person under our thing. Or number three, you can just go on working for us and not work with Marc and have your own life. But what we can't have is you come in, having Marc sitting on your lap all the time; this is really uncool. So within minutes Marc had left.

Before that I'd already talked to Marc and said: Look Marc, you're doing really well, you're doing these shows with Peel and things and it's going very well, your first album's doing quite well. The problem is you're sitting cross-legged on the floor with an acoustic guitar with a microphone, and you're trying to get monitors so you can hear yourself sing and play, but they're feeding back because you're just using an ordinary Shure mic and an acoustic guitar and it's feedback nightmare, so people can't hear you. You're sitting cross-legged and most of the stages are not very high so they can't see you either, and even if they're reasonably sighted, they can't see you. So I recommend, Marc, that perhaps you should get an electric guitar and stand up so that people can see you. It would make an awful lot of difference; it would really help.

So then the row carries on with June, and June is not happy with the suggestions. A note comes in, which to this day I'm really upset I never kept, but it was a note on a tiny, torn out bit of paper by Marc, saying, Dear Peter, I'm leaving Blackhill because you started to interfere with my creative work by suggesting I should go electric. It was more cutely phrased and shorter than that, but basically I was accused of getting him to go electric, and getting involved in his music. Three months later he was riding a fucking white swan.

CARL LEIGHTON-POPE, Sixties Mod

We all started taking a handful of pills on a Friday and in those days, and I think this is really what's most interesting about that time, is that the people that I hung out with, my age, none of us took drugs because we were drug addicts, we took drugs because we didn't want to miss anything. I think the key to all of it was that we took drugs because we wanted to spend a whole weekend awake. So Friday night we'd take a handful of pills and then we would go to the Marquee Club, then we would go to the Scene in Ham Yard which was a Mod Club in a little yard in Soho just off Shaftesbury Avenue, then we would go from there to the Flamingo for Georgie Fame or John Mayall or anyone of the great Blues bands; get there about one in the morning, 2 o'clock maybe. Then at 3 o'clock you'd go to the Roaring Twenties which was Count Suckle's club, which was the only black club in the West End, and that was in Carnaby Street. The reason that the Roaring Twenties was great was that the music was just sensational, very black, low lighting; I mean, you couldn't see anything in there anyway, everybody was dancing, and also they had one of those mirror balls with the lights that nobody else had. So it was kind of cool.

But we were all drinking Coca-Cola; in fact we were all so stoned we were drinking everything because we were dehydrating like crazy. We were dancers. In my era, in the late Fifties, early Sixties when we all started jiving, if you could jive with two girls, which I can, you were kind of one of the guys. Then the Twist and all the other dances came in, and you were cool if you danced. In those days cools guys weren't the guys that were standing at the bar; cool guys were the guys who were dancing, who were dressed and looking good, they were the cool guys. In those days you took a load of pills; you just danced on your own, so it didn't really matter.

About five in the morning, Saturday morning, I would walk home. I used to wear Tonic mohair suits, hand-made boots, I just looked the part and I would walk home to Swiss Cottage. I would let myself in the newsagent shop about six in the morning, and then I'd hang my suit up and put a white coat on and then mark up all the newspapers for the rounds. Harry Greenbaum in Edgeware Road made my suits, he'd kill me if I got printers ink on my suit, it would be sacrilege. So then I would put my white coat on and do my paper round with no trousers on because I didn't want to get any print on my trousers.

JEFF DEXTER,
Disc Jockey

During the early Sixties we'd set off in many directions. We'd taken record shows on the road, we'd opened clubs in Greenwich Town Hall in South London which became a huge success. We worked at other Mecca Ballrooms bringing in lots of people, Hammersmith Palais, the Empire Leicester Square. The ballrooms were still the mainstay of the masses who went dancing. But the whole point in those days was that they weren't going to listen to the band, they were going to dance in front of bands and in front of records. That was how it worked in those days. I think out of all of those clubs as various factions came together, the poets came in, artists came in, and that all kind of got distorted in what eventually turned into the alternate society and Psychedelia.

The early Mods discovered late-night clubs, and in order to be able to stay up all night, the main drug of the day was a purple heart. You could also get something that lasted a bit longer, called a black bomber, and that was all pretty easy to get hold of in Wardour Street in those days. There was always someone around with a box of pills you could buy a few. As the Mod thing developed everyone was trying to jump up on the cart, and a friend of mine, Peter Meaden was working with this group and his whole idea was right at the start of the Mod explosion. It was the time when Carnaby Street really became something else other than just a street with two shops for men, one for gay men and one for young boys who wanted to be slightly different. Peter had the idea of dressing the group up and turning them into Mods. Keith Moon himself already had a good idea of what he was. He was into surfing, so he kind of liked that whole West Coast, Brian Wilson look from the Beach Boys, so he already had a certain edge on it, but The Who weren't actually Mods to begin with, but they were marketed as Mods. In my terms of course latter day Mods, but of course by that time we were doing Mod-style clubs all over town and all over England. The Mod thing exploded I guess round about '63 or '64.

BARRY DICKINS, Booking Agent

The Howard Davison Agency was a massive company, and they looked after Frank Sinatra and Judy Garland, had Tony Bennett and all those sort of people. He had The Dave Clark Five, The Applejacks, The Mojos, I can't remember who else they had, but quite a few bands. I started off there, and that's really when I started to do quite well. I was a kid and I was prepared to learn, and if you went out on the road with a band you'd kind of see what it's like from their point of view. It's easy sitting in an office sending them up and down the motorway. But if you go out on the road with them you suddenly realise it's not all fun, especially in those days. It wasn't suites in hotels, it was two of them sharing a room and we were staying in Bed & Breakfast type places; it wasn't that much fun, although we had a laugh. It was just different times.

I went to Eel Pie Island, I went to Toby Jug in Tolworth, not many people have been there. The Black Prince of Bexley; The Blue Moon at Hayes; Leyton Baths; the Crystal Palace Hotel. I can remember all these weird ones; there were hundreds of these places then. The Roundhouse at Dagenham; we did them all. The Mojo Club Sheffield was Peter Stringfellow who now lives in the same block of flats as me. People go: Do you know Mr Stringfellow? I say: Know him? I knew him forty odd years ago.

Tuesday nights I used to go to the Marquee Club, I had The Who on there and I can remember The Nice, which was a band that I was involved with at the very beginning, they actually started off life as PP Arnold's backing band. We went round and we found this band and we found a keyboard player, which was Keith Emerson; we found a guitarist, Dave O'List was in The Attack, which had a little bit of a following. We got Lee Jackson who played bass. I remember he was from Newcastle; I think he was in some band in the Cromwellian. The original drummer, I can't remember, it was Ian somebody who played drums with Chris Farlow. He left after about a year and then Binky Brian Davison took over, so that was The Nice. They used to play Tuesday nights and I can always remember Chris Wright and I used to phone each other up, I think Jethro Tull played one night, one Tuesday, The Nice did another one; Ten Years After; and we'd go, how many did you do? We all used to lie; oh, we had a thousand in last night; oh, we only had 980 or something. Oh well, The Nice were always bigger than Ten Years After, or Jethro Tull or whatever. So yeah, spent a lot of time there. Started off with The Who; that's where I first found them, not found them but where the success started. There was actually a great band there called The Action that were really very popular but never really made it. Reg somebody was the singer, but they really could. At least my recollection is they were very good.

The Who had a tour manager, they nicknamed him Cyrano; his real name was Dave Langston but he had rather a large nose. Which was good because so have I, but he had an even bigger one than me. We played around in this hotel and I think it was Cy who came up with this idea of hairspray and a lighter equals flame-thrower. So what he did, he goes whoosh, and it burnt a big hole in these net curtains, and this window is like the biggest window you've ever seen, must be eighteen feet, this is my memory, I could be wrong, but it was pretty high. We go: Oh my God, what are we going to do? What we'll do is, we'll take the netting down so instead of two we'll just put one, and no-one will know. This is a bedroom that John Entwistle and Keith Moon are sharing and I am the tallest, so I have to get up onto the dressing table, climb onto the wardrobe, get a chair, get onto the chair to get this. For some reason I get as far as the wardrobe and I'm not doing very good. So somebody says: Oh come on, get down, we'll do it. So I jumped off the wardrobe onto Keith Moon's bed and bang, it broke; that was quite funny.

BILL SHEPHERD,
Booking Agent

I was introduced to Chris Farlowe and I became his tour manager. I liked Chris Farlowe, he's a really nice guy and we got on well together, and he's a good singer too. Then there were two brothers who ran the agencies, Rik and John Gunnell. I ended up working with them, and I went on the road with them sometimes and we had great fun. I was the tour manager, you're going to be appalled by this but I had a white DB5 convertible. Mick Jagger actually quite liked me because of that, because he had a green DB6. I became part of management then, I think the Gunnells liked me and liked my attitude and I was still young; we were all young really. So I tended to take over more of a sort of role of junior management. I then thought, well I'd quite like to do some myself, because I felt they were, in the nicest possible way, slightly what I would call looking backwards in terms of history. In terms of what was going on, rather than having the sort of child-like enthusiasm and innocence that I had about going, hey why don't we go and do this, or that. They'd been there a long time and they'd been established and were doing. You want to go and do something you've got to go and do it yourself.

I started Circle Agency, I found Ed Bicknell and I found Rod MacSween and I found John Tobin, and we just sort of started. Anyway they all came to work for me. I think I was very fortunate. I left the Gunnells and opened my doors, but that's what happens, certainly at that time. What was really going on was like a village. It was a small number of people basically who were involved in it on a major level, and I was part of that. So the leaving thing, okay I wanted to go and start something. I think people went, oh it must be alright because he'll be working with the Gunnells, Georgie Fame and some of the other people I worked with and everything else, and they just thought, yeah, okay, great; you want to do that we'll come with you. I was lucky in getting Ed Bicknell, Rod MacSween and John Tobin and saying, come on let's go and do this. Out of a naïvety I think, but a genuine sort of enthusiasm, thinking, yeah, I'd really like to do this; I think this would be great fun, it would be good to do. We could help people's careers and whatever;

let's go for it. When this first started out I was completely gob smacked in that I couldn't really know what was going on. Roxy Music ended up playing in my garage one evening for me, Quintessence were another, The Pretty Things, and I was managing Home. Obviously all kinds of things were going on that were there which I've forgotten about. That wasn't because I was doing a lot of drugs or anything; no, it wasn't that.

ED BICKNELL,
Booking Agent

There was no planning, nobody in the management game ever came in with a plan. You never ever met or co-ordinated anything with a record company or anything like that; you just put in gigs. Bands gigged; they didn't tour. Tours have a beginning, a middle and an end but the bands of that era, even the biggest bands, gigged. You would try and get them five or six gigs a week; you might get them £125 on a Monday and a Tuesday, and they might get £350 on a Friday and a Saturday. They all had percentage deals written into the contracts and nobody ever bothered to ask how many people had come, what the ticket price was. It was totally different to how it is now. Now it's become a science. Nobody had riders; nobody said we have to have 'x' amount of power, or the clearance of the stage has to be this, or the stage must take this amount of weight. You just turned up with a Transit van, with three amps and a drum kit, you didn't have any lights probably; you probably used the stage lights that the university had or maybe the Birmingham Odeon had.

One of the things I always think that has never really been acknowledged, or detailed, is what an impact the development of technology had on the live side of the business. I'm talking about how sound systems became bigger. My memory of the whole people we're talking about was Marshall stacks. I remember when I put The Who on at university, Pete Townshend had the Marshall stacks which he would crash into and knock over; the speakers had been taken out of them, because they weren't going to spend the money on replacing the speakers. So he had empty Marshall cabinets that he would push his guitar straight through. Again, that's the romance of it.

I was a huge fan, and still am, of black soul music of a particular period, which was the James Brown, Isaac Hayes, Motown, Eddie Floyd, Sam & Dave period, Wilson Pickett period. But back in the early Seventies when I was working with Barry Marshall and I'm twenty-six years old and I've got hair down to my waist, well one day he calls me and he sends me off to France I think it was, or Belgium with Ike and Tina Turner. It was the days when everything was paid in cash. Ike would put it all in this briefcase with certain other paraphernalia that he had, and a gun. This is before we had the security stuff at airports, and I'd never seen anybody carry a gun; and Ike Turner had a gun in his briefcase, along with his paraphernalia and wads and wads of cash.

I remember we were at Brussels airport, and because the musicians of that period, both black and white, were generally pretty tight, there was no tour manager, so Ike was checking everybody in at the front of the queue. There was a scam in those days where people would have briefcases with false bottoms and they'd place it over the top of another briefcase, operate a click, and that's what happened to his briefcase. He had all the tour money in it, and he had a gun, and he had some paraphernalia; and of course we were not about to report this, kind of rock and a hard place. Amazingly he didn't go nuts. I mean, he was pretty nutty about it, but he didn't actually punch anybody in the face or anything, and what I remember was he paid everybody.

I loved working with those artists. I also did Bill Haley and The Comets. What was interesting about Bill was, it was the same deal as it was with the black acts. I would go round to the hotel, and I would have £1,000 in a freshly sealed plastic bag from the bank. I would give it to Bill, he would then count it on the bed, because they didn't even trust the banks, then go and put it in the safety deposit box in the hotel, and we'd get on the bus and we'd go. Provided you did their ways you never had a problem with them.

JOHN REED,
Musician

It was great in Germany in the late Sixties because all the hookers used to buy the bands beers. There was never any 'you know', because business was business. They knew we were all basically starving, and there was kind of a good relationship between us and they would mother us, if you like. They'd say, come on boys, there's a beer. Cheers, thanks very much. There was a clause in the contracts that you're not allowed to smoke on stage, and some of the club owners were unscrupulous. The waiter would say, I saw him smoking. Right, that's 100DM off your contract, they'd play all these little tricks.

We'd heard about this guy Jimi Hendrix, and Bob our guitarist's mum used to send us records out so that we could learn them from a little portable record player. One of them she sent out was 'Hey Joe'. Well, we're playing the Top Ten Club this particular evening; it was early on, we used to play one hour on, one hour off, and we'd play six or seven hours every night, very arduous to start off with. The Beatles talked about Hamburg throat, and when you go out from England, where you were spoilt doing two forty-five minute spots, changing to five or six hours a night was a bit of a culture shock to most of us. But it did tighten up your harmonies eventually, and of course we all drank and smoked as well, so it wasn't exactly the healthy lifestyle.

The drummer was normally either stage left or stage right; well I was left of stage that night, and playing away and I suddenly caught in the corner of my eye coming in through the doors this guy who looked like he'd come from another planet. He had the big Afro, he had this huge military jacket on, the sort of Hussar's jacket, and I always remember he had a spliff out of his lips that was about the size of a drumstick; it was huge. Followed by Mitch Mitchell, Noel Redding, of course, then I recognised Chas Chandler from The Animals. Things started to click because we'd heard that Chas had been managing this guy he brought over from America. Bizarrely, in the party also was Chris Barber. They'd parked up, because they were doing a one-night stand at the Star Club that night and had met Chris Barber who was doing a gig on the Reeperbahn, and had said: oh we're going in here for a beer, do you fancy coming in? So we had The Jimi Hendrix Experience and Chris Barber, who came and sat to my left, at the nearest table at the side of the stage.

Of course we automatically knew there were Brits and when we finished our hour, we came off and, hello lads, how are you doing, you know, fancy a beer? So we sit and join them at the table and we all got chatting. They said, we're doing a one-nighter at the Star Club, which was just round the corner; and as luck would have it Jimi Hendrix was on at midnight, and we were doing the eleven till twelve set here. Job done. So we said to Chas, can you put our names on the door? Yeah, yeah, no bother. So we finished our set about a minute to twelve, off we went, and we legged it down the Reeperbahn round the corner, into the Star Club, and we're just blown away. I mean, in those days it was still very much that Mersey Beat era still, I mean, we used to wear shirts and ties; okay, they were Ben Sherman shirts and paisley ties, but all the bands still wore suits, and it was all that sort of thing. Then you see this guy playing a guitar with his teeth, and left-handed too. It was like, what?

ROLAND RENNIE, MD Polydor Records

Chas Chandler, I had met in EMI days, and we made a deal for Jimi Hendrix just like that. My great thing was not the artist really: it was the managers. Forget all the disc jockeys and the pluggers and so forth; it was those guys like Kit & Chris, Chas Chandler and his lot. They were incredible. It was the managers I went for all the time. They came in and talked, and I'm pretty good with people. Of all things, I don't think I'm in any way creative but I always was a good catalyst, that guy and that guy; put them together, see if it works. They were very good in those days. I could see Robert Stigwood was good; I'm not just saying that but it was obvious because what he'd done and how he'd worked.

The Who, now this was a deal with Kit & Chris. They wanted a label; it was Polydor's but we just 'gave' them a label. Ego? I don't know, but it worked. That was alright. I didn't have anybody in the company with their nouse to deal with it. They were there for the money thing, and they knew all the angles, so why not get them to do it?

We used to have arguments with the managers about sleeves and stuff like that. There was that Hendrix sleeve with all the nude ladies on. I just said: I don't know. So I took it round to everybody, does this offend you at all? They said: No, so we let it go. It's a long time ago you know, it's not like that today.

That's what the extraordinary thing was; it was a revolution and not only in music. I always remember being at EMI and Lockwood sent two of his bright boys over to America, and they came back to tell us all about America. What a waste of time, and a waste of time for them too. They didn't do anything, or tell us anything; it was extraordinary. But that's what it was like then, yes sir, no sir, three bags full sir; one of them.

A lot of these guys then became the norm, as it were; they became the establishment. I remember one night when Eric Clapton and Jimi Hendrix were playing together in the club; it didn't mean a lot to me then, it was just how it was in those days.

£££

DAVID ARDEN, Manager

There's one thing I will put right, for the record. Seeing that Mickie Most has admitted Don gave him The Nashville Teens, but actually the old man set him up as a record producer too. Absolutely no ifs, ands or buts; because Mickie and Don knew each other when Mickie promoted Gene Vincent for Don in South Africa. Then Mickie left South Africa and came back here still working as an artist. The old man used to put him on, opening up on all the tours. When I say tours, he did at least three or four tours. Mickie was awful actually, he was, he used to be embarrassing; he'd open up and roll on his back.

Anyway, I digress: Peter Grant had heard about The Animals and he'd told Don that Mickie wanted to be a producer, let's do a record company now, and all the rest of it. Because the old man had got a bit pissed off, he hadn't realised what had changed. He used to promote all the artists' records; he'd bring in Brenda Lee, John Lee Hooker and he'd promote them, do the record company's job for them. They'd have the hits and he got nothing for it. Then all of a sudden the penny dropped. So when Peter said Mickie wants to be a record producer and let's have our own record company, all of it. It was: Great, let's do it.

I remember this night as if it was yesterday. We'd heard about this group The Animals, Peter was all excited and said: Oh the rumours are this, that, and all the gossip. They're coming down and they're doing the gig at the Scene Club, which was just off Great Windmill Street, owned by Ronan O'Rahilly. So we go down there, Mickie, Peter Grant, Mickie's wife, dad and myself, and on come The Animals. Of course Eric Burdon, what could you say? He had the old man drop-jawed, because he loved talent. That's what people didn't realise, he adored talent. When he heard Eric open his gob, you know, that was it. So they go backstage, backstage, well the cubby hole at the back of the club and Don marches in announcing: This is Peter, this is your producer, Mickie Most. Not like, um this is your producer, um Mickie Most. There was no Mike Jeffries, no nothing. Just: Right, we'll send up all the contracts, Bye.

We got out and everybody's excited and Mickie's going: I can't believe them, oh my God. Then he said: Oh, I just want to ask them something about one of the songs that they did, I'm just going in to see them, I'll be right back, and we continued walking on to our cars. Five minutes later Mickie said: Don, Don, Peter! Yeah, what's the problem? He said: Fucking Ian Samwell's down there talking to The Animals about being their producer. Over my fucking dead body. Down there; fuck off. That was that.

The God's honest truth, that was it; Mickie was the producer but there was no record company with dad, Peter Grant and Mickie. The old man was promoter and agent and when it came many months later or eighteen months later, or two years later he went, where's the record company? Mickie was: Oh, bye. And that was it. But that is the God's honest truth. So the old man, and Mickie Most, well I have not seen anywhere where Mickie says the old man gave him The Animals. But I swear to you that is the God's honest truth, and sometime later of course that's why he wrote, The Animals were the first, because the old man felt very bad about Ian Samwell. That's why he got him to produce The Small Faces.

I don't want to ruin Dad's image but he had a big heart. But what people don't realise is if you have talent, and that's what I've been brought up to believe, if you've got talent you can do whatever you like, almost anything you like, and get away with it. If you haven't got talent he'd go: Fuck off or I'll knock you down them stairs, piss off. Talented: do whatever you want to do.

ARTHUR SHARP, Singer

Like everything else you'd all intermingle, and word got round: Hey what have you done? Well, we've just lost our drummer. Oh well I know a drummer, blah blah blah, and all of a sudden there's six guys playing together named The Nashville Teens. The great Don Arden found us at the Jazz Cellar, Kingston, and within weeks Mickie Most was introduced to us and we recorded 'Tobacco Road'. Because Arden was bringing in the likes of Jerry Lee Lewis, Chuck Berry, that was our first tour. After Lewis then came the Chuck Berry tour, and this is all under Don Arden's guidance.

Jerry Lee Lewis, bless him; he's a country hick. He never spent a penny on the entire tour. You think he might buy a drink now and then but no, not he. There's a wonderful story about revolving stage. Hey, what happens here? Right Jerry. We're out at the back setting the gear up, he said: There's going to be a problem here. Why? The piano is on the left. Yep, that's the way you like it. Yeah, but when it gets round there it's going to be on the right. No Jerry, it's on the left and it stays on the left. To Cecil, his cohort he asked: What do you reckon? No, it's going to be on the right when it gets round there. We had to drag out the electrician; right, follow your piano. We followed it round the door, we're now in the auditorium, it's on the left. Huh. That was the end of that, just couldn't handle that at all, the brain would just not pick that up.

Chuck Berry would only do his allotted time, and Patrick Meehan Senior, Patrick Meehan Junior eventually ended up managing Black Sabbath, but Patrick Meehan Senior was on tour with us, and Berry would come off and say, Hey, they want an encore. Pro rata. So he said: well, do ten minutes. Bang, bang, bang, counting out the money: Yup that's about right. He'd go out and do another ten minutes.

Carl Perkins, bless him, there's some tracks of the Nashville Teens backing him as well on Decca Records somewhere, he was a nice guy. He was on the Chuck Berry tour, and you'd go by coach; everything was by coach. Overnight you'd go from one gig to another and you'd sleep on the coach. Well Chuck Berry took one look at the coach and said: I'm having the back seat, because that was a bench. Carl Perkins said: That's about right, boy, because I ain't having him up the front with me, I'm a Southern boy. He was bringing that up. I said: you can't do that here; this is not down south, you're in England. He said: I don't give a damn and that was it. Berry didn't mind because he was in the back with Caroline Attard and Jemima Smith of The Other Two. That was a grand tour. The package tours were great, we had recorded 'Tobacco Road' by the second and we did three package tours in '64. We went to Kingsway Studios with this guy called Mickie Most that Mr Arden had introduced us to and recorded 'Tobacco Road'. We went in with three tracks: 'Parchman Farm', 'I Like It Like That' a Chris Kenner record, and this one 'Tobacco Road', which if you listen to the original was John D. Loudermilk with a guitar, folksy and slow. We just beefed it up with drums. We did 'I Like It Like That', Mickie Most went, hmmm. Also in attendance was Peter Grant, who went on to be Led Zeppelin's manager, he worked for Don Arden as a heavy, a kind of chauffeur. We played 'Parchman Farm', he went, Er, okay. Got any more? Yes, we've got another track called 'Tobacco Road'. We played it, and both Mickie Most and Peter Grant, they both said almost in unison, That's the one.

Going back years, we'd never got any royalties, courtesy of one Michael Hayes, alias Mickie Most, because he had signed the contract, not Don Arden. Mickie Most signed the contract with Decca Records, so they paid him. He then should have paid Don Arden who'd have paid us. But that never came to pass. That went on for thirty-odd years, until our drummer phoned me up and said: Hey, there's a new Common Market thing about copyright; you can actually sign an indemnity form to whoever's paying out the money and they can bypass who they've been paying before if you are the guy that wrote the book, wrote the song, or actually performed the record. So we all signed, and EMI said: Right, from here on in we pay you guys, and if Mickie Most turns up and says, where's my money going, he can sue you, not us, because you've signed this. He never did turn up and ever since we've been getting our royalties.

£££

MATTHEW SZTUMPF, Manager

I suppose the reason Madness never made a huge amount of money then was they didn't crack much of the rest of the world, they did okay in some territories but you only ever really make money if you crack it globally because you're just repaying all the costs in the UK, aren't you?

Then they didn't get paid, but what did come out of it was that we managed to get the entire back catalogue. Maybe it was just my own naïvety, because, how old was I then, twenty five when I first started managing them? But I had no concept that the business might continue in the way that it has done, because all that I'd seen of it thus far was that a band was successful, and then they went away. Individually they might go on to form different acts or whatever, but once a Madness split, you didn't have reunions in those days. The only thing that you could compare it to were the sad cabaret acts where there'd be two members of a band that would go and play the Bailey's circuit for a while, but that wasn't the music industry as we knew it. That wasn't anything you'd want to do. So to my mind it was like, well once a band has split up that's it. You couldn't conceive that even in five years time a band could get back together and be bigger than they were when they'd split up, if you see what I mean. We didn't make huge amounts of money; the deals were bad; the licensing deals were even worse, obviously, Stiff Records were licensed by whoever in Germany or Japan and the amount that would come back is minuscule.

But even if you didn't get huge advances, later on when I managed Swing Out Sister, I think we did 1.2 million albums worldwide on the first album, and you're still un-recouped. You'd think, well, how many fucking records have you got to sell, you know. It's bizarre. Once the marketing costs became so high and the recording costs, and then the producer costs, all those costs escalated and made it more and more difficult for everybody to make money. Because with every record came a video, and with every album came possibly three videos. Yeah, the studio costs, the producer costs, everything else. You'd get to a point where in this day and age it's very easy to be like four, five hundred thousand pounds un-recouped by the time a young act has gone out and made two or three videos, an album and done some touring. How much is the cost of a billboard, and everybody has to have billboards now. The old days were when you'd just get a load of posters and get them slapped up around town overnight.

The first time I got involved with The Smiths was when 'Meat is Murder' had come out and they were going to tour America. Their agent Mike Hinks called me up and said: I've got The Smiths and they're going to America in, I think it was like ten days or maybe two weeks time, and they've fallen out with their manager. Anyway, they were in a mess, they didn't have anything else booked, just the gigs were booked and that was it. So I went and met Morrissey and had a chat with them and got on board on that, put the tour together. It was a bit of an eye-opener actually because I think Madness had never done the sort of shows that The Smiths were doing. We'd always done ballrooms and stuff like that, whereas The Smiths were exploding out there. Suddenly I was going to these 'sheds', as they were called then, the sort of half-covered, half-open shows in the States. There'd be like 15,000 people there. It was the first time I'd really come across the large amounts of money that acts could make on the road in America, which was kind of unknown here because we didn't even really have arenas then. The sheds were a great idea because you'd have like 5,000 under cover, so that would seem like an ordinary gig, but then you'd have a grass bank at the back that they could just stick another 10,000 people onto. Yeah, you could make huge amounts of money.

There was always somebody around that could cope because nobody ever managed The Smiths. When I say nobody managed them, certainly I didn't have a contract. I got involved when they were injuncted by Rough Trade and I sorted the deal out with Rough Trade, because basically they wanted to get off Rough Trade and go to EMI. But as I recall, what happened was they split up before they ever got to the end of the deal. They might have delivered one more album. Then Morrissey went to EMI and I got involved with him again. It seemed like every time they were in a bit of trouble they'd come back knocking on the door. They were the first band that were really cracking it globally, very much in that student market I suppose, or bedsit market or whatever people called it. But yeah, very exciting times.

DAVID COURTNEY,
Songwriter

My first time of arriving in America was staying at the Beverly Hills Hotel with Adam Faith. He showed me the way, this is how you do it, this is where we're going, this is where we're going to be. Being in the Polo Lounge of the Beverly Hills Hotel when all the film stars are in and out, and it has been like that since the Golden Age of film; spotting people like Sophia Loren walking past, that was quite amazing. Anyway, we were there, this is my first time in America so it's quite mind boggling to be in the middle of Hollywood and this whole thing, and we are there off the back of a successful UK album with Roger Daltrey, and the Leo Sayer one just starting. We were there to discuss the release of the Daltrey album with the record company in America. So we're on a real vibe here and we're meeting lots of other people and I'm making friends with people like Irving Azoff who was managing The Eagles, and we were all together. It was wonderful, and I'm taking this all in.

Then, we suddenly get tipped off that the record company are going to purposely bury the Daltrey album, because they feared that if it was a success that Roger would leave The Who. Now, this was quite frustrating, you can imagine. So we start making phone calls back here to England to Roger: Do you realise what they're doing? He went absolutely…. well you can imagine. This album was very precious to him and for them to do that was quite disturbing. So he then got on to Kit Lambert and Chris Stamp who were the managers of The Who, and it started to blow up.

The next thing is that Adam and I are summoned, and I say summoned, to a meeting in the Polo Lounge, this is like something out of a movie, right, with, I won't say the name of the person, a very high up person in this major label, and they were… let me say there's always been two types of Mafia in the industry record-wise: Warner's were more the Italian type and the Jewish Mafia was the MCA's and all those sort of things. So you're dealing with people, they're hardball. Anyway, so this guy summoned us to this meeting, we didn't know why, we just thought we were going to talk about what they were going to do with promotion. I'm sitting in there in a booth and Ringo walks in, he sits down, we're having a chat: What are you doing here? He says: I'm here to attend this wedding. And literally there, on the patio area of the Polo Lounge, is a full-blown Godfather wedding going on.

He's going off to the wedding, we're waiting for this meeting with this character, who then comes in. Basically we were warned off, to say you've got to stop making phone calls, you've got to let this go. Now, this was my first taste of major success and I'm told we've got to stand back, and watch this album just be killed off. It was just starting, the record was getting played and you could see it was going to go up the charts, and they pulled the rug. There was nothing we could do about it, and it was almost like: If you don't stop making the phone calls you won't be going back to England, it was almost that. I started to get a bit vocal and I got the kick under the table from Adam to shut up, be quiet, you don't know what you're dealing with here, this is not something to get excited about. But it was a terrible, and Roger, who wasn't at the meeting obviously, would confirm the story because he was at the other end of it. It was the most frustrating, terrible thing to have happen, because you knew you were a hair's breath away from cracking it big in America. We later did but to have that done to you is not very pleasant is it?

JEREMY LASCELLES, Virgin Records A&R Manager

We signed Culture Club, and they were brought in by Danny Goodwin and Richard Griffith from the publishing side; Danny was Richard's A&R guy, and he had found this band who were great. We heard some songs and thought it was pretty good but no-one else was interested in them. Tony Gordon, who was the band's manager, was desperate to get a record deal. We subsequently discovered the band had hired him on a 'get us a record deal in three months or you're out' basis. So he would have done a deal with anyone just to say I've got you a record. There was a rehearsal they set up for us all to go down to, and I specifically remember Simon Draper, Jumbo and myself plus Danny and Richard, I think maybe Steve Lewis went down. They were playing away and the songs were really good, and I was moving my head around, thinking, yeah, this is kind of pretty groovy. After two songs, George turned and said: Will you stop doing that, why are you shaking your head, are you telling everyone that we shouldn't be signing? No, I'm just moving my head because I think you're pretty good.

We put out two singles, the names of which escape me right now, which weren't hits, and George was getting a bit desperate. Then he wrote this song which we'd never heard at this point; it wasn't the song we signed them on, it was called 'Do You Really Want To Hurt Me'. As soon as we heard that song we all went: This is your first big hit. I remember absolutely clearly being with Simon and coming back from lunch and meeting George on the corner of Portobello Road, just bumping into him as he was coming out of the office and we were coming back in. We all just said: 'Do You Really Want To Hurt Me' has got to be your next single. This conversation took place on the street, George said: I don't want it to be a single; it's too slow. If I go on television and Top of the Pops I won't be able to dance to it properly. I remember him saying, over my dead body will this be our next single. Well it was, and he's still alive.

The three artists I remember working with all roughly at the same time at Virgin, who I thought were people that really inhabited a different planet than me, were: Captain Beefheart, Scott Walker and a wonderful, wonderful Canadian singer called Mary Margaret O'Hara, who made one of the great records, the only record she's ever made, called Miss America. Those who know it, love it. Having conversations with each of them was a pretty surreal experience. Beefheart would spin you out on this surrealistic sort of word trip and he was so mesmeric and charismatic that he was playing games with you, because just when he thought you actually were losing what he said, he'd ask you a question about whether you were paying attention earlier on. He would definitely play those kind of games.

Scott Walker was a lovely guy but quite a troubled individual I suspect, and would come up with the most extraordinary excuses as to why he would postpone the start of making this record. It would all be to do with the alignment of the stars and whether it was the lambing season or whether the leaves had turned a certain shades. I suppose my favourite story about Mary Margaret O'Hara, having very laboriously and with extreme difficulty, made this first record. So then we started making the second and she kind of panicked halfway through making the record. She had a real phobia about recording; I think it was a bit like how some remote tribes have a fear of having their photograph taken because it captures their soul? I think she felt like that about committing her music to permanence on tape. She felt it killed the soul of the song or something. So she kind of decided she couldn't go through with this recording process, and we've still got the tapes of this half-finished record. But she had no problem touring live, playing in front of people; so I said okay, let's do this in a way that's going to make it easy for you, let's just record a succession of live concerts or let's just find a room that you like, just playing with your band, so it doesn't look like a studio but like a kind of remote recording facility, whatever.

I said: Where shall we record this record? She said: How about recording it in my head. I didn't really have an answer to that. Then she actually said to me: I don't really need to make this record because I know what it sounds like.

SIMON DRAPER, MD Virgin Records

Virgin Records was nothing to do with the Music Business. That was what was so unusual about us. There wasn't a single person working at Virgin who had ever been in the music business before. On principle we would not hire anyone who had been in the music business. We didn't want to know about the rest of the music business at all. It's very arrogant but we thought we were doing something different.

I'm probably slightly exaggerating because of Tom Newman, but he was an artist. He'd been in a group called July, and Tom Newman did the Manor Studios for us. But all the people we hired were from elsewhere. I can remember when we first hired a professional person, which was when the company was bigger and we needed a new Head of Promotion. We suddenly realised we weren't going to be able to train someone up from nowhere. We have to get someone immediately who knew what they were doing, and so we hired someone who had been working at Chrysalis or maybe it was Island; whatever. I remember Steve O'Rourke, the Pink Floyd Manager, before he got to know me, he thought we were all like the Moonies; forget the Masons, the Moonies! We were like a gang of people who had really come from somewhere else.

'Tubular Bells' was the first record put out on Virgin Records. Richard Branson got Sandy Denny's contract and amended it. I was there. Richard asked me to start a record label and so the mail-order moved out of South Wharf Road to above the Notting Hill Gate shop, and they left me in South Wharf Road to start the record label. Going from a packed office of like-minded, dope-smoking individuals, all great fun, I was suddenly sitting in an office that used to contain six people, and it's been redecorated so I've got a desk by myself. It was horrible, I didn't know what to do really.

I had no idea how you started a record label, so I had to sort of improvise. I started vaguely looking. I begged Richard to be able to come back and I went back and had an office in the Notting Hill

Gate shop, right outside the loo on the upper landing. Nik Powell was down below me, we had a spiral staircase, and I had a reel-to-reel tape recorder to listen to tapes, and a desk. Well I started looking for artists I suppose that must have been '72, and I thought that I'd be able to sign the music that I was listening to, which was American.

You suddenly realise you're not going to be able to sign American artists; there's no mileage in it. It had to be English artists, and what artists are there, and you start looking round. Most of it wasn't very interesting, I didn't think.

Mike Oldfield was at the Manor because Blackhill Enterprises were trying to promote this black American guitarist as the new Jimi Hendrix, Arthur Louis, and they needed a backing band. Because of the Kevin Ayers connection they got Mike up there to play, rehearsing, and Mike left his tape with Simon Hayworth and Tom Newman. Simon and Tom played me the tape and I went, wow, this is going to make us; this is absolutely right on the button. I think he started recording it in July '72, and we launched the record company in May '73. We wanted a range of records, so we signed Faust, which came out of our Kraut Rock involvement with the mail-order; Kevin Coyne, because Dandelion, John Peel's label had folded and we looked through to see what was worth picking up and Kevin was the most interesting to me. Gong, which came out of the whole Soft Machine thing, and because we were importing Gong records from France.

Signing Mike Oldfield was interesting as we didn't know what to do. Richard made what possibly was a mistake then, but he signed him to personal management; we signed his publishing, his agency, and his recordings, all using template contracts, Sandy Denny's contract. I think we looked at it with a view to getting royalty rates, that's why Mike started up with a 5% royalty as that's what she was getting. Later on Mike's lawyers pointed out that this could have been a bit of conflict of interest when Richard was managing him and signing him to his own record company. We renegotiated his contract a number of times over the succeeding years. But the thing with Richard was that he grasped some very fundamental truths.

He's an amazing bluffer, but he knew that if we started a record label we needed to control as much of what went on ourselves, otherwise other people would be making money out of us. So we went to get distribution. Island wouldn't offer us a distribution deal even though that's where we wanted to be, we wanted to be with Island; they represented everything we were trying to do. But Island already had Chrysalis and Charisma and EG. They were all on licence deals and Richard was holding out for a distribution deal and they wouldn't give us a distribution deal. So we went to CBS and they would. We went to CBS to sign the deal and there was Maurice Oberstein sitting behind the desk, flanked by Robert White; and we'd gone thinking we were signing the contract but they hadn't got it ready. So we thought bit of a waste of time all this, we'll come back tomorrow. Island got on to us overnight, realising they were going to lose us and gave us a distribution deal, which opened the floodgates because after that Chrysalis went in and said we want one, and so did EG and so did Charisma. But Richard knew, and he knew that you've got to have worldwide rights for your artists, why sign an artist for the UK only?

JOHN GAYDON, Manager

As fortune had it, there was a comedy trio signed to Decca who Noel Gay represented called Giles Giles & Fripp and we were working for Noel Gay. Robert Fripp came in one day and said to David Enthoven and I: Look, we've got this little band together, rehearsing down the Fulham Palace Road in the basement, would you come and have a look at us. So we went down and it's King Crimson obviously, and they played us the whole of 'In the Court of the Crimson King' from beginning to end.

In those days bands would stop for a fag and a beer and whatever; they were all dressed in black. Fripp was on his stool: Mellotrons, the whole works, and we're sitting there completely blown away, as you can imagine, hearing that whole album from beginning to end. So we stuck two fingers up at Richard Armitage and Noel Gay and set up EG.

Robert Fripp was very together, very organised he knew exactly what he wanted to do. He sort of told us the deal we were going to do with him, and he said: look, we'll do a 70/30 split of the costs and all the expenses, whether it be staging, touring, whatever it is, and all the profits. So we get 30%, band gets 70%. Which was pretty novel in those days. I don't know where he learnt it, he was just a very bright cerebral character.

So we borrowed £4,500 from Barclays Bank in the Gloucester Road, well David did, because his mother had bought him this mews house, and we finished the album up at Wessex Studios up in North London, which was incredible. Then we met Chris Blackwell, also an old Harrovian, and he said: you've got to do a lease-tape deal; this is the new way business is going. You pay for it, you license it to me, and you own the underlying rights. This was all pretty novel too at the time.

By this time we knew Chris Wright and Terry Ellis, and Chris had a flat above Safeways in the Kings Road; we used to go and smoke dope with them and get out of it. So we were all starting at the same time. We borrowed the money, finished the album and did a lease-tape deal with Chris Blackwell for the world excluding North America. Then David and I fly off to New York with the album cover, which was a killer, and we met with Jac Holzman, Armet Ertegun, Mo Austin; the main players.

They were all wining and dining us and wanting to sign the deal, and eventually we agreed $100,000. I can't remember what the royalty was but Ahmet Ertegun was Mr Charmer, he was the coolest of them all, so obviously we're going to go that way. He had a great label obviously, and he said: I'll pay you 12% or 14%, whatever it was in retail, and you mustn't tell anybody because I'm only paying Aretha Franklin this much. The usual story, I'm sure that's happened hundreds of times before.

I remember David and I, we got the $100,000, we jumped in the lake in Central Park and we were off and running; this was it.

ROGER WATSON, Chrysalis Records A&R Manager

I was in the right place at the right time. I'd hit twenty runs off Chris Wright on a Sunday I remember, at his house, at the cricket game, and I was in the lift with him in the morning and I said: Oh Chris, sorry to make mockery of your spin bowling yesterday. He said: Oh don't worry about that; why don't you come and see me at lunchtime. This was a Monday, and it was 1975, and he said to me: What do you think about America? I said: Well, how do you mean? Is it like moving there, or is it trying it? Suddenly there was a leaving party on the Friday and I went. I was on the plane on the Sunday morning and then I arrived in LA and stayed at the Sunset Marquis. I think they met me with a big spliff and we went and had daiquiris and we went to see Russ Meyer's Supervixens, this was Los Angeles during the mid Seventies. Then the next morning Terry's secretary arrived in her car to take me to the office. Boom, and I was there.

It was new; it was just a few people. I was living in a bedsit at this time in South Kensington and I'd split up with a girlfriend recently and I was a bit bruised, so I was ready for a change, and I was twenty-eight. I happened to know the guy who ran the LA Budget Rent-A-Car, Arnie Graham, lovely guy. I went into see him and he was: Rog can we get you a car? this sort of thing. He was a very friendly guy and I said: Arnie, I think I'm here for a while, how can I find a house? He got Violet on the phone and he called her: Violet, what are you doing? Got a friend here, we're coming over, we'll be there in five minutes. They took me over there, and Violet said: Let's see... Anyway they took me up to this house at lunchtime, and this is on the Monday. The guy in the mailroom took me up there, and it was way up Wonderland Avenue, up Sunset Plaza Drive at the very top of the Hollywood Hills. I'm just going, wow, I'd been in a bedsit and stuff. This was part of the experience of arriving in LA in the Seventies. On the steps of this house was a guy who looked a bit like Peter Fonda, and it turns out he was Peter Fonda's stuntman. But these guys had been earning big money in Hollywood doing stuff and they bought houses, that's what they did. Anyway, he showed me round the house and it had a shag carpet and it was nice, big doors overlooking the valley. It was really on the top. That's where I stayed for seven years. The whole LA scene, as you drove down Sunset Boulevard, the Strip, it was all billboards about music.

I found a guy on one of the tapes, a guy came into see me and his name was Nick Gilder, and we had our first Number One with Nick Gilder and Mike Chapman. Mike Chapman played a big part in what we were doing at the time. I mean, this is an Australian guy who'd had all these hits with Nicky Chinn here in the UK, with Mud, and they had ChinniChap and he had an office on Sunset Boulevard. So I managed to stay on for a while as it were, and then I met a guy called Bob Brown, who managed a group called Pablo Cruise. They were signed to A&M, and Bob was a good guy; he managed Huey Lewis. He was a stockbroker from San Francisco. Huey, I went to see several times and really got on with him well, and who wouldn't, he's such a lovely guy; real anglophile character, because he used to play with Nick Lowe and stuff. Anyway, against much competition, because of my relationship with Huey, he signed to Chrysalis. Terry Ellis only got to see Huey Lewis because we found him a restaurant nearby; it was a little bit like that. I kept trying to get him to come to gigs, and it would sometimes revolve around the restaurants that were in the area. Which I quickly learnt to play. And yeah, I found one near where Huey was playing. Incredible.

DAVID HOWELLS, MCA Records A&R Manager

We did MCA for three, four years, and fortunately rebuilt the company. Musically there were some great things going on, and the Average White Band particularly was a good success for me. The first album was 'Show Your Hand', but then a few things went wrong at the end of the period. Mike Maitland had been the President of MCA; he was wonderful, we broke a lot of American stuff over here that hadn't been worked on before. Then he moved on, whatever, politics or whatever changed, and suddenly again it was: Well, we need to know what you're doing, and what's your projection on this. They went through a period in America where they signed two or three acts which were dead and gone, and they spent a lot of money on them. I got, again lucky, Jeff Wayne came in to see me, and he'd been working with an act called Vigrass and Osborne, Paul Vigrass and Gary Osborne, and we were doing stuff with that, and I said: What else are you up to, because you're obviously busy. Well he said: Yeah, I've just found this guy David Essex. I said: I'll sign him. He said: You haven't heard anything. I said: No, no, no, I've been following David Essex for three years. I started watching him as this young drummer growing into this figure, and by this time he was in *Godspell*. I said: That guy is definitely a major talent whatever it is you're doing. Jeff said: Well, then you should hear the track, and he played me 'Rock On'. Well, I fell off my chair; it was just amazing. I would very rarely ever go out on a limb but I said: This is a Number One, but this is a Number One. He said: Great, we'll do a deal. At the same time I just delivered the second Average White Band album, and Richard Branson had asked me to go and see this concert with Mike Oldfield, because he'd done 'Tubular Bells', and he was interested in doing something in America.

So for the first time now I have to apply to America for a budget to sign acts, and the David Essex deal wasn't expensive: a phenomenal deal. MCA America then turned down the second Average White Band album and just said: No, we just don't get it; the first one was not really... and well the second one, what's the point of having six white kids from Dundee playing black music. We've got loads of this stuff. And at the time it was selling everywhere but America. Then they turned down the David Essex budget; they said: No, we don't see this kid. I said: Well you wouldn't; you're over there – we're over here, this is how it works. You just have to allow us... and they said: Nah; we just don't see it.

So at that point my partner Derek Everett and I just looked at each other and went, let's start our own company, this is madness. It's their money, their decision, their right, but you can't do this kind of stuff. I'd already tipped them off about Mike Oldfield and Richard Branson. So we put in our resignations and I went to America to finalise stuff with the Los Angeles office. We told Jeff and David Essex about what we were going to do and they said: Great, we'll come with you. I said: But we have nothing, it's literally two blokes and a dog and we're going to open this office. And they said: No, no, this is great, this could really work.

At the same time Ahmet Ertegun heard the Average White Band album, which is 'Pick Up the Pieces', basically, and he went: I'll take this. So he took that. Richard Branson had just got married to his first wife and then when I was flying to America I said: Come and spend your honeymoon in Los Angeles. They've got this amazing hotel on the lot, the Sheraton; I'm sure we could get you the Presidential Suite or something for a couple of days, come over and meet these guys. So he came out with me. I said: Although I'm leaving it's still a good company in America, their distribution is second to none. They were very hot; they had Elton John, they had The Who, a whole bunch of stuff apart from their own successes. So they were very good at handling English stuff. Richard, his wife and myself flew out, I went in, I took them in the company the first day and I said: Look, this is going to be one of the most exciting things you'll ever get involved with, played the record, everybody went this is great. I took photographs of him and Artie Mogull shaking hands on the deal by the pool. Richard had never been to America before. By the way while we were there, I said to him on the second day: I'm going to show you a record shop. You think you're in the record business, come with me. I drove him down to Tower Records on Sunset and he went into the shop and went: Oh My God; it was a megastore. When he came back he turned his shops into megastores. So Richard cancelled all his appointments with A&M and Atlantic and everybody else, because he's got a deal, and I think it was the third day or the fourth day and Artie Mogull called us in and they all sat around with the accounts people and everybody, and they all said: If this 'Tubular Bells' had lyrics on it, it'd be a smash.

So as an A&R man usually you maybe sign one major act a year if you're lucky; maybe one every three or four years. I've been very lucky, I usually tended to get involved with one a year. But to have the potential to be involved with The Average White Band, David Essex and Tubular Bells, all in a couple of months, and see a bunch of Americans go: Nah. So then Derek and I started Gull Records.

TILLY RUTHERFORD, Magnet Records A&R / Marketing

A&R at Magnet Records was for a while a different ball game with Darts. You listened to thousands of Doo-Wop tunes and looked around and went to see the band loads and loads of times before you signed them; looked at what they were doing and how they performed, and got a few ideas of producers in mind; did a few demos with one and a few with another. It was phenomenal; it was great, it was like self-indulgence at a real level.

The Darts thing was great because we brought Tommy Boyce in to produce, who was one of the great songwriters; worked at the Brill Building with Phil Spector, worked with everybody. This guy was like, God bless him, he was just one of those people you never thought you'd meet in your life, who did Dick Clarke's Bandstand at fifteen. As a kid growing up in Coventry you'd only heard of Dick Clark's Bandstand. Now you're drinking and eating with the guy who sang there, and wrote 'Pretty Little Angel Eyes' with Spector, 'Under The Moon Of Love', who's got these great records, and you go, wow. He had so many stories, of course he already had The Monkees by then, so you got all The Monkees' bits as well. He was wild man, such a wild guy, I loved him. He's a sad loss to the music industry.

We brought Richard Hartley in to work with him, the conservative Richard who was a great musician and did lots of shows and things like that. Richard was at public school. Then we've got Boyce and him together, and it worked; it worked fantastic. That was a phenomenally successful period, and then in the next year it was The Matchbox. I went to see them at the Royalty in Southgate, and I thought, could you do to Rockabilly what you did to Doo-Wop, because we'd already had five or six hits with Darts by then, starting with 'Daddy Cool'. So I watched this band called Matchbox play and I thought these were fantastic. I just thought this is exciting. There was loads of people dancing and jiving; I'm thinking such a throwback, and this is 1977. So I called a friend of mine who'd been doing jingles to see if he wanted to have a look at the band about producing and that guy was Peter Collins, THE Peter Collins, who later became very famous as a Rock producer. Matchbox was his first ever successful production. It was just an extension of a hobby, you were just searching; the first Matchbox single was 'Black Slacks', the Joe Bennett and The Sparkletones classic record, which is totally self-indulgent. It wasn't a hit.

The records were great records, they actually sound good today. If you listen to the Darts and the Matchbox albums now, because of the productions, because of the people doing them, they sound really, really quite cool. Then of course the next year was Bad Manners in 1979. I had tried to sign Madness; that's who I wanted to sign, and I got gazumped by Dave Robinson and his oppo Jake Riviera. So I thought, fuck this, we've got to get one of these Ska bands. So I went to see Bad Manners at the Rock Garden, Covent Garden, and there was millions of maniacs on stage and I thought, this will do me. Dougy Trendle, Buster Bloodvessel. So the next morning I got them into Magnet and I said to Michael Levy, sign these; and he signed them that day, seriously. They did the first album in Coventry, back in my hometown, with my good friend Roger Lomas, who'd just had a hit with The Selecter. These are cheap deals, of course they were cheap deals.

October 1987, that's when the PWL label came about, because I did the deal with Trevor Eyles at Pinnacle for the label which was Mandy Smith, 'I Just Can't Wait'. Because PWL2 became Kylie Minogue, 'I Should Be So Lucky'. But in that interim period obviously we had all the stuff that went through RCA, through Peter Robinson, so I got heavily involved in that, and I went to America to launch Rick Astley and all sorts of things; it just really started to be great, you know. That's how, if you like, the label came about, because we wanted to put records out ourselves, so they came back with the Mandy Smith really, the first one. But the Kylie was, not made, it was sort of half-made; we were trying to sell Kylie on because she'd already had a hit in Australia with 'Locomotion' the previous summer.

But as David Howells quite rightly said: nobody was interested in Kylie at all. They went: Fucking stupid name, who's that? Because nobody really knew what *Neighbours* was; I had no idea. David and I were the only two people to meet Kylie I think when she first came out. The boys wouldn't speak to her, ignored her, till the last day when she hummed over 'I Should Be So Lucky' to a drummer and bass line that Matt whipped up, you know. Peter Pitstop, our club promotion guy, thought up the name, because he went oh I should be so lucky; that's how it came about. You can't believe how successful that became, and really it was down to one TV in Australia, Christmas Day, *Noel Edmonds' Christmas Special*, that Michael Hurll had shot driving around Melbourne in a car. He knew all about her because the BBC had *Neighbours*; we didn't know what he was talking about. It was phenomenal.

The 'Kylie' album was the album of the year that year: 2.3 million in the UK. I know, because I went and picked the award up at the Music Awards. Then the following year we won it again. I said: we'll win this again next year, like as a joke, and of course the next year we picked it up with Jason Donovan.

STEVE MASON / PREBBLE, MD Pinnacle Distribution

The thing mostly I remember was with Rod Stewart and The Faces when they came to Mr Fox at the Greyhound, Croydon. This was obviously when they were top of their drinking thing. They arrive late, they were drinking and they got on stage late. It was a Sunday and to promote on a Sunday it was strict licensing laws, finish at ten, everybody out by twenty to eleven. We used to have 600 cushions on the floor in the Greyhound, Croydon. So, they don't go on stage until 10 o'clock, something like that. It get to 10.35, the manager of the pub comes up to me and says, if they're not offstage in one minute's time, you'll never promote in here again. So, I had to walk on stage, go up to Rod Stewart and say, you have to come off right now or I'm pulling the plug, because I'm going to lose this venue.

Rod turns round to the crowd and says: Well, we want to go on for another forty minutes, but this bloke says we've got to stop now, so goodnight. He turned round, walked offstage. I had 600 cushions burying the stage immediately. I got hold of Rod, I put him up against the wall and said: right, you've had all your fun, now I'm having mine, no money, clear off.

We had opened this really cool record shop, Mr Fox of Croydon with listening booths, chairs downstairs and stuff, and did quite well. Then the first WH Smiths ever to sell records was WH Smiths in Croydon. The top end of all our sales, Led Zep 2 etc, just went out the window, so we started doing imports and then I left, and started Windsong Exports.

I just became an exporter; that was it. Certainly we were the cheapest country in the world at that time to buy your records from. We had started at kind of similar times and so I started Music for Nations with Martin Hooker. 20% inflation, that was the Labour Government we had then, 20% inflation and 20% hikes and interest charges, that was it. But that was just right at the beginning of Punk and the independent labels.

We ended up at Pinnacle, and when I went there, I just said to them: Look, I'm going to give you my distribution but don't like the stories going around about your financial wellbeing, so I want a Directors' meeting so you can contra anything that I buy for Windsong, against what you owe me as a label. So when they went bust they owed Music for Nations £20,000 or £30,000. So that's why I ended up buying Pinnacle. It was £150,000, or £140,000; this was October. I said to the Receiver, every week you are here and I'm not, knock, £5,000 off the price. It took them six weeks to make up their mind, and I bought it for £110,000.

The first thing I did when I moved into Pinnacle was a stock take. At the back of the warehouse, all the warehouse staff were walking through the back of the warehouse into the car park for lunch, and more records went missing out that back door than you could shake a stick at. Within the first week of me getting there, I locked that back door and five people had quit. They were back to warehouse wages, not nicking it.

My problem there at Pinnacle was that Our Price had £100,000 worth of returns to come back. This was obviously the problem of the old company, or the Receiver. Our Price came to me and just said: We ain't buying from you until you take these returns back. I said: well I'm not selling to you. I got six months in and I said to my accountant can I afford to get out of this company? And they said: No you can't.

I think the big turning point with all that was there was joint distribution agreements; remember that 4AD went through Spartan and Rough Trade; Factory were through Rough Trade and Pinnacle, Mute were Spartan and Rough Trade. Our three biggest labels actually had joint distribution. I put my foot down and said: this doesn't work, because we're getting a new New Order record, all the Rough Trade guys are on the phone, and we're all on the phone too phoning all the shops: The new New Order record, how many do you want? I went to see Tony Wilson and said: this is a nonsense; you spend months recording, designing a sleeve and everything and it's sold in on a Monday morning in an hour and a bit. So I said: we're going to be exclusive. Tony Wilson being Tony said: nobody tells me what to do, and put the gauntlet down. I went up to see him in Manchester; I always remember his comment. He opened the door and he said: Fuck me, you ain't got horns. Because obviously he'd been sold this bill of goods from Rough Trade that I was the devil incarnate. He said: What do you want? I said I've come to tell you that, unless you are exclusive, we can't be your distributor anymore. So he said: You know what I've said about that, don't you? Yeah, but I can't, this doesn't work. We are an exclusive arrangement and it's not fair on anybody else. So he said: You've got the balls to come up here and say this to me? And I said: yeah. Then he said: Then you're my distributor. Typical Wilson. So he phoned Rough Trade and said: I'm really sorry, I wanted the strongest distributor and Steve came up here and said it.

MARTIN HOOKER, MD
Music For Nations

Twisted Sister, had sent a tape to Gary Bushell, and Gary had passed it on to me at Secret. I just loved it so much I phoned up literally that night and flew out the next night, because I knew if I didn't something else would come along. Literally from hearing the demo to flying out there to sign the deal took about a week.

I mean, they couldn't even get a deal in America. The day I signed them I flew out to America to see them and they were playing in Poughkeepsie of all places, and it was snowing. There was over 3,000 kids, and you're thinking, and this band can't get a deal? Then merchandising rolls up in a big removal lorry and it's packed; and when it went away there was just like a torn poster in the back and that was it. Dee rides up on stage on a big Harley Davidson and all that and you're thinking, I can't believe this band hasn't got a deal. Of course they were fantastic.

We went backstage afterwards and they had more money on this table in cash from the merchandise than I've ever seen in my life, in piles everywhere, I'm not kidding. I thought, holy crap, I've got no chance of signing this band. I was tied in with Gary Bushell at the time, he was helping me with all the Punk and the Oi stuff, before he got the reputation that he's currently revelling in. He said: You've got to sign them, they're fantastic, they'll do really well. So I said: Let's talk about a deal then. Then their manager kind of went out to the toilet and the band said: Just make us an offer, we're really cheap. Oh, okay. In the end they weren't really cheap but it was a good deal for all of us, and we sold a shitload of records from them, and then I helped them get a deal with Warners and the next album did five million.

Later on I thought, I'm going to start another label, and I'm just going to do Heavy Metal. I thought, you can sell it to every country in the world; it never goes in or out of fashion, the fans stay loyal forever. That'll do for me. So I thought, I've got debts up to here; I'd just toured The Exploited and Twisted Sister on my Amex card and I suddenly wasn't getting any of that back. I owe tens and tens of thousands to Amex, who were always really friendly and helpful in that situation.

So Steve Mason said: What do you want to call it? I said: I want to call it Music For Nations. So, okay, that's what we did. In February we released our first record, which did like, 35,000. The second record was Ratt, who ended up being enormous, and the third record was Metallica.

With me, obviously one of the pivotal things was signing Metallica; it kind of changed my whole life, because it led to so many other things, Christ, I've traded off it forever. It could have been so easily missed because it was one of many I'd got to listen to that day, and most of them were absolute rubbish. This one came in, a little cassette with 'Metal Up Your Arse' on the front and a hand with a sword coming out of a toilet. Nowadays you'd look at that and go, no thank you, and you probably wouldn't even get it. A lot of the companies of course don't even listen to unsolicited tapes. I listened to tape after tape after tape and they were all just dreadful. I put this one on and it wasn't very clever quality, and it could so easily have been, after thirty seconds, Nah; and for some reason I stuck with it and thought, actually this is really exciting, and played it again, and did the deal. But one of those pivotal moments and it could have gone completely differently and your whole life would have been different.

TERRY MURPHY, Landlord, The Bridge House, E16

All the family's always been into music but it does help, doesn't it, being a boxer. Especially with me and Canning Town at the Bridge House, because all the customers, I knew their fathers. I used to say: Hey, behave yourself or I'll tell your father.

To keep control of the old Bridge House for seven years without any serious fights was phenomenal really; of course there was fights, that happens everywhere. But I think it was because of me and my sons and my family: my brother John's a well-known boxer and my brother Mick was a well-known boxer; brother Jim is still at West Ham now. So we were a boxing family, and I guess it helped. Because you knock them out quick see, when you're a boxer: you knock them out and take them out. The biggest thing that ruins any business, especially the entertainment business, is fighting and trouble, so we were there to stop it, not start it. If you hit someone on the chin then you're starting it, so you've got to make sure that nothing happens inside.

Stevie Marriott's manager was a lovely bloke called Laurie O'Leary. I'd known Laurie since the early Fifties, boxing and stuff like that, and his friends, Ronnie and Reggie; we used to meet his 'friends' often. So Stevie said: I want to do a gig, I want a gig. I said: well, you can play next week if you like, STEVIE MARRIOTT ex-Humble Pie!! He was sensational, sensational.

The police were waiting to arrest him. When he'd gone to the States he had a recording studio with some guys and they were obviously, well I don't know whether it was on the book or what, they got all this equipment in and then someone sold it and Stevie vanished to America. The police must have heard that he was playing the Bridge House, but it was billed as 'Blind Drunk'. The gig was billed as 'Blind Drunk', Stevie was called Red Wine, they all had different names. So the police said to me, Stevie Marriott here? and I said: I don't think so, no. The pub was packed, 800 people there and the police want to arrest him. Anyway, I got to him; I was driving round, he'd gone to have something to eat and I found him and put him in my office upstairs. I don't give an eff about them, he said. I said: I don't know about that, but they'll bang you up. Apart from this gig you don't want to be locked up. So he said: Oh, I've got some stuff in my pocket anyway and I don't want them to see. Anyway, I phoned Laurie and he came straight down and spoke to the police. It was not a criminal thing actually; it was completely over the top. He soon sorted it out and Stevie was back again. He'd done four weeks on the trot for us.

Ronnie and Reggie Kray, well we grew up together; we boxed together, we were all boxers together. Amateurs together, and professionals together and stuff like that. I used to see them in the dance halls; I was always dancing when I was a kid. Pop Pacific was one of the places. It was their place and we used to go there, and our place would be the Public Hall Canning Town. It was all sort of gang orientated, even in them days. We'd have our gang up Canning Town and they'd have their gang over Bow and stuff like that. You'd meet and then you'd go and have a fight and stuff like that. But through knowing them, you didn't fight with people you knew.

Charlie Watts Big Band played the Bridge House, I think they just wanted to be treated as ordinary people in the end, because the Stones were major stars all over the world. He came down the pub, he'd done all his own roadie-ing and stuff like that, which is unheard of, a major star doing roadie-ing! He set his drums up and got the sound; he was amazing, he really was. We used to have lovely drinks after time and all. Of course Mick and Keith came down and wanted to take us out; everyone kept looking at Mick Jagger and saying, Mick Jagger's brother's here. They just wouldn't believe it was Mick Jagger. I said to him: do you like this type of music Mick? He said: No, I hate it. Jazz, wasn't it! He said: I hate it, we've just come down to support Charlie.

BRYAN MORRISON,
Booking Agent

I was actually quite fortunate because one day I bumped into someone that I'd known for a few years, a guy called Laurie O'Leary, and Laurie was always dressed in a blue suit, white shirt, tie; smart. Quite bright, nice guy, never heavy. He came to see me one day and said: Bryan, a couple of my mates want to start a theatrical agency, they want to start booking bands. But they've done a bit of time, nothing important, and can't get a licence from the Greater London Council. He said: Would you mind issuing the contracts and splitting the commission with them, you take 5%, they take 5%, and all you do is type up the contract. I said: Yeah, alright, why not? I mean, how much effort is this going to be?

Besides managing my bands all day long, I used to go out every night round every new club, finding the manager, chat him up, talk to him, can I have your 'Sole Booking' for the venue; and it would takes weeks to get it agreed. So I said to my secretary: If these contracts come in, keep a separate pile from then and just take a note and do it. You're going to get one contract a month probably. Well within about six weeks or two months, there's a huge pile, this high, and there's a small pile. What's that lot? That's your friends, she replied. What are you talking about, how come they're doing that much business?, I wondered.

I start looking at this, and every day they're getting new 'Sole Bookings'. They're getting them daily. Every club open anywhere in England, or southern England anyway, these boys are in there. So after about five months of this, I rang up Laurie and said Laurie, I want to meet your mates, because by now I'm managing four of the top bands in England. I know how to chat up club managers and it's taking me a month at a time to get a 'Sole Booking' and they're getting one every three days. So he said: Alright, good; yeah, they're at a gig in Essex tomorrow, a new club in Essex they're going to see tomorrow, why don't you come along there?

So I roll up at this place and it was a big barn-like place, and I walked in this door and down the end there was a bar, with a staircase, and above the bar there were three offices, or three doors above this bar. I walk over to the bar and there's these five guys, backs to me, and Laurie. He says: Bryan's here, how are you, what do you want? I said: gin and tonic. He says: blah blah blah, Ronnie, blah blah blah, Reggie blah blah, and something just clicked. We talked for two minutes, and one of them says: Brysee, be back in a minute, just got to go and see the manager. Two or three of them went up the stairs; silence, just talking up there for a minute or two, then suddenly, bang. I looked up, and there's this geezer bouncing down the stairs, stopped halfway down, they pick him up, kick him down the rest of the way; the two or three that were still with me ran over, they all kick him in the head, walk back to me, and one of the guy's says: Another 'Sole Booking'. Well I tell you, I had this gin and tonic in my hand, and the bubbles were going up my nose, and I thought, what the fuck have I done here, it's The Kray Twins.

I tell you what, I spent about forty eight hours in a complete mental state, because my philosophy has always been from the very beginning, that there's a line; and I don't mind bending the line, but I never cross it – and this was crossing the line. So I rang up Laurie on about the third day and said: I've got to see you. So he came in, and I said: Laurie, I don't want to do this anymore, I'm out of this. He said: Bryan, it's the Twins. I said: I don't give a shit who it is, I'm out of this. He said: Look, leave it to me son, leave it to me. Two days later he rings me up, he says: I've someone on the phone for you and this geezer says, I can't remember which one, Ron here, or Reg here, Brysee, don't worry about it, it's not a problem son. If we can do anything to help you, Laurie will give you our number, feel free to call. Click.

Years later I said to Laurie, why did I get off so lightly? and he said: Because you were a star, because you were managing four or five of the big bands, you were bringing in all the stars. The Kray Twins loved it, I mean, Rock and Roll was like football is today; it was the only thing, everyone wanted to meet Rock and Roll stars in the Sixties. You know, you're there, and that's why I got out of it.

But the great thing about it was, by now of course, in the six, seven months I'd been doing all their work, word's gone round that I'm working for the Krays, so no-one bilked me. So for the next ten years I got paid, never had to get on the phone and say: Where's my money. It didn't occur to me until years later why it was, because everyone knew what I didn't know.

DAVE HARMER, CBS Records Salesman

In those days my CBS van was bright orange with all these artists' names down the side, and doing the East End of London, I had Barbra Streisand, I had Ray Conniff, Tony Bennett, 'I Left My Heart in San Francisco', all those sort of things. The Clancy Brothers, Bob Dylan of course. I was at the concert in the Royal Albert Hall when he brought The Band on and everybody booed him. The whole sales force were due to meet him afterwards and because he was so angry with the reception they had had, he refused to appear. Talk about cutting our own noses off, we decided there and then, as he wouldn't meet us, that we'd boycott his albums for about a week. So every time we went to a record shop they said: oh, have you got this Bob Dylan – 'Freewheelin'', and 'Bringing It All Back Home'? We said no, sorry, they're out of stock. Of course at the end of the day we suddenly realised the only people losing out were us. We weren't earning any commission on them, so we soon stopped the boycott.

My very first sales conference I can really recall was at the Hilton Hotel. It was a CBS conference. I was very young, married with a young family; never ever drunk spirits at all, never been to anywhere like the Hilton Hotel. We got called in, had the meeting, and it was great. The Peddlers performed, Sly and the Family Stone were there, Johnny Mathis, and Alf Garnett, because we had a deal with Allegro Records, we used to sell and distribute Allegro stuff, and he was part of it as well. We had a great day, it was absolutely fantastic, just surrounded by all these stars; it was just wonderful, a big cabaret. Then we went to the tables, there were tables of ten with ten bottles of spirits, all the mixers all round. We sat down and guys were saying, I'll have that, I'll have that, and I ended up, at the age of twenty I think I was, or twenty-one, with a bottle of whisky; never drunk it in my life. So I drank three-quarters of a bottle of this whisky. Then the conference came to an end and somebody suggested that we go to the top floor of the Hilton to have a look at the view. They put me in the lift, pressed the button, and as the lift went up I just went down; my legs just wouldn't take the speed of this lift, and I collapsed on the floor.

I was driven home by Brian Champion in this wonderful Ford Corsair he had, and he was dropping Mike Edwards off in the East End of London as well, in Leyton, and we drove down the Lea Bridge Road and I said: Brian, you've got to stop, I need to go to the loo. So I got out of the car, and it's exactly the place now where the Ice Rink is in Lea Bridge Road; it used to be a wood. I've gone to go into the wood and I said: Brian, you won't leave me will you? He went: 'course I won't. Of course the minute I've gone in behind the tree, brrmm, brrmm, I hear. So I'm running up Lea Bridge Road with my old boy in my hand, saying Brian, come back! The next minute I heard brmm, brmm, brmm, I look, and there's a policeman on a noddy bike alongside me; he's going: what's going on here? Champion, who'd had a skinful as well, got out and said: It's all right officer, he's with us, we're only having a game with him. He said: Get him in the car and get him home. This was a Friday, and because the next day was a day of calling on all our best accounts, being the sort of guy I was, I told a lot of them I'd be there on the Saturday morning. I woke up and I was still so drunk and I took my three year-old daughter with me to keep me awake to drive this van. I did five calls and had to call it a day. I spent the rest of the weekend in bed.

TREVOR EYLES,
Director Pye Records

I started as a salesman at Pye Records at a quite young age, and I worked my way through there. Just by hanging around and as people left I managed to get a better job every time. So I ended up first as Sales and Marketing Director and then General Manger of Pye, but by then it was called PRT. There really was no average day, but they were long days, you drove in early in the morning. I used to get in really early and I used to work with Louis Benjamin, who was like a legend in the theatre world, and he was Chairman of Pye. He'd like a little chat in the mornings about how it was all going, this sort of thing, and then you've got your turnover figures and things like that.

Then about half-past eleven, twelve, Benjie would call you into his office, which was huge and palatial, and hand a key reverently to you and you mixed him his first Bloody Mary of the day. We'd have a toast together and then often I used to go to lunch with him or some of his cronies, because he knew all the people at London Management, and people like Max Bygraves. Don't forget Pye Records had a huge 'Middle Of The Road' business, people like Max Bygraves would come in for lunch, and Des O'Connor and all those people. We used to go over to the Cumberland Hotel and do these great big lunches with these artists.

Having said that I had a cocktail bar bigger than some local pubs, you know. When I was made Director I got a contract and in there I had to have the ability at home to entertain at very short notice, anybody from overseas. We used to just phone up a company called Christopher & Co and order cases of champagne, wine, and so my garage looked like a branch of Threshers half the time. There I was, I was thirty, Mary was about twenty six, and we had a lovely house in Marlow, and we used to just have massive parties at Christmas with the staff, then cleaners would come in and all this sort of thing.

I would say 1974, 1975 was the time when we were really romping away with stuff. There was a time we had Barry White at Number One in the UK, Carl Douglas who was a UK signing, at Number One in America. Peter Prince was incredible, I think he was probably one of the most underrated A&R guys around; he just made the company a huge success. He left to run Motown in the UK, I think he was made an offer he couldn't refuse. That really I think was the start of the decline of PRT/Pye Records.

We had a sales force of sixteen; I think most companies did, between twelve and sixteen. I think most of the companies had about that, between twelve and sixteen, some up to twenty reps; all these independent shops, you know. Just amazing. I know all the reps were home by 4 o'clock. I used to catch them out sometimes; I know it sounds evil but just once in a while I'd go to somewhere like Lincoln and be outside a rep's house at 8 o'clock in the morning, see what time he left home. To see their face when they leave at eleven and you're sitting there. You only did that once in a while and the word went round and they all started watching themselves a bit.

PAUL KINDER, GTO Records Marketing

There was an ad saying 'Messenger Wanted for Music Company', so I applied for it. I got to this place and it's called the Gem Toby Organization, it was a music company, not a label, and it managed people. In this building were people like Mike Leander, a very Tin Pan Alley songwriter called Tony Macaulay and these people wrote for artists that I hated, there was Gary Glitter, there was The New Seekers. Then I heard that they were starting up a label with this guy called Dick Leahy who used to run Bell Records and was hugely successful. Bell Records had Gary Glitter, had The Bay City Rollers, had David Cassidy, had The Partridge Family, had Dawn. He left Bell to start up his own label called GTO, which were the initials of the company I was working for, the Gem Toby Organization, with his partner Laurence

Myers. So I sort of hung around to see what all this was going to be about. When they moved to their offices in Mayfair they asked me to go along, so that's how I started working in records. I stayed there for about seven years, and it was fantastic. This was 1974, Dick was at the height of his powers I suppose, and there was only six people there but there was quite a bit of money, and I started off as being the messenger, then eventually I worked in promotion, in marketing, in international, and ended up in A&R working very closely with Dick, sitting in with him in all his meetings, learning contracts, seeing how he dealt with artists, writers, producers.

Once we were sitting there and he was in a foul mood; I was in the meeting, I can't even remember who the person was, he put this tape reel on and he pressed play, and he lasted I think about forty five seconds, and he pressed the rewind button and said: This is fucking crap. He then spun off the reel, took it out and he threw it out the window. This poor kid, he was just mortified, and then having realised what he's done Dick apologised, only to discover that they'd landed on the roof of a van, and the van took off down the road. So this poor kid is running down the stairs. I don't know if he ever got his tape back; we never saw him again.

We had some fantastic artists. I worked with Billy Ocean, Donna Summer, The Walker Brothers, Heatwave. Dick was an amazing teacher because, working for a small company like that, you learned everything. So what it taught me, apart from the business, it taught me about music, because I was probably quite narrow-minded in many ways. I thought I was cool and I liked all the cool things, and I didn't really understand certain elements of Pop music that actually were very valid.

IAN McNAY, Bell Records Financial Controller

I saw this advert one day in the *Evening Standard* for a financial controller for Bell Records. I thought, Bell Records: they were pretty successful. They were just breaking The Bay City Rollers and Showaddywaddy and Gary Glitter, and they had Partridge Family, David Cassidy and Terry Jacks from America. I thought this would be fantastic. So I applied, this is obviously all pre-email and pre-fax; it was a handwritten letter I think. I got a call saying: Do you want to come for an interview? So I went to an interview with the accountant, Alan Smith, the guy who was leaving. That went okay and then I got called for a second interview with the big boss, Dick Leahy, who was a bit of a legend because he'd signed all these bands, or most of these bands anyway, the English ones. I had an interview with Dick and we kind of got on okay and I obviously wasn't asking for too much money and he felt I was competent enough to do the job and so he gave me the job. Then he said: Oh by the way, I'm leaving; I'm going to start a new company and I'm taking some of the staff with me. Anyway of course I joined Bell Records, which was maybe July '74. I got there and it was very strange because Dick had left, the Head of Marketing had left, the Head of International had left, the Head of Production had left; they'd all gone with Dick to start GTO Records.

So I remember looking at the accounts the first month I was there; I looked at the accounts to see what they'd done the previous month so I could work out the first month I had to do, and they'd made over £100,000 profit. This is going back a long time, more than thirty years I think. I thought, this is extraordinary, this handful of people and this quite small office in Charles Street was making all this money. The third or fourth week there I think they had something like nine singles in the Top 40, and I thought, this record business, it must be a doddle making all this money, because Dick hadn't paid a lot of money to sign any of these acts. But the deals that Dick was doing were clever in one way but not so clever in another way because he was doing lease-tape deals; so the company wasn't owning the masters. He was getting them cheap, which was great because they were becoming successful and making lots of profit, but it meant that after five years or something the rights all reverted.

A few weeks after I got there, I remember *Music Week* ringing up on Monday morning and them saying: Do you know the new Bay City Rollers album has gone to Number One? No-one had thought to check. Somehow people weren't that on the ball there, here was the new Bay City Rollers album, it ships a few thousand, that was all okay. In those days for a record album to go in at Number One was quite exceptional, especially as it was the debut album by the band going in at Number One. So the Rollers thing really took off, and every time the band were going to come in, or some of them, there was a mini scene when the band arrived. The funny thing was I was in a stationery shop round the corner from the office just the other day and they had these fridge magnets, you can put notes underneath them, they had one of The Bay City Rollers. I said to the guy behind the counter, do people really buy these now, this is over thirty years later? He said yeah, they sell really well The Bay City Rollers ones.

It was an extraordinary thing at Bell because you had The Bay City Rollers and you had Gary Glitter. The whole story about 'Rock and Roll Part Two' was that it wasn't even Gary Glitter singing on it. Mike Leander made the record, 'Rock and Roll Part Two', which was the first hit and Mike Leander was singing. It took a long time; it wasn't like now, singles either happen or they don't very quickly. It was a real club record, mailed out to clubs; it took a long time. Bell Records, what you did then was, you had these paid plays on Radio Luxembourg; it was all totally legal, it was £20 a play, and they had two or three a week so they were really hammering that as well. So when 'Rock and Roll Part Two' became a hit, they had to find an artist, and that was when they got Paul Gadd and changed his name to Gary Glitter, because it came out as Gary Glitter, that's when Gary got involved. But the early records were basically Mike Leander. Same with Alvin Stardust's, 'My Coo-Ca-Choo'. It was Pete Shelley singing and who also produced it, not the Pete Shelley from the Buzzcocks, the other Pete Shelley who had a hit with 'Love Me, Love My Dog'. He came up with this Alvin Stardust idea and again that was a hit, and they had to go looking and they found Shane Fenton.

CLIVE FRANKS,
Studio Manager

The Troggs used to come up to Dick James Music and we'd speak and have a few laughs and I would cut demos for them and everything. Anyway one night I was engineering there; this was after I'd moved back from Island Studios, I was now the studio manager, and they wanted to do a master recording, which they hadn't done at DJM before, but they wanted to do it. They didn't have a producer with them, and Dennis Burger, who was one of the A&R guys in the office was just there to oversee it, and of course it was that same studio room as before but now we had decent, better equipment but, I still couldn't see the studio from the control room. They couldn't see me from the other room where we had Reg Presley, because he was playing acoustic guitar, so we were all separated. The studio had the drummer, the electric guitarist and Tony the bass player; I was in the control room with Dennis, and Reg was in the other room, and none of us could see each other. They started trying to put this thing down and it went on and on. It was hilarious what was going on. So I thought, should I, should I, or not?

Well, we had some two-track tapes so I put that into record mode, and I let the tapes run through the whole session. When they came back in the control room to hear what they'd done and talk about it, I would sit with my finger on the talkback button because the 'ident' would then go to the tape. Anyway this session went on for three, four hours maybe, and it just fell apart totally, and we abandoned it at two in the morning and everyone went home. I was tired; I just turned the studio off and went home.

The following day there was no session booked in; as I say, it was only a demo studio so we didn't work all the time. Well I had three, four or five reels of 1/4 inch tape that I'd recorded, and I'm thinking, I wonder if it was as funny as I thought it was yesterday. I had marked them as tapes 1, 2 3, so I put the first one on and listened to it; and there's lots of talking, lots of blank bits, lots of door slamming, people going in and out. So I would just listen to it until I got to a funny part, and I'd cut out that funny part. Then I would listen to the next bit and there'd be five minutes of nothing or just boring talk, so I'd pull that bit out, and then the next funny part would come along so I would join it up. Now, I kept joining all the funny bits, never intending to make anything but just to have all the funny comments.

I went through it and it took me a couple of hours, all these reels, cutting out, long stretches of nothing and then hearing funny bits. But it was as it was, I never got to a bit and thought, that would be good in that bit, it was just as it happened through the evening. At the end of it I had a cup of tea and I played it back. I thought, oh my God, that is unbelievable, and someone came into the studio, one of the guys who worked there, and I said: listen to this, and he fell about and said: Give us a copy, and I went, alright. It just went from there. I was the guy that recorded The Troggs Tape, but not too many people know that.

I started doing tapes for people, I thought, I shouldn't be doing this, but people wanted tapes, and of course they'd have a tape and they'd copy it for their mates and this, that and the other, and it went on and on. Anyway time went on, and a few months later Dick James came into the control room and said: I've heard that there's this tape going round of The Troggs; do you know anything about it? I thought, oh, that's it, I'm dead. I said: actually yeah, I do. He didn't ask questions, he said: Do you have a copy, and I went, yeah. He said: Could you do me a copy because they're coming up; they've heard about it too and they want to hear it. I thought, oh shit; that's it, I'm out of the business.

So I made a copy and I was very, very worried. They all came in, and Reg came into the studio and we were talking. We didn't talk about the tape; he said they had a meeting with Dick, he didn't say what it was about. Anyway I'd given the tape to Dick James earlier, so they all went in the office and had this meeting, and the office was just round the corner from the studio. Well after ten or fifteen minutes I came out into the reception area where Dick's office was and I could hear the tape; they'd just started playing it. Now, all of them are in there, Dick, all The Troggs, and the tape. It's going on and suddenly, this was the incredible thing, I heard Reg's voice louder than the tape, yelling at the drummer saying, I told you, you were fucking wrong;

you can't fucking play it, can you? I told you. Now they're arguing again over the top of the tape that was the argument. I'm thinking, should I run in with a mic and do a follow up?

It was just incredible that they were arguing and laughing while listening to the tape. I thought, well this is interesting. So I stayed around for a little while and there was quiet again, and then there was more arguing, so I went back in the studio. Anyway after about another twenty minutes, maybe half-an-hour after the meeting was over, I was out in the studio thinking, oh God, Dick's going to call me and all hell's going to break loose. Reg came into the control room and he went, Dick just played us that tape; it's fucking funny. Can you do us a copy? And that was it; that's as far as it went. They loved it.

A few years later I was on the road, we were up in Birmingham and before the gig I was in the green room or dressing room, there's loads of people in there, and a guy I hadn't seen for years, who actually engineered Kiki Dee's first album that I produced with Elton, the 'Loving & Free' album, a guy called Richard Dodd, he came up to me. He said: Well, I came to see the show but I'm up here working with Jeff Lynne: we're doing an album for him here in Birmingham. So we talked for a while, and he said: George is here. I hadn't noticed, George Harrison was standing in the corner and he said: Have you met George? I said: oh, years ago when they were signed to Dick James Music and one thing and another, but he wouldn't remember me. He said: I'll introduce you to him. So Richard took me over and George was talking to somebody and when they finished talking Richard said: George, I'd like you to meet an old work friend of mine from way back: Clive Franks – he did The Troggs Tape. That's what he said to him, that was his opening line. George came back and said: You did The Troggs Tape? Let me shake your hand, you've given me and the boys years and years of pleasure. I was gobsmacked. I said: hang on a minute, you're George Harrison, I'm supposed to be saying that to you, you've given me years of pleasure. So that broke the ice, and we started talking about The Troggs Tape.

TREVOR CHURCHILL,
Rolling Stones
Label Manager

I've always been a fairly lousy employee, I just don't like people telling me what to do. I like to do it the way I like to do it. So what happened was I just answered an advert in *Music Week* and it was for Label Manager for the Rolling Stones, so I thought that sounds good. I went up and Mick himself did the deed. I'll never forget this interview, the guy can't sit still, you know. He was on his feet all the time; there was a table in the middle and he was walking, strutting round this table asking me questions, walking around like he was on stage, you know, it was amazing. He was a good bloke. Anyway I got the job and I did that for about two-and-a-half years; I can't seem to last any longer than about two-and-a-bit years in most jobs. Again at the beginning, before they started the label, I started work there. The first record I worked on was 'Get Your Ya-Ya's Out', which was the last Decca album, and I helped them get that tongue logo. I happened to know John Pasche who was working at Chrysalis at the time, and he was doing freelance work as well. I don't know why I chose him or what happened but anyway he came up with this logo, they loved it; it is another icon.

John Pasche, he's famous for having done it, we just paid him a measly fee for doing it as well; it didn't seem like anything at the time, it was just something to stick on the label, just to make it look like something instead of a blank yellow label we would just stick this logo on it. They wanted something to go on the label; they hadn't even got the name by then. They just ended up calling it the Rolling Stones Records, which was a bit of a cop out, we had long lists of names we wanted to call it, proper names, but nobody could decide on anything. That's why I never really signed any acts, although we were supposed to be signing acts and making a record label out of it, a proper one, but they could never get that together. They had half-a-million dollars I seem to remember that was on the table there to sign acts with and they could never decide anything so they just took the money and shared it out amongst themselves. I think John went back in after I'd left and they did have the decency to pay him some more; I don't know how much more, I wasn't there.

The other interesting thing there was finding these tapes; they had a rehearsal studio down in Bermondsey that Ian Stewart was in charge of and all the equipment was kept there and stuff, they used to rehearse a bit there. In the corner I noticed a whole pile of multi-track tapes; I thought, what the hell are they? They weren't even marked properly or anything. So I asked Mick if I could just take them down to Olympic Studios and just put them up on the board, not mix them properly or anything, just put all the faders up and make a rough mix and stick it on cassettes, that's what we used to listen to in those days, cassettes. I waded through all these tapes and sent them all cassettes and sure enough there was some good stuff on there. The ones they picked ended up on 'Exile on Main Street'; that's been fairly well documented now and you can tell which ones came out of that pile of tapes. I guess they had too many tapes in Olympic and they just had to take them out or something, I don't know. Anyway that was quite good because they got extra money for a double album, well I thought, that's paid my wages, so walked away from there in a fairly decent frame of mind.

JO MATTHEWS,
Sixties Child

My father was a musician. My mother was a violinist and she was yay high; and my father was an alto-sax player and he was tall like this. Guess who ruled the roost? He'd be upstairs playing and she'd be at the bottom of the stairs going, stop that filthy jungle music! I got very heavy into Jazz and Blues before anything else. Of course when the Stones started coming out with this white version I thought that was absolutely marvellous, with that dirty looking Mick Jagger; you really wanted to, anyway, there was just something about him with that big mouth. He absolutely blew me away. He was tiny of course; all the Rock stars seemed to be so small in those days. You look at them, really narrow little hips, tiny little things. You fancied them until you got to meet them, then you went right off them.

The first time we went to Eel Pie Island, oh God, it blew me away. It was tuppence on the chain ferry, because the bridge wasn't there. So you'd get on this chain ferry, this guy would be up winding away like crazy; you'd get to the other side, and it was a very hot night, and it was Alexis Korner was playing, and I thought, wow, this is absolutely fantastic. Of course everybody is drunk as a skunk and dancing bare foot on the lawn of the hotel. Then I went back to see the Stones, I wasn't that impressed at the time; it was later on that I really, really, you know, thought these are really good. There was something very dirty and sexy about them; up to then you'd had, I don't know, Dennis Lotis and all those vile, clean-cut, singing ballads. I didn't want ballads; I wanted something to be able to get the juices flowing. I loved the *6.5 Special*, absolutely loved it, and when *Ready Steady Go!* came out I thought that's it. I went along to a couple of those sessions, the one I remember really distinctly was when Simon and Garfunkel came here, actually it was just Paul Simon, came over, and he was on *Ready Steady Go!* I was just agog. It was like when Hendrix was on the Lulu show, incongruous to the nth degree.

I was down here but then I met Art Blakey. My mother used to say, my God, she's fallen for a little fat black man. It was the scourge of

126

the family, apart from my father who thought it was wonderful. My daughter lives with Art Blakey. I went off to New York with him; I was sixteen, just before my seventeenth birthday. Went off to live with him but because he was already a big established star, he pampered me, and I could come back to England any time I wanted, but people in those days just didn't cross the Atlantic as freely as they do now. So I was, you know, bit of a brat really. I said: Oh, I want to go back to London for a bit. Sure thing honey, get your ticket. Always first class. So yeah, I kind of got used to that.

FRANKIE LEIGH,
Personal Assistant

In the Sixties I worked for Keith Goodwin, *Private Eye*, NEMS Enterprises, Simon Dee; I mean, I was an 'It Girl'. At all the hippest parties, there was something going on every night of the week and I remember going out never earlier than 11 o'clock at night. London was a small buzzing place; we used to go from the Whisky A-Go-Go to the Discotheque to the Flamingo, to the Scene, to the Last Chance, to the Speakeasy, to the Bag of Nails; I mean, all these incredible clubs that were hopping every night of the week.

Simon Dee came from Radio Caroline, he was offered his own talk show and he did very well. Simon Dee was the first radio personality to get his own television show, and working for Simon was like working for Royalty. I remember driving down Park Lane with him in his Aston Martin, in his DB5 red Aston Martin, with the roof down, and he would drive 100 miles an hour down Park Lane. Stepping into the Aretusa or any restaurant and literally getting the red carpet rolled out. He was a superstar. He started at the BBC and then they got into a big feuding war with him because, as he used to say to me: It's my name that's up there, it's called the Simon Dee show and if they want to put a guest that I'm not interested in and the interview falls flat, it's still my name up there and they're going to say, it's the Simon Dee show and it stank. So he used to fight for what he thought would be an interesting show and what the public wanted to hear.

We used to have a flat that I used to work out of in Stuart Towers in Maida Vale, on the fourteenth floor where I looked over the whole of London. It was quite glamorous. Pluggers would be on the phone to me every day plugging their artists; I mean, relentlessly. I was his personal assistant, and that carried a lot of weight.

I'd go to Biba a lot. Biba was my drug of choice. I used to have to go to Biba at least once a week and get a new outfit.

JON NEWEY,
Magazine Publishing

Certainly in around 1960 or '61 I started to get very interested in listening to *Pick Of The Pops* on a Sunday because this was the only kind of show where they played modern records really on the BBC Light Programme. I was also tuning in to Radio Luxembourg on a crystal set that my father had bought me; one of those fantastic little crystal sets that you bought from Headquarters and General Stores up in High Holborn, London, these wonderful stores where everything seemed to be advertised with the tag line, *Latest Russian Miracle*. The other tag line was when it went: *Fantastic Volume, From a Whisper to a Roar, Enough to Fill the Largest Hall*. But of course you ended up listening to it on these tiny headphones. Tuning into Radio Luxembourg and listening to that phased signal under your bed sheets. Well funnily enough there was an offer on there advertising the *New Musical Express*, and you could send off for a copy by enclosing a stamped addressed envelope. You hardly ever saw it for sale in the shops, and the idea of a Pop music weekly absolutely fascinated me. So I sent off for it and sure enough, two weeks later a copy of NME arrived. It was all Cliff and The Shads and so on and so forth. I remember it was before The Beatles came out so it was still 'Beat before The Beatles'. There begun a really lifelong fascination with the music press, and I've spent the last thirty years working full time in the music press, but that was where it all began.

The first gigs I started going to were in the Sixties at the Silver Blades Ice Rink in Streatham, because I grew up and was brought up in Streatham, and I can always remember the first gig that I went to on my own was the very Monday that The Kinks' 'You Really Got Me' went to Number One, and I actually saw them that night. They did what was called a 'personal appearance'; they actually came on and played for half-an-hour. I remember I was thrilled because I got their autographs that night, and I must have been then thirteen years old, so I started going to gigs on my own at thirteen. Over the weeks at Streatham they had Nashville Teens, The Pretty Things, all manner of bands really. The Kinks were, along with The Beatles and Stones, absolutely my favourite bands. Then when The Who came out, and certainly The Pretty Things as well, but it was The Who, who really grabbed me. I think because I was studying Art at school and their whole thing with the feedback, with the quite aggressive sound and also all the pop art and op art imagery. Of course the clothes too, because it was I would say the more attractive end of Mod, because there was quite an unattractive side of Mod, which was the whole kind of bullying side to it. The whole front that The Who put across I think was, well, it was just everything that you kind of ever wanted really. Then we actually started to go to Locarno in Streatham as well where they had bands on, so we'd go and see The Small Faces. I remember a memorable performance by The Who in December 1966, where they wrecked all the gear, and it was at the time when 'Happy Jack' was out, by which time their sound was becoming more innovative and of course The Yardbirds were doing all these innovative things with sound. I was really drawn to feedback and weird guitar breaks, and Eastern modes on the guitar. Then of course by that time I discovered The Blues as well, mainly through John Mayall and Eric Clapton's Bluesbreakers.

TONY POWELL, Manager, The Witch Doctor Club

This might not sound right, but I was standing on a corner at the end of a street in Hastings in the Sixties and this big blue American car, I think it was a Ford Thunderbird 500 or something, pulls up, soft top down, man driving it, middle-aged bloke with a very good looking young blonde woman by his side. Left-hand drive, pulls up alongside: Excuse me, do you know where such-and-such is, which was Marine Court in St Leonard's. I said: Oh yes, you can't go wrong, you just go along the sea front and it's a building that looks like a ship; still there to this day. He said: Are you from round here? and I said: Yes, he said: Do you need a lift or anything? Yeah, that would be nice; I've actually got to go that way. So I jumped in the back of this American car, I wasn't going to miss that opportunity was I? We just made idle chat, and we got to where it was, and he asked: What do you do? I said: Well, I don't do anything, I've just lost my father. He asked: Do you like music, do you follow music locally? I said: Oh yes, we have the Hastings Pier, we have some of the big acts on. Then he asked: What else is there in Hastings? I explained: Well there isn't anything really, there's a few coffee bars but as far as gigs and places to go, it's very difficult. It's just Hastings Pier, we go Friday and Saturday night. Oh, he said: I own a nightclub in Manchester but I'm maybe looking at this place here that's maybe opening a dance hall place to put bands on. I said: Oh, that'll be brilliant. He said: Well, we might need some bods to help out when we're doing it, give me your name and address. So I did, didn't think any more of it and off he went.

About four weeks later a letter dropped through the letterbox: we've decided to do this, I've given your name and address to the person who's going to be setting this up, please go along and introduce yourself, I'm sure he could find you a little job to do. I go along, walk in, meet this guy from Manchester; he explains to me what he's doing, they're putting in a floor which has got square up-lighting, they're going to call this place The Witch Doctor. So I met this guy who was going to manage it. He said: We've got to paint it, we've got to decorate it, we've got to do all this. I was on the payroll. Within about a week he said: I've got to find some bar staff because we're opening in about three, four weeks. He said: We've got to build the bar, and do you know who the local breweries are? So I sort of put him in touch with a few people. About two weeks before the place was ready to open he said: I think you should be in charge of the bar. I went: Well I've never done anything like that. He said: It's not a problem, not a problem. So that was my job, I had to get the bar sorted out.

Right, opening night's coming up; first act on Friday night is The Nashville Teens. They're coming down straight from *Ready Steady Go!*, and they're going to be on, and of course that week the record went to Number One. So on the Friday night they had *Ready Steady Go!* and then they are to arrive at this club where I'm head of the bar. All was going swimmingly until the day before The Nashville Teens were due to turn up; the guy who was running the club, decides he doesn't want to run the club, he wants to go back to Manchester. So there's a guy drafted in who was doing the Maidstone ballroom to run it. He comes over to me and he says: Forget about the bar, I need you to do other things; you can be my assistant. So I became the assistant manager of the club before it even opened. We opened, first night The Nashville Teens, the place was absolutely rammed. I can remember it was so hot, even before the act came on. I ended up having to go on the microphone, which I'd never picked up in my life before, because part of the role I now had to do was to put the records on between the bands. All I had was a Dansette Junior auto-changer and a microphone, and as one record finished I started talking and I had to stop before the next record dropped down. So I went on this microphone and just as a flippant thing I just said to the kids: If you get hot there's always the sea outside; just run down have a dip and come back. Well with that, half the place emptied; everybody's rushing down, diving in the sea and coming back, and they're all completely and utterly drenched with water. Oh My God! But everybody had such a magnificent night that first night, and they had The Nashville Teens on; it was just like, Wow.

The place just went from strength to strength. We were opening every night, we were putting bands on. Saturday nights were our big band nights, or Friday nights: two bands. You'd have a reasonable band and then some local band, or somebody who was on a tour. Sunday's we do a sort of Souly, Jazzy night, which would be all the acts that had most probably played The Flamingo in London the night before; so you had Geno Washington, Zoot Money, Georgie Fame, all those sort of people on a Sunday night. Wednesday, then we used to do a mid-week special where again you'd have the up and coming bands. Anybody who was anybody with a transit van at the time would be coming in and you'd be paying them like £10 a session or something like that. That was all fun, and the amount of people we had through the door, like numerous other places, because everybody was on the same circuit, you name it, from The Moody Blues, to Them, to Dave, Dee, Dozy, Beaky, Mick and Titch, who started off as Dave Dee and The Bostons and acts like that. If only I had that list of all those people. Obviously during that period it was the Mods and Rockers thing as well, so that gave it all a focal point and an emphasis.

SID CHASE,
Road Manager

The Hellraisers were with the Jim Godboldt Agency, which was the same agency as The Swinging Blue Jeans. We go back to what, 1964, '65, yeah? We got the engagement to play The Witch Doctor club in Hastings, which was right on the sea front, it was a circular room with a glass floor and a glass ceiling, which had lights in both, flashing lights. All round the room were pictures of witch doctors; you can imagine when the lights started flashing and everything else, it was quite good. I was road manager for the group and we arrived there, I was taking all the gear in to set it up. On the left hand side I noticed was like a little cubicle, which is like the old cinema, the ticket came out of the slot, and they had a notice up there which said 'Entrance Fee 12/6d, which includes two Aspirins'. I spoke to the girl who was just inside, I said: Do you work in the box? and she said Yeah, so I asked her what the two Aspirins were for, and she said The Hellraisers are on first, followed by Screaming Lord Sutch. Just hang around for a bit and you'll find out, and I did. Screaming Lord Sutch came on and I found out what the two Aspirins were for and I went outside and stood by the sea, and you could still hear him from the other side of the road.

We started off gigging on the Friday night and we'd gone down somewhere on the south coast. We'd ended up going from the south coast touching on to the parts of Devon, and were to end up on the Sunday night at Kings Lynn in Norfolk, supporting this group, which I thought was one of the best R&B groups at the time, a group called Missing Links that came from the West Midlands, Birmingham area. They went down really well. Then when we got to Kings Lynn, I got out of the van, found the manager, explained who I was, got the dressing room set up and all the rest of it, but there was no lock on the door. Our group by now being stars of television after doing BBC2 *Beat Room* were the headline group and Missing Links were the supporting group to us. So they'd done their bit, The Hellraisers done our bit, and we've gone back to the dressing room. Well what I've done is stood with my back against the door, and the door's being pushed from the other side by these heaving, panting females. I'm standing there, and my mate, then the drummer, said: What are you doing Sid? I'm keeping the door closed. Why? Well, there's at least twelve girls the other side of this door trying to get in. Yeah? So I opened the door and I went out to the van.

PETE DELLO,
Musician

Then we decided that we'd like to start our own Skiffle club, so we did do that. It was quite good really, we had about an average of about four or five people on a Saturday night, on a Thursday night, until we discovered that everybody was going down this place called the 59 Club run by Father John Oates, which was a really big place; all the stars used to go and play down there. In the end we all trooped down there just to look at the competition. The first thing we saw was about a thousand kids in there; and then secondly they had a proper stage. Downstairs they had snooker tables and everything, it was a real going concern. It was opened by Princess Margaret. The Shadows were down there; I've got a lovely photo somewhere of Hank Marvin's foot coming up and just missing her chin with one of his kicks.

Adam Faith and Cliff used to come down there a bit, Vince Taylor, all the big stars at that time used to come down and play for nothing because Father John was like that. He's still like that; he still gets you doing things for nothing. I remember him saying to us: You can start on Sunday. I said: Oh, I didn't know you did anything on Sunday. He said: Yes, we have a free one, but everybody's got to go to church. Then we found out we had to go to church as well. But it was quite interesting because it was High Anglican, you know, with the incense and I found it quite enjoyable really. I can't say I got religion or anything but the interesting point about this is the amount of work the church used to do in the community. They didn't have all this 'church in the community' stuff that we got in the Seventies, which all became sound bites and things like that. They actually used to do it because where I lived there was at least three or four church clubs that really did their job, and it was somewhere for you to go. The 59 Club was of course the epitome of these because it got a very rough district; it got everybody coming in to that area, coming towards the club and getting involved.

We used to do trips down to Clacton and it was always well publicised in the Evening Standard and Evening News and all that. So it was a really big concern, and that really was the beginning. I think if I hadn't actually gone to that I wouldn't have progressed really in music. I said to him, Rev, what do you think of our band? Well, he says: It's alright, but what I like to do is to get two of my best bands and put them into one group. That's what he did, and that's when this little group called Red Talis and The Talisman I think it was, became Grant Tracy and The Sunsets, which became a little bit more like a proper group; everybody had equipment for a start. Then he sort of took us over and he took us on lots of gigs and everything. He used to do everything for us, we did a few TV things, and he was really sort of in it all, he'd put the make-up on us if we did the TV and put the little dots; he was really completely au fait with show business and everything, and quite a wonderful bloke really.

CHAS HODGES,
Musician

When we started getting bits of hit records in the charts, then of course the rest of the country had heard about us, so we started doing gigs in like, Bristol and Manchester, and Shrewsbury; long way away, and there was no motorways in those days, wasn't even the M1 as far as I can remember. The M1 might have just started, but there was no other motorways; everything was like, the old A4 you went to Bristol, and it took ages. I remember we used to work it, average, and it works out right in those days, wherever you were going, if it's a 90-mile trip it's an average of 30 mph so it would take three hours. That's normal traffic, with a stop at a transport café. So that was it, and that was our first taste of being on the road and being bored on those journeys.

We were on the road with Heinz and his band, and we had bought some cheese rolls or something, we just went past and chucked them at him. It was so exciting that at the next town we stopped, and it was

Ritchie Blackmore's idea, he said: Let's get some flour bags. Well we bought these little half-pound flour bags, all clubbed together, and he was a better shot that me. When you're going along in the van that way and someone's walking the opposite way you've got to just know when to throw it. We'd always pick hard nuts; we never picked any old people or kids. We'd pick the Teddy Boy who thought he was going out for the night really done up to the nines, and chucked the flour bag at him, just these clouds of flour. We just used to fall about, it was just hilarious. I remember doing it once, there was a bloke looking under his car bonnet and we just went past and sort of dropped it on his head, and it just whap, just like it does in the films. He must have had the fan belt going. But he jumped in his car and chased us, we're going around, and we end up going to Swansea. We were about ten miles out of Swansea going around all the back doubles trying to miss him. We were with Gene Vincent then at the time. He finally caught us when we were sitting outside the gig. He comes out of his car and he was a statue, just pure white. Oy, cunt, he says to Gene Vincent in the front. What Sir? No Sir, not me. He give him a right bollocking, but he didn't do anything; there was too many of us there in the car.

Ritchie Blackmore hit on the next one, he was good at thinking of things like that. Buying these big bags of goosegogs and a catapult. I remember Gene Vincent; we stopped and I can see it now like it was a video, we'd pulled up at this level crossing and Gene Vincent always had the best seat, the passenger seat, while we were all stuck in the back under overcoats and all that. Ritchie Blackmore leant over behind Gene and there was this woman walking towards us. I remember she had one of them Sixties PVC macs on, that was sort of draped down. Ritchie Blackmore went boom, and it went whap, hit her in the back. Didn't hurt her because it was like a slack bass drum, and of course Gene Vincent fell about and this woman came back and she grabs hold of Gene, shaking him: Not me M'am, not me. With that, the level crossing gates open and off we went. But Gene told that story to everybody. He loved it: Whap, it went.

BOB SOLLY, Musician

In the early Sixties I was asked to go professional by a band called Band Seven, a seven-piece band, and they had saxes and so on, and it was one of those showband type of things where you wear a tuxedo and a dickie bow; I was a guitar player then. So that was the start of my professional career and they were based in Maidstone in Kent. There were a couple of fellows in that band, who had the same thinking as I did, so we left and formed The Manish Boys. We had a contract with Dick James Music. We went to see Dick James and he lined us all up against the wall and said: Look, you lot, one thing, no booze and no girls; I won't tolerate it. Now you can go and see Leslie Conn. Leslie Conn was a manager in another office, he was a real character. He said: I've got a great thing lined up for you; I'm glad I've met you all because I've got a singer who's ideal for you. His name is David Jones.

We said no more singers, because we all sang ourselves; I started out as a singer actually, and he said: Well, he's made a record and he's very good, plays a saxophone, you've got saxes in the band. I'll come down with him at the weekend and you can give him a trial. So we did. He came down one summer weekend, he came in the back door with Davie, and that was it. We thought, wow. He had long hair down here, and buckskin and everything, and we thought, oh yeah, he's great, he'll do. So we make a place for him in the band, but we didn't really want him at first, we didn't want anyone else. That's how that David Jones/Bowie happened.

Eel Pie Island and the Marquee, we seemed to play in all of them. Then quite often we would rehearse in these places too. Not necessarily Eel Pie Island, but in Soho, some of those clubs, they've got rehearsal rooms above and you'd rehearse in these places. Next door might be The Moody Blues, and over there you've got The Downliners Sect, all in the same place. Of course in those days you could go into the coffee bars around Soho and in a minute Jimmy Page would walk in, and Rod Stewart would come in, someone like that, and there'd be a whole coffee bar full of these future superstars. They were Jack-the-lads round town in those days. You might have Rod Stewart come in and he'd say: Are you lot working tonight? And we'd say: yeah, then he'd say: I wish I was. It was great. We've even played as a group with Bowie as the lead singer in a field where no-one, absolutely no-one turned up. It was a Harvest Festival thing and just no-one turned up. No-one, zero.

We recorded for Mickie Most. We auditioned for him at the Charlie Chester Casino in Archer Street, which was a favourite place to audition for people like Mickie Most and other agents in the afternoons. We got down there and set up on the little stage in this room downstairs and we were playing away and Mickie Most came in and sat down opposite and listened to us. When we finished a couple of numbers he came up and stood in front of us and said: I really like what I'm hearing; do you want to make records with me? And we said: oh yeah, absolutely. So within a day or two he'd booked a Decca session for us and we had 'Duke of Earl', 'Hello Stranger', 'Love is Strange', and one other I can't remember. We did it I think in Regent Sound in Denmark Street. But it was never released and presumably the tapes got wiped. Tapes were quite a valuable commodity so no-one hung on to them. Probably the next day Mickie Most would have heard it and said: No, can't use that, or something of that nature and they would have immediately just wiped them.

In the Fifties, and previous to that I suppose, you became a musician because you wanted to be good at what you're chosen thing was. Nowadays of course it's the fame, the fortune, the stretch limousines and all the rest of it: the celebrity culture. But there was none of that in the Fifties. You would appear on stage in the clothes you'd been walking around the street in during the day, and probably slept in the night before. So there was nothing glamorous or glitzy about it at all. It was the music that counted 100% really. Except, one of the other driving factors for people wanting to play music was the girls, and of course you got many, many more girlfriends if you actually could stand on stage and give them a wink and play 'Poor Little Fool' or something. That was really another motivational force. So it was the music first perhaps, and then impressing the girls later.

TONY HILLER, Songwriter

My great grand blah blah came from Poland, came to the East End of London. As my father and his father got a bit older, the boys, his three sons, went to America but they left Sam, my father, behind as he was the youngest one. The sons all did very well actually, very well, in the music business, or very successful agents. Then they called for my father and my father went there apparently in 1912 as a young man, and they got him a job in a company where the late, great Irving Berlin worked. In fact my brother Irving is named after Berlin so there you are. Then my father came back and as we got older we'd hear these wonderful stories. Now my parents were not professional players but they were musicians without playing instruments. All I heard as a kid was harmonies; I didn't know what thirds and fifths were but I heard harmonies and we were always singing. I was one of eight, and the four girls were older and they were always singing, so I always heard music.

As we got older, I'm talking now about eighteen, we started to play at writing songs, and there was Irving Hiller, Tony Hiller, and a boy called Danny Newman, and the three of us wrote, and over a period we had about twenty-six cuts, which was very good those days. That's what we did, that's really how we started. Irving and I would write songs, go down Denmark Street and sell our songs. We sold many songs for thirty quid or twenty quid, or if we were lucky fifty quid. When I say sold, it was just an advance royalty; you never sold the copyright. That's what we did. So that's how I became a writer, and Irving became a writer. We also became a double act, The Hiller Brothers and we worked with probably every major act of the period. In fact I became a London cab driver, and so did my brother Irving because it enabled us to be able to work at nights and go down Denmark Street in the daytime. That's really how we started.

We worked in Germany as an artist; we worked in France. We worked all over the place, had a fabulous time. We worked with the biggest but we weren't big, but the getting there was just so exciting.

It was the background of my father and hearing about these great writers and us loving, and my father and mother were always singing and harmonising; always. I was: What song is that dad? And then as we got older we became very, very learned; we knew every record, every writer, we looked for the mechanicals. We knew everything, who the writer was, who the publisher was, who the arranger was, who the producer was, who the company was. So we had a lot of knowledge. We used to go every day and sell our songs, and we would meet all the other writers, and also the greats and have our tea at the cafe. We'd see Dick James and see everybody. By going round and trying to sell our songs, they knew us and then they'd say: Do you fancy doing a demo for us? So we were getting a living out of it. We did well because I was a good harmoniser, and we really worked. We weren't nervous and we sold songs, and we got twenty quid or thirty quid or whatever.

LES REED O.B.E., Songwriter

In London's Archer Street the musicians were my big friends, a lot of heroes. But somebody, I think it was Kenny Baker, who's a wonderful trumpet man, knew that I was a bit of a composer, and he said: Why don't you go down to Denmark Street, all the songwriters are there; it may suit you. So I strolled down to Denmark Street, and immediately I went into Tin Pan Alley I felt at home. I don't know what it is but I felt home. I looked up at the windows and there was publisher, publisher, publisher, Regent Sounds Studios, and there's the little café, Julie's Café, down the road.

I'm looking at some of these guys thinking, he's a famous songwriter that guy. So I went into Julie's Café and I'm sitting there drinking a cup of tea and all these old war songwriters were sitting in the corner. I actually didn't know them but I knew who they were. But Tony

Hiller, who was a publisher then with Mill's Music, came in, he said: Hi, you want a cup of tea? He immediately became very friendly. I said: I'd love one thanks, who are you? He said: Tony Hiller, I'm of The Hiller Brothers, my brother and I do an act but in the meantime I'm working for Mills Music as a plugger. I said: Les Reed, I'm a musician trying to get into the popular song business. He said: I'm your man. So we sat down, had a great talk and a cup of tea together, and I said: who are these guys over here? He said: You'll never believe it, Jimmy Kennedy, I said: Jimmy Kennedy? He wrote 'South of the Border'. Yeah, he said: and others; and he named half-a-dozen other songs, 'Harbour Lights', you name it. I said: the other guy? That's Michael Carr, he wrote this, that and the other. I said: gee, I've got to meet these guys. So I went over and met Jimmy and Michael Carr and we became really, really good friends. In fact Jimmy, over the next few years, became my mentor and taught me all about commercial songwriting; all about it. Of course I was a big fan because some of the songs, 'South of the Border', was done by Les Brown who was a big band man; he wrote some wonderful stuff. He took me on basically and taught me everything I know today.

I went out and worked with Geoff Stephens and a couple of other writers, Jimmy Duncan, Mitch Murray. We came up with a few songs and Burt liked what we'd done; they managed to get a couple of records on some of these songs, not least of all The Applejacks with 'Tell Me When', which was a massive hit for them, which I wrote with Geoff Stephens.

Later Barry Mason used to come down to my place in Woking and one Sunday afternoon we were going to play golf, but it was raining so I said let's do some work. He had got there about half-past ten in the morning on this Sunday and we actually started eight songs. Out of those eight songs, five became hits, and others became album tracks. 'The Last Waltz' was one of them; 'Les Bicyclettes de Belsize', 'Kiss Me Goodbye', 'Love Is All'. There was one other, 'I Pretend', by Des O'Connor; they all became hits over the next few months or few years. To this day I think it's a magic story because I don't think there's anybody else that has produced eight songs. Even though we didn't write them all in that day, we took time to finish them; but all the ideas, the germs of the ideas, were there that day. We had a title here, and a hook, put that aside, we'll start that next week, etc etc. that's how we did it in those days, and came up with these eight songs, five of which became very big hits and the other three became lovely album tracks for other people.

Our way of working was, we'd start with a cup of tea, always a cup of tea. It's ironic in a way that we were pop writers and we didn't get the bottle of whisky out, or the drugs or anything else that goes with our business. We were tea men, literally, and we'd probably get through half a dozen cups in a day, probably more, and some biscuits or whatever. When people hear this they say, oh cute; nothing stronger? No, nothing stronger, ever. So it's become a bit of a joke in the business, the Tea Men. But on that tea we wrote one helluva lot of songs.

I just want to put one thing on record, because, love him as I do, my old friend and partner Barry Mason, always takes credit for some reason for the title of 'The Last Waltz'. Really how it happened was that, when I was a kid and the War was on, my mother would go to a dance over the allotment and you could hear the music coming from the old village hall there, and I used to listen out round about 10 o'clock at night, and once I'd heard the last waltz playing, which was 'Who's Taking You Home Tonight'. These women were all dancing together, the men weren't around, they were all in the War, and I knew that I would get my supper within ten minutes. I was telling Barry this story, and he says, Les, has anyone ever done a song called 'The Last Waltz'? I said: Well, that's why I explained the story, because I thought we've got to write a last waltz! Indeed, a couple of weeks before that I'd offered it to Geoff Stephens, this idea, and I'd already done melody, and he was watching the England/Australia cricket match in his front room, and he'll verify this, and we'd just written a beautiful song, and he said: I want to watch the cricket. I said: No, No, I've got one more idea. He said: What is it?, I said: It's called 'The Last Waltz'. He said: No, no, next time. So I thought well, blow you and I took it, and that's when I gave the idea to Barry; but he still insists he came up with the title of 'The Last Waltz'. But I love you Barry, I love you.

JOHNNY WORTH, Songwriter

I remembered years back, Buddy Holly, when I was in the Oscar Rabin band. When you finished the gig it was 2 o'clock in the morning and if you didn't have a car, and nobody did as you had to be a millionaire to have a car in those days, so you had to catch the all night bus home to Wandsworth, and then walk from Wandsworth High Street to Southfields, which is one tube station away from Wimbledon. You didn't get home till three in the morning. What you did was, you went down to the Embankment and you stood under Hungerford Bridge, because the bus stop was under the bridge, and if you're old enough to remember, nearly every railway bridge in England leaked like a sieve. They never worried about rain pouring through; so wherever you stood there'd be rain coming in under Hungerford Bridge, so you found a place where it didn't hit you. But it made puddles, and I used to stand there night after night and listen to this noise, it was like somebody playing. Well I thought, yeah, that's Buddy Holly, that is. That's when I started to write 'What Do You Want'. When I say write it, I just made it up as I went along. I thought, hey, that's what I'll do, I'll have pizzicato strings in it somewhere. So I got on the piano with one finger, because I could hear what I wanted.

Adam Faith, I'd got to be very friendly with, well they used to make him sing Rock and Roll songs, and I sidled up, like you do, and said: You are a small person with a wonderful presence and a great face, and you shouldn't be singing Rock songs. You should be singing love songs, and then every granny, and every mum, and every kid are going to fall at your feet. He said: Oh, do you think so? He already had two records released, neither one of them was a hit, they were with Top Rank, and they flopped. Well because we used to go out in the break in rehearsal rooms and go and have a coffee or leaf through vinyl records, the conversation would go on and on about his future; so naturally when he was asked to record for EMI, Parlophone, he asked: You got any songs John? I said: Yeah, but I haven't got it on me, I'll bring it in tomorrow.

I had to get somebody to write it out; so I got Les Reed to write it and I told Les put the pizzicato strings in and I'll write the lyrics under those notes, like footballs on sticks. So he did, and when John Barry did the arrangement as Les was the pianist, John said: Can we have pizzicato strings? John Barry said: Yeah, sure, and he did it. So that's how it got there. Then I did probably the most important thing I did for myself and for Adam. I said: What I want you to do is sing in a way that no other people sing. Not lunacy land, but you need to have distinctively your own style, and if I can say that without insulting you, is you're not a very good singer, and he took it. I said: What you've got is charisma, massive charisma. So what I want to try to do with you, if you'll go along with me, is to create something different in your vocabulary, the way you sing. I had noticed that he had this top tooth over the lip so 'what do you want...' became 'vot do you vant...' You can't say it now but you could say it then with clarity – it was different. They are always the songs that are massive hits, the ones that are 'different', so we've got to find something 'different' that you can do. And then it hit us. We twisted 'baby' into 'bay-beh' You sing that to anybody and they'll love you. It's easy to be clever after the event. It was just an idea, and we're extraordinarily lucky that it hit. He was bloody well right. It wasn't just Number One, it was Number One for sixteen weeks, and it's still selling today. It never stops being played. I can't understand it, but I am ever so grateful.

GUY FLETCHER, Songwriter

We wrote a song, I don't even remember when it was, in the Seventies sometime. We're sitting there and I'm playing a Fender Rhodes and I come up with a few notes and a tune, and I say to Doug: You know what, this would be great for Ray Charles. We sat and wrote this song called 'Is There Anyone Out There?' It was a song that we sat down and wrote for Ray Charles. I made a demo of it, which was extraordinarily slow and about four-and-half minutes long, which was interminably long for a Pop song in the Seventies. It was at least a minute longer than anything else we'd ever had. Anyway we made the demo and, to make a long story short, we went to Los Angeles, doing some stuff with our publishers, and I said to Doug: Let's get this to Ray Charles ourselves. So we rented a car and drove to Watts, south of Los Angeles and this is an extraordinary naïve thing to do and I had no knowledge because being brought up in England you don't have this innate knowledge of Harlem in New York, Watts in Los Angeles and what that means; those communities don't mix, they're quite separate, or they were then.

We didn't think about it; we got in the car and drove to Watts all because Ray Charles had a little company called Orange Records, which was right in the middle of Watts. We drove there, and when we got down there I looked round us and I thought, this is a very strange place. It was entirely black people everywhere, there weren't any white people. I even looked at the billboards and the cowboy riding the horse smoking a Marlboro, saying Welcome to Marlboro country, was a black guy. This was an extraordinary revelation to me; I'd never seen it before. Didn't think anything of it, so we found Orange Records, went in, walked in through the door, they were gobsmacked to see Doug and I, two little white guys from England come in. They said: Can we help? I said: Yeah, I've got a song for Mr Charles, is he here? They said: Well no, he's not actually here, but we'll get someone to talk to you. They went out the back and got Big Dee Irwin, who was at that time head of A&R for Orange. He came out, he's a massive, big old Rock and Roll singer, I was thrilled to see him. He came out and he said: You better come in. He took our acetate and put it on the turntable, and this was a very slow song, very slow; it took probably half a minute to get to the first line of lyric. Anyway he only got fifteen seconds in before he took it off and he said: Thank you very much coming, Mr Charles will not be recording this song. So that was the end of that, and we went away.

We got back, crestfallen, in the car, drove back up to our publishers in Hollywood, and we walked in and said: We've just been down to Watts and seen... and Lance Freed said: You Did What? You Went Where? What did you do that for? and we said: Well, Ray Charles, dadada. Anyway, they told us how stupid we'd been and we were lucky to escape with our lives, and you're never going to get a song recorded down there like that. So we gave up. They submitted it via one of their black music specialists, and it was turned down. Then the following year they submitted it again and it was turned down.

Five years went by. Suddenly I got a call from this guy called Shelly Weiss who said: I'm now working for A&M, I've just found your catalogue and this great song in here that would be marvellous for Ray Charles. I said: Yeah, tell me about it. It's been turned down for five years. He said: Leave it with me, and he went out and got a Braille lead sheet done. He ran across Ray Charles at some event, said: I've got this song for you, have a feel of this, sort of thing and Ray Charles said: I want to hear it. They played it to him and he recorded it one week later. So five years it took. It's still the same song, it's just that he'd never heard it up until then.

MALCOLM FORRESTER, Music Publisher

I was always quite pally with Tony Caulder. I knew Andrew Loog-Oldham but not that well. So eventually I decided to throw my lot in with Immediate Records, because they were an exciting place to be. I kept an element of my publishing catalogue, Getaway Music, the song 'Getaway', Georgie Fame and some other things; so I kept an element of that and threw my lot in with Immediate. They had the Beach Boys catalogue and stuff like that, and all The Faces thing, and Michael D'Abo a great writer, brilliant, still is a fantastic writer. That was the beginning of it although I'd been on my own for two or three years before going with Andrew and Tony, that was the big learning curve for me. That was most probably Andrew getting towards the tail end of his relationship with the Rolling Stones, but he invested a fortune in Immediate, Andrew. I know people slag us all off and we get it on the Immediate thing and we're all a bit Svengalis to certain age groups, but under our watch I thought it was a superbly run company. There was Andrew, who would come in every now and then; Tony ran it, basically, with his wife Jenny.

When we had The Small Faces at Number One in Germany, Andrew, myself and Tony, went out to Berlin, they were playing in some arena thing. So we turn up and we're in the foyer of the hotel and somebody comes up to Andrew and says: Did you know Little Richard's playing down the road? Now we've got this biggest act in town. But Andrew says to me and Tony: Have you ever seen Little Richard? No. Shall we go there first? Oh, what a great idea. We had limousines in those days, went to this club and we saw Little Richard. Fantastic. How good's that? We saw Little Richard and we come out of there late; so we go to this auditorium, like a kind of Earl's Court type thing, we go there and there's no-one, they're wheeling out the hot dog stalls, they're coming out, there's no-one around. The Small Faces were so pissed off with us, oh dear oh Lord.

But I stayed up with Andrew all night, that night, because it was after Kennedy had done the famous speech and that platform was still there. We went round the corner there about 4 o'clock in the morning and we go round, and we say to the driver: What's that? He says: That's where JFK spoke. Well we walk up, as you do when you're pissed, and are looking over the Berlin Wall, there's the wall, and we're looking over it. It was a big thing, it was important in our lives, the Berlin Wall, big thing. Andrew was dressed in robes in those days, he says: I'm going to bless them. I thought, oh okay, here we go. All of a sudden I see this machine-gun, or whatever, some piece of kit was aiming at me. I was down those stairs, in the car, round the corner; he says: No, I'm going to bless them, and I thought, you can bless them as much as you like Andrew.

TONY HALL,
Record Promoter

Brian Epstein I knew pretty well. I had a flat in Green Street in those days, in Mayfair, and two of The Beatles, George and Ringo, were living right across the road from me and I was very friendly with them at the time. They came and introduced themselves to me once. Anytime they wanted to come over to my place, they had to call me first; they had to because of the fans outside in the street all the time. They had to order a radio taxi, which pulled up outside their flat across the road; they then had to go half-way round the West End, change taxis, come back and stop off at my side, and I'd be waiting in the dark with an open door and they'd dash in. Crazy.

But we used to give fantastic parties at Green Street on Friday nights, generally after Ready Steady Go!, and literally everybody who was anybody in those days used to come. The Beatles would be there, the Stones would be there, Dusty, Cilla, Eppy, Andrew; they were quite notorious. We also gave a party there when The Beatles wanted to meet The Ronettes, and so that was laid on. It was strictly The Beatles and Ronettes, plus Andrew Loog-Oldham and Phil Spector, and it ended up being a very weird evening, and John Lennon ended up disappearing with Ronnie Spector upstairs; we never saw him for a while. Phil disappeared and came back later. All very odd.

I think that same night, there was a terrifying experience with Phil Spector and the chauffeur-driven car that Decca were paying for him to ride around in town in. There was a big restaurant, somewhere in Mayfair. I can't remember the name. Phil pushed the driver out of the seat and took over this car, and he's still so small that all you could see was this head over the steering wheel, and the car was much too powerful for him; and he drove this through the West End at a rate of knots, scattering people left, right and centre. A pretty terrifying experience that night, thank God I wasn't in it. I saw it but I wasn't in it.

In the same era, did you ever hear 'Fuck You Sir Edward', which is recorded by The Stones, Andrew Oldham, Phil Spector and Gene Pitney? It's a sort of twelve bar riff that they recorded in Denmark Street in the legendary studio there. I had a copy once but I don't know what happened to it. It was in a drawer once, it may still be. A BBC producer asked me to let him have my copy once and he taped it. I don't know what happened to the tape though.

£££

STUART BATSFORD, Manager

It was August 1986, I've gone as far as I can go working in a very small independent import record company called Shigaku. A couple of relationships had fallen apart, I'm ready to make a move, and I'd become very friendly with an American musician called Phil Seymour. We stayed in touch and one particularly sour, miserable day I called him and was telling him of my woes, and he said: Why don't you come to Los Angeles, and you could be my manager and get me a record deal. Well it seemed like an incredibly appealing idea. The day after I got into LA something very strange happened. We were driving in the car and he received a phone call from Phil Spector's secretary, who suggested that he come and see Phil because Phil would like to record him. He asked if I was able to go too and she said that was fine, so within twenty-four hours of getting to LA there I was invited to the Spector mansion.

We turned up a week later, 22nd August 1986, 8pm. We got there and we were greeted by Phil's man, George, who looked after his house and his cars and his grounds, and ferried Phil around from place to place, and George invited us into the living room where we sat. I can still remember now walking through the hallway and at the end of the hallway was one single very large mono speaker, with a 'Back to Mono' badge pinned to it, and it was playing Fifties doo-wop. You double-backed at the end of the hallway and came into the living room, and at the end of the living room that you entered was a white piano, which had a Christmas card on it, although this was August, and I believe the Christmas card was from 1970 or '71, from John and Yoko, saying: Happy Christmas Phil, love John and Yoko.

So we sat there, and after a few minutes another couple of people entered the room and one of them was a guy called Art Fein, and he had a girl with him called Mercy, whose surname I don't recall. But it transpired, after we introduced ourselves to this pair, that they'd been invited up by Phil too. Art was managing Mercy and Mercy had been asked to sing with Phil Seymour, even though in the invite there was no mention of anyone else going there. So anyway, we sat there and we talked, and we listened to very loud monaural doo-wop recordings for the next half-hour until Phil Spector finally made his entrance. He entered the room and the first thing he did was to shake Art's hand and say Hello, and was introduced to Mercy, kissed her, said Hello. So after those introductions obviously Phil introduced me to Mr Spector and, it's very difficult to describe this but it went something like this: This is Stuart. What? Skewered? No, Stuart. Skewered? Stuart. What kind of fucking name is Skewered? It's not Skewered, it's Stuart. What do you mean Skewered? What the fuck's Skewered? It's Stuart, S-T-U-A-R-T. Oh, okay, okay. Pretty much from that point on I realised I was in for a bit of a rough ride.

So Phil sat down and talked to us and explained that what he wanted to do was record this song, which John Lennon had recorded actually, called 'Grow Old With Me'. Phil was going to play the piano and he wanted Phil Seymour and Mercy to harmonise and just see how they sounded, with the possibility of maybe cutting a record at a later date. This process of checking out what they sounded like went on for about eight hours. We were there at 8pm and I think, actually it was ten hours; we left at 6am the next morning. In between all manner of little incidents occurred, the most memorable ones being that he demanded that I play the piano, which I'd never done in my life before so I found it quite difficult. When I protested that I actually don't play the piano Phil, sorry, the response was: What do you mean you don't play the fucking piano? Everyone plays the fucking piano. So he sat me down and he said: It's easy, you just play E. I said: Well I don't know what that is. He said: It's this and showed me. Can you do that? I said: Okay. Well that's what I did, I played the piano in my fashion and he played the melody, and Phil and Mercy sang. So while we're doing this he said to Art: I want you to record this, Art, and he produced this very old fashioned Panasonic cassette player; I still remember it now, and he said: Right, when we start playing I want you to record it. So we started playing, Art began recording, and after a couple of minutes he stopped and said: Right, I want to do this right. OK Art, I want you to record it now. Art said: I thought you wanted me to record then, but I couldn't get it to record, Phil. Are you an idiot, Art?

Well this became the tone of the next few hours, which I was very relieved about because it meant that I was off the hook and Art was going to get proverbial piss-taking. We found out that the cassette that he'd given Art had had the tabs removed, so it wouldn't record. Art stated this to Phil and Phil said: What do you mean Art? What are you talking about? What do you mean tabs? I don't know what you're talking about, I don't know what a tab is. Art replied: Tabs on the cassette Phil. Really? Is that what happens? This is the great Phil Spector, the renowned producer, who may have been taking the piss, or may indeed not have realised that once you take the tabs out you can't re-record onto a cassette.

Then there was a moment when Art was kneeling next to the piano stool where we were sat, and while Art was on his knees attending to the cassette player, Phil leaned over to his head and pointed his fingers into the shape of a gun and made shooting noise. It was an incredible night, to be there. I wouldn't say he displayed deranged behaviour but he was very, very odd, and on the edge of something that I've never experienced before with anyone.

HARRY PITCH,
Musician

I came back to London halfway through 1942. I was already quite a good trumpet player and I started playing with various bands in London on trumpet. In those bands there were people like Ron Goodwin, who ultimately became a very famous conductor, but in those days he was just another trumpet player. There was also just another trombone player whose name was Geoff Love, and he became a very, very famous orchestral conductor.

When they made *Bridge Over the River Kwai*, the very first thing that they wanted was somebody to play the harmonica for the film. As the guys marched into captivity they were whistling 'Colonel Bogey', and they wanted one of them playing the mouth organ with it. Ron

Goodwin remembered that and he mentioned it. So they got me to do the soundtrack playing the mouth organ, and then Ron Goodwin did it again on a record with EMI, and that was the first thing I ever did at EMI, and it was such a knockout, it went so well, that I became within a very short space of time the harmonica player for EMI. When Frank Ifield did his 'I Remember You', he used to yodel in it, and Norrie Paramor thought of putting that introduction of a harmonica playing wah-wah-wah-wah wah wah, and that took off. After that everybody, all the singers, anybody who was anybody in the singing field, Dusty Springfield, Kiki Dee, Cliff Richard, John Leyton, so many of them, they all wanted a little bit of harmonica. So I was going from studio to studio just putting on little bits of harmonica.

I was just sitting there in the Abbey Road canteen one day having a cup of tea and these two guys, it was Paul and John, came in and sat down, they knew who I was. I think it was just after I'd done that Frank Ifield thing that they'd said that they'd heard it, and John Lennon asked me: How did you do that? I said: Have you got a harmonica? He said: Yeah. So I said: With this one, all you do, you put it in your hands like this and I showed him. Anyway, he asked me how I got a certain effect, and he said: I'll try that. He tried it and it worked, and that was that on 'Love Me Do'.

ROLAND RENNIE, EMI
Records Licensing
Manager

I used to get stick from people like George Martin saying; why can't we get something going for The Beatles in America, and in the early part of '63, Sir Joseph Lockwood and L.G. Wood sent me to America to find out what could be done. So I went over. We had a good lawyer called Paul Marshall, and I went to New York and then said what I thought should be done. Got back to England and told L.G. Wood and Lockwood, and he said: You better go do it then.

So in August of '63 I went to America and with Paul Marshall we set up this company called Trans Global Music, which was my company but without EMI it would have collapsed. They sent me over for this period with furniture, wife and a kid. Don't forget that The Beatles had started to break and George Martin was creating, and rightly so, about Capitol Records. Later I read about one of those guys in America at Capitol, and he called himself the guy who discovered The Beatles. I just kept getting cross because it was so difficult to get anything through to these Capitol people at all.

I mean, at that time, 1963, very few people went to America from here; everybody goes now but in those days it wasn't common, and it was quite an experience for me to be sent on my tod really to get this thing going, and that was amazing. I learned a lot and it was great when I eventually came back to England because you learned a lot in America then, about people's attitude. For example, you could go and have lunch with the bank manager and ask him how business was, whereas you couldn't do that in England, not then with your bank manager; my word, he was sacrosanct.

There are various stories about how The Beatles really broke in America. There was a lot of buzz, we got a lot of buzz going with it anyway, but in my opinion what happened was the TV News in America showed these people in England doing silly things with this group, and that's how their thing started in America, really started in America.

Brian Epstein came over and there was this hotel in Central Park, a very old big hotel on Central Park, the Plaza. It was extraordinary because it was very like Palm Court, this hotel; all these nice people, a very posh hotel. I went there with George Martin, to this place. Brian Epstein had booked them in under their real names I think, and you can imagine all the kids.

The radio stations in New York were extraordinary with The Beatles, extraordinary. They had never met people like them. Prior to that, if you got an artist on radio it was we are just good friends and so forth, but The Beatles were different, they'd just chat to anybody. It was incredible for them.

Of course the radio stations knew where they were staying. So the kids would go to this hotel, and the Plaza had hired these Pinkerton men who'd look after things. The kids were running up the corridors and all these old dears were having their tea, and all these kids running everywhere, such an extraordinary situation that was. Then they had a concert, The Beatles, in Carnegie Hall. The balcony was moving up and down, somebody fell off the balcony, oh dear oh dear. You wouldn't believe half the things that went on, it was extraordinary it was.

MERVYN CONN, Concert Promoter

Derek Taylor left The Beatles and went to live in California. When I went to America on my very first trip, I went and met with Derek, because he was living in Los Angeles, and he said: I want to take you and show you a group called The Byrds. They could have been called anything for all I knew. Well we went to the Troubadour and saw this group, and they were very good. He said: I want you to take them to England. I thought: I can't take them to England, because it was not a low fee, plus the airplane tickets, the hotel, the sound, the lighting, all the whole rigmarole that you have to do to put on a major production. I said: Well I'd better have a word with Joe; so I phoned Joe Collins the following morning in England and I told him. Well he didn't know them, they could have been called The Fairies for all he knew, or The Flowerpot Men. But I booked them, and of course by the time they got here they were Number One with 'Mr. Tambourine Man'.

Lonnie Donegan I managed at the end, in the last few years of his career. A very, very talented man. I think he could have gone much further, but I think he was his own worst enemy; artists usually are. He was long in the tooth in the business and he needed to take a little more direction in certain respects. A talented man, very fun to be with and a good performer on stage, and once again, very underestimated. He had a booming career at one time which could have gone much further. Maybe if it had been handled proper, but that was before I got involved in his career. I had him in the latter part of his career, like Matt Monro, but it's about taking direction, and when an artist is a little late in their life they don't want to take too much direction.

What happened with the PJ Proby concerts was that he'd been warned. Three times he split those trousers, velvet trousers, and they split. If you don't wear underpants you're going to be in trouble, aren't you? I can remember quite clearly that night, there was Joe Collins, John from Granada, Cissie Williams from Moss Empires, Stan Fisherman from Rank, and some guy from the ABCs. These were the guys that controlled all the theatres. I went to his apartment with his agent, a fellow called Tony Lewis, and Tony Lewis worked for John Hayman. For John it was a secondary thing in his office because he managed Elizabeth Taylor and Richard Burton and now Proby was becoming a bit of a thorn in his agency's side. We got there at 11 o'clock; at 12.30 he eventually came down, bottle of Chivas Regal in one hand and some bird in the other. Hi Mervyn, great to see you, great show. I said: Yeah, it was a great show, but tonight will be the last show for you, because if you do it again tonight you will be out of the business. Oh no, no, I promise you, this that and the other.

We come to the show and he does exactly the same thing again. Well not only did they drop the curtain but in the theatres at that time they had an iron curtain and they dropped that on him as well. He never performed again for years after that. At that time Tom Jones had just got in the charts and he was Number Three then with 'It's Not Unusual', I think was the first major hit he had. We put him on but it was a bit early days for him.

I did the first concert with The Who, I've got the poster upstairs actually; I just hoiked it out. They were on with The Bachelors. They were the opening act, I paid them £35. But that's show business. I think seeing The Beatles open at the Odeon, now the Apollo Hammersmith on the Christmas Tour show, extravaganza, that you couldn't hear one note of any music. To me that was one of my most incredible theatrical experiences up till then.

ROD DUNCOMBE, Liberty Records Label Manager

I was having a bit of a relationship with this woman called Barbara, and she was the assistant to PJ Proby at the height of his fame. He was doing a show at the California Ballroom in Dunstable, right at the bottom of Dunstable Downs, and this ballroom had balconies both sides of the room, which overlapped the stage that he was appearing on. I was at the side of the stage with Barbara, it was in the time when PJ Proby was causing this mass female hysteria and there was a girl that we both noticed that was looking a bit 'out of it', and you think, she's going to launch herself. Well this balcony wasn't that far above the stage, and she did it. She launched herself, she jumped onto what she thought was going to be the stage. Even in those days you had bouncers that kept the audience away from the performer, and PJ was in one of his, I don't know, 'There's A Place For Us', or whichever one it was; and she jumped onto the stage and went bang, like that, and without breaking rhythm he just stepped over her and carried on with the song, and a member of the road crew or two just sort of gently collected her but she must have damaged herself.

Nowadays that just wouldn't happen. The road crew wouldn't let it happen; the security, the health and safety, none of that would be allowed, because you have all these things in place now. In those days you didn't have curfews; the act went on until the owner of the ballroom or whatever it was pulled the plug. Or for as short a time as he could get away with.

We're having lunch one day; there's me and Simon Platz and Paul from Holland. And Marianne Faithfull's in there, and she walks past our table and I stop her. I say: Marianne, it's Rod, Rod Duncombe. I said: Marianne, do you remember when we worked at NEMS and we put out that album with Patrick? She said: Oh, those bastards. I said: Can I introduce you please, this is Paul Smith from Holland and this is Simon Platz, and she said: and what do you do Simon? He said: I'm your Music Publisher, Marianne.

MARCEL STELLMAN,
Decca Records
International Manager

Mick Jagger came into my office and asked: Are we going to Paris? I said: Yes, you're booked to star at the Olympia. Will there be a mob at the airport? I replied: I don't know, but I hope so. Well he said: We like that. I know you do I replied, I'm sure there'll be somebody there. When we got to Paris airport, Orly was jammed with kids. I was scared out of my wits; the limos were there, the motorcycles were there. I was sitting with one of the boys, not with Mick, in another car and we were driven to the hotel. That was my introduction to going abroad with the Rolling Stones.

Mick knew exactly what he wanted, he had a lot of management and a lot of people who were very demanding about everything. They were entitled to demand because they knew how big they were. They knew that we all earned a lot of money out of them. Now I remember there came a time where they were going to leave us, and Ted Lewis said to me: What are we going to do? I said: We've got eleven titles of the Stones. He said: What do you want to do? I replied: I would like to release an album with the twelve singles. He said: You can't do that. I said: Yes, we can. How do you know? I said: The contract says we have the control of their records, but they owe you three albums and they won't make them. He said: Why not? They're lazy; they don't want to work, they'll do it when they want to. You'll never get another one out of them. He said: You believe that? I said: I can't say it's true but I would be risking the fact that I would put a lower-priced album with only the singles on it. He said: They won't like it, they won't allow me to do it. I said: You can do it, they will take the money.

The first album came out on EMI, and we came out with the big hits, 'Satisfaction', 'The Last Time', all their big hits on one album. On Deram I think it was, it wasn't on Decca. When the cheque went for the release of the album, I said to the old man: Did they take it?, and he said: I think so!

KEITH ALTHAM, Journalist

In those days you became a kind of specialist journalist with certain bands. I was the Stones man on the *NME*, I probably interviewed The Rolling Stones more times than any other journalist in the world. The formula on the *NME* was once you hit the charts you did your first interview – Top 30. You did a second interview if the record hit the Top 10, and then another one if it went to Number One. You'd start with an interview with Mick Jagger, then the second one would probably be Brian Jones, and the third one would probably be Charlie or Bill, or Brian again. Hence you'd do three interviews on the Rolling Stones for one hit record. They were knocking out a hit record every three months, so you can see how the interviews soon added up, and you were always the Stones man. Alan Smith at the *NME* at that time was the Beatles man, I was the Stones man. I think I got to interview The Beatles maybe three times in my life because of that arrangement, which is silly really because you got bored with talking to the same people all the time.

I got on well with them, I liked The Stones enormously in the early days. Mick was great fun in the early days but wasn't much fun later. I used to come back from lunch, there'd be three messages on the switchboard from Reg Parsley of The Cloggs, who had rung. I knew exactly who it was. Can you ring back Reg Parsley of The Cloggs? Oh alright, I know who that is. He was good fun, and so were The Stones and also they were in those days, anti-authoritarian, which we kind of all were to a degree; we were all at the same age, I was the same age as The Stones or The Beatles. You were kind of in sympathy with them because they were getting knocked about and spat on by the national press to a certain extent, as being unclean, and dirty, long-haired louts. You only had to meet them for five minutes to know they were extremely bright and not at all loutish; well-read. I went out on the road with The Stones, travelled in Europe with them a bit. Slept with Mick in Nice, in the same room – not the same bed though. He used to wake us up with The Beach Boys. This is what I call wake-up music. Oh nice Mick. Just what I want to hear at half-past seven in the morning, 'Help Me Rhonda'; help me God.

In The Stones' case I travelled with them a fair bit because the guy who used to be their roadie lived in Epsom where I lived, whose name was Ian Stewart. He was actually the sixth Rolling Stone, he was the guy who was aimed out very early on because his face didn't quite fit. He had this big chin and he refused to conform to the long haired look, he looked a bit like a kind of Desperate Dan figure. He was a lovely, lovely man, a Scot and a boulder of an individual. Andrew Oldham fired him because, as he said: The great British public cannot add up to six when it comes to a band. Stu was given the option of either becoming the tour manager or the personal manager, and he worked out very swiftly by being the roadie/tour manager that the equipment does not answer back. And you don't get the Brian Jones problem, Brian was becoming a problem. So he took to looking after the equipment and they trusted him implicitly; he was the one guy that The Stones would always listen to. You got the truth from Stu. It was pretty much as Keith Richards once said, years later when Stu died sadly with a heart attack: Who's going to tell us the truth now?

I used to drink in the same pub with Stu in Ewell so I got the inside track on The Stones all the time, and if there was an option to travel with them somewhere or an interesting gig to go and see them play with The Ronettes or something, I'd go in the van with them, and drive in the fog all the way up to Aylesbury or somewhere. Terrifying, before the motorways. There was one gig I drove with them, to see The Ronettes, in the fog, and as we're driving, Stu suddenly says, Oh well, there goes Brian the other way in his Cadillac, we are now a quartet. He had this kind of laconic humour. We'd carry on driving, we'd gone about another five miles, and we'd suddenly go boom, and we've hit this roundabout in the fog; silly place to put a roundabout in the middle of the road. Keith Richards who was in a sleeping bag in the back, shot up, banged his head on the roof. Oh Keith; he's just larking about being silly. We thought it was just that; five minutes later we arrive at the gig, we all tumble out, Stu goes round, opens the back door to the van and Keith Richards rolls out unconscious. Stu looks down and he goes: Right, I'll attend to the talent mate, you go and explain to the promoter we're now a trio. They did the gig that night as a four-man line up without Brian Jones, Keith came round with a big lump on his forehead, he was alright. They were quite good as a quartet that night I have to say, without Brian Jones.

160

CHRIS WELCH,
Journalist

The local Rock scene was taking off and I started writing about all the local bands because I loved the music and there were lots of clubs. I think it was Bern Elliott and The Fenmen who were a local band, and then there was a band called The Pretty Things, and then The Rolling Stones from Dartford, so I was writing about all these local groups. The first time I saw The Stones was 1963 and they were playing in a tent at the Richmond Jazz Festival, and right at the back of the Festival, not even on the main stage. The main stage featured bands like Acker Bilk who were playing really nice Traditional Jazz and hundreds of people were watching him, and then suddenly you heard this announcement, 'The Rolling Stones are going to play in a few minutes', and the whole audience turned round and ran away from Acker Bilk, ran to the back and packed into this tent, and there we saw The Stones playing live; first time I'd seen them live and it was one of those historic moments, you realise that Trad Jazz died at that moment, and R&B took off. In fact the compere Bill Carey who was a Canadian guy, shouted this announcement: 'This has been Rhythm And Blues; this is The Rolling Stones'. 1963, it's like a historic moment, the big breakthrough. After that they weren't playing in tents any more, they were out on the road doing cinemas and theatres.

After about three or four years people kept saying to me, you like writing about all these bands, you should work for a music paper. So I wrote off to *Melody Maker* and they said: Ah yes, the letter writer, because I'd written lots of letters, abusive letters, to the readers' column. I got an interview at the *MM*, and that was 1964. I did write to the *NME* first because they were advertising a vacancy and they wrote back and said: I'm sorry. I think it was already taken, so I missed that one. But I was glad I got the Melody Maker; they had a vacancy too, somebody was leaving. They didn't have many young Pop writers then, very few; they were all older writers brought up in Jazz and Dance Bands. The *Melody Maker* as you knew it originally started as a Jazz and Dance Band musicians' paper. They desperately needed somebody to write about all these groups so having written articles about The Stones and been to see them play one of their early gigs, that helped a lot.

I found in the garage recently some of my early stories that I wrote, because I was quite pleased and excited about doing these stories and they were on slips of paper, it wasn't a full A4 sheet, it was like a little quarto slip, and you used carbon paper as well of course. Well there'd have to be at least one carbon copy and of course if you made a mistake you could just tear it up and do it again, so that's why it was all in short slips, and for the subs to edit it as well. The maximum for a live review would be about 300 words and a feature would be, if you were lucky, 1,000 words. You had to compress everything and you had to have a very strong introduction, and an angle. You couldn't just waffle away and transcribe a tape, you weren't allowed to do that. In fact we didn't have any tape recorders at all; all the interviews had to be done with notebooks. I had to type at speed with people breathing down my neck, like the editor or the news editor.

My first day was a nightmare I have to tell you on Melody Maker, because I was used to the jolly atmosphere on the local paper; it was news day on a Monday and you had to do all the news stories, which meant that you had to ring everybody up, get quotes from the bands and the managers and the PRs, and write it very, very quickly. They were screaming down your neck if you hadn't got it done on time. Like for example, what's The Beatles new single going to be? Can you get a quote from John Lennon? Well I don't know where he is. He's at Heathrow Airport, he's going off to America. Ring the airport and page him over the tannoy. You had to do stuff like that, get a quote. So the first day was a nightmare compared to my happy days on the *Kentish Times*. I went out for a drink with one of the staff afterwards in the pub and he started being very pessimistic and saying: You know the music business is finished, don't you? *Melody Maker* is probably going to close; circulation is terrible, it's only about 15,000 a week and you've come at a really bad time. It will all be over soon. I think he was winding me up. I was so disheartened after this terrible day of hard work and drinking too much and smoking too much, I was probably sick in Fleet Street outside the office, and went home and thought, do I want to go back there? I thought, well I've signed the contract, I can't give up now.

162

So I went back the next day, Tuesday; totally different vibe, all the people who were shouting at me had disappeared. Of course they were all at the printers and I just sat down and relaxed for the day and it was very jolly. Wednesday was a planning meeting; and I realised it was only one day a week that was really hard work, so after that, having thought I'd leave after the first day I stayed for fourteen or fifteen years I think it was. Every day was exciting I have to tell you. It was good because people were keen to write and everyone was involved in the music and they wanted to champion their particular artists, whoever it was. In my case it might be The Yardbirds or Georgie Fame, or Zoot Money, or The Who later on, because we thought these were the new upcoming groups and you'd want to see them on the cover. But you had to convince the editor, who wanted somebody on the cover who was going sell lots of copies.

MUFF WINWOOD, Musician

We played together in a band and we started to put the Ray Charles numbers in the little Trad-Jazz band thing, and of course people started to talk about it. Then we met Spencer Davis, who was a Folk singer who did Blues songs at Birmingham University, when we were playing a gig there. I don't know how we got round to it but afterwards, talking, we decided we'd get together and do Blues together. So Spencer Davis, and Steve and I used to do a little Blues thing. Then a drummer from Birmingham University, Pete York, joined us, on and off. So that's how we started a group called The Rhythm and Blues Quartet. Everywhere we played we'd turn up with our hacked old equipment, this was only in the Birmingham area of course. Steve was still at school, and Spencer and Pete York were still at university. Everywhere we played, we would turn up at 6 o'clock to some pub or some little club somewhere, and there'd be queues down the street; it was unbelievable. Everywhere we were playing was packed to the rafters and we realised that we were doing something that everybody really wanted to hear.

Millie Small was playing at Birmingham Town Hall, she'd just had a massive hit with 'My Boy Lollipop', and she'd been brought to Britain by a young man called Chris Blackwell. Well he was with her that night and he said to somebody, which is typical Chris Blackwell: Is there any action in this town? Is there anybody any good we can go and see? Well somebody said: You've got to see this Rhythm and Blues Quartet, they're fantastic. So he came down to this club after Millie Small had finished and saw us, and fell in love with us and wanted to manage us. He wanted us to be his first white British group, because he managed quite a lot of Jamaican Reggae artists, including Jimmy Cliff and Jackie Edwards and Millie Small, and people like that. His whole business was selling Reggae records to the British/Jamaican contingent. I always remember him telling us that it was a fantastic business. He said: Do you know what? You'd get a house with about five Jamaican families all living in the same house, and when they've got a favourite record they *all* buy it. He said: The household doesn't buy one, all five sets of families buy their own copy. That always stuck in my mind; what a businessman. Anyway, he became our manager and we had to change our name, because The Rhythm and Blues Quartet wasn't a good enough name. Spencer Davis had such an interesting name, and he also loved being the front man in terms of doing interviews and everything, while we just wanted to stay in bed; we hated interviews. So in a mad rush we said we're going to call ourselves the Spencer Davis Group, and that's what we called ourselves.

We played a lot when we were in London with a lot of the Jamaican artists; that's how we got to know people like Jimmy Cliff and Jackie Edwards, who was a very popular artist in London in the early Sixties, and Jackie wrote 'Keep On Running' for us, which was our first Number One hit record. I remember recording it, and you know, it's very interesting but it helped me a lot in my future life as an A&R man. We went to Phillips Records, this would be about 1963, and this really was a time when people in record companies wore suits. It's a joke; they're called 'the suits' but they haven't worn suits for thirty years. But in the Sixties they did, they wore suits and the guys that worked in the recording studios wore white coats, which is the other extraordinary thing. Anyway, we went to see the A&R man with our 'Keep On Running' record, which we'd recorded, and he listened to it and said: You know what, this is a good song, but it's got no intro. It's got nothing of interest to make you stop what you're doing and go, what's this? He said: If only it had a proper interesting intro, then it would work. We of course went out of there thinking, what does he know? Who the hell is he? This bloke sitting there with a suit telling us what to do; he's got no clue. Chris Blackwell said: Well we've got to try. He said: Have a go, see what you can do, and don't worry. If it doesn't really work, I'll talk him round.

So we went in the studio and I always remember that someone had given Spencer the first fuzz box that had been made in America to fuzz guitar sounds, and it was called the 'Big Muff'. My nickname is Muff, and so we were laughing about this thing called the Big Muff, so I plugged it into my bass; it was for guitars, but I plugged it into my bass. I played my bass with it and it made this fantastic sound. So I kind of worked out a silly little bass line, and the guys said: Hang on, let's try that in the front of this 'Keep On Running' song. We did that and Blackwell heard it and said: Hey, that sounds really good; it's so interesting a sound, nobody's ever heard a sound like that before. Of course, we took it back to the A&R man and he said: That, you see, is exactly what I was telling you. I always remember that because there were many, many times in the future where I was going to have to do very similar things to other musicians, and I knew how I felt at the time when I was told, and how I realised that, give it a go, because the guy might be right.

ADRIAN KERRIDGE, Lansdowne Studio Engineer

During my time at Lansdowne with Joe Meek, he would work all night; he was fanatical. I was quite naïve in those days; he used to give me 2/6d and say, go down the chemist and buy Preludin. I didn't know what they were, they were slimming pills but they gave him a high which kept him working. I only learnt that later when I spoke to somebody about it; I had no idea what they were. But Joe didn't do anything harder than that. Then one day I get called up to one of the offices, and Lionel Stephens, the money man and Denis Preston were there, and they said: We've sacked Joe. Oh. Can you take the studio over and run it? I said: Yeah, I'll do that. That's where it all started with me with Lansdowne, effectively. So Joe set up his own flat locally and then he moved to Holloway Road, and of course 'Telstar' was a big hit and he had other hits too. The reason he left, walked out, was because he was always pestering Dennis to record his 'artists'; and when you're on a session where the producer is concentrating on an Afro-Cuban band, Jazz, you don't need an engineer pestering you. Denis used to have Mach 1, Mach 2 and Mach 3's, in anger, and I think he probably had a Mach 3 with Joe, and Joe walked out. He really could be quite excitable.

The Dave Clark Five were sent from Keith Prowse Music to the studio to do a demo. That was the big thing at Lansdowne. Because of Skiffle in the period from late Fifties, early Sixties they were all looking for groups. I did a demo and I thought, this group's pretty good. They were obviously green as heck, you know, but so was I, I was only a kid in short trousers almost. I said to them: This is great, have you got a record deal? They said: Nope. So I introduced them to EMI's A&R department, they signed a contract and it went from there. We did something like nearly 100 million records worldwide over a ten-year period. I don't think Keith Prowse Music actually took the group up, well, obviously they didn't, and I had said to Dave: We've got a studio, let's do a deal. That was my responsibility then because by then Joe Meek had left, after the big row with Denis Preston. Denis had an agreement with EMI for his Lansdowne series records so to me it seemed logical to recommend Dave Clark to go to EMI, because we knew the blokes there, and he'd more likely get a deal.

We were doing some work one time with Dick Rowe at Decca and we had a small control room downstairs. He was sitting next to me and I said: That's a fantastic take, that's it. Dick looks at me, and he had his pipe, and he walks through the door in the studio and says: Guys, that was great but can I have one more just like that. So some wag, obviously the drummer says: Oi, what was wrong with it then? Nothing, so we did one more just-like-that, which of course wasn't as good, and I was not impressed.

But we turned out hit after hit after hit after hit; out of that of course came Spencer Davis Group – 'Keep On Running'; Craig Douglas, Adam Faith – 'What Do You Want' etc; Emile Ford and the Checkmates – 'What Do You Want to Make Those Eyes at Me For'; Richard Harris – 'McArthur Park'; Mille Small – 'My Boy Lollipop'. Sid Dale was an arranger/conductor, and he knew Chris Blackwell of Island Records. Sid and I got on quite well together and I was invited down to meet Chris at his home. We played 'My Boy Lollipop' and Chris said: What do you reckon? I said: Well, we can do this alright. It was still four-track, so very little room to manoeuvre. So Millie Small comes into the studio, we put a voice on, it was very quick, she was well-rehearsed, and that was great. Chris decides that he's going to put a harmonica on it. I thought, where are we going to put the harmonica? It was a very tight drop in, it was one beat, drop in, drop out. I've never forgotten this session, it was 11 o'clock in the morning; a half-session of course which was two hours in those days, union rules, you know. In comes this guy, I thought, you're very young; looked a bit scruffy, just a harmonica player. He did it in two takes, we dropped in each time.

CLEM CATTINI,
Musician

I'd had enough. I got to the stage where at £20 a week I asked for a rise, £20 is not enough to live on and pay all the expenses. It's funny because I went up to Larry Parnes's office and he brought some people into the office with him in case I was going to jump over the desk and hit him. I said: Well that's it, and I left. I don't know what I was going to do, I hadn't got a clue. I thought, well, I've had enough of this, I'm not going to travel round the country on tour. Health-wise it wasn't good touring, I had terrible chest problems, mind you that was probably down to smoking at the time. Anyway I pissed off; his offices were in Oxford Street, so I went up to the 2i's, because that was like a labour exchange at that time, and next door was a pub. Went in there and a musician I knew said: What are you doing? I said: I've just told Parnes what to do with his job. He said: Oh, are you looking for something? I said: Well, if there's anything about. He said: Well there's this guy in Willesden called Fred Heath; he's got a group Fred Heath and The Nutters, but I think he's changed his name to Johnny Kidd and The Pirates, and he's looking for a drummer and a bass player. Do you want me to ring him? So he rang John up and he said: Come over and audition. That was it: the start of Johnny Kidd and The Pirates.

He'd already got a deal; he had released 'Please Don't Touch' before I joined him. The first one I did with Johnny was 'Shakin' All Over' and that was originally the B side. Peter Sullivan the producer decided, No, no, because the A side was supposed to be 'Yes Sir, That's My Baby', believe it or not. Then he decided to flip it, and there you go; the rest is history.

There is just the matter of the drum break in the middle, it was a complete and utter mess up from me, I made a complete cock-up of it. I was supposed to do one bar drum fill into the guitar solo and I got into this thing which I couldn't get out of. Eventually I managed to get out of it and it came out as two bars instead of one, but Peter Sullivan said: No, no, keep it in. I said: I can do another one. No, no, that's great, leave it. It just shows you how mistakes can work and that's it, I still can't play it to this day. I did this thing, and, oh crikey, how do I get out of this, and I was going to stop and force it but I didn't. We carried on recording and then I thought, oh sheepish look, and, No no, keep it, it's great. I could probably never do it again anyway. It was at EMI, well, EMI then we used to call it, it was Abbey Road studio number two, before The Beatles. This was in the number two studio and that was before The Beatles were even born I think. The thing is, people don't realise, but there were a lot of hits coming out of EMI, or Abbey Road, way before The Beatles. They didn't suddenly invent Abbey Road.

I never had the greatest memories of Abbey Road Studios, because of trying to get in the place to load your stuff in: Oh you can't park here, oh no, no, no. And the times I've said: Right, I won't park here, I'll go home and tell the producer, I'm working for George Martin, tell him I've come and I can't get my gear out and I've gone home. Then suddenly it was: Oh well get your stuff in and then you'll have to move it. I'd say: Alright. But I never did, just used to leave it. A couple of times the guy would come: No he can't move his car, he's in the middle of a session, so I got away with it. At EMI, you had to finish recording at 10 o'clock, because in Studio Two, which is Abbey Road Two, or whatever they want to call it, they had an echo chamber on the back of the building and the thing is, it disturbed the neighbours so they had to finish by 10 o'clock each night. Silly isn't it?

RAY RUSSELL, Musician

Then, people were accessible then. You could phone somebody up, as their number would have appeared in the paper, it wasn't like 'your call is unimportant to us', and you could do it. I was working then, I was seventeen or eighteen, and basically I had had two jobs in a year-and-a-half and I was bored by it. I was doing kind of local band things, and I saw an advert that said that Vic Flick was leaving the John Barry Seven, and in my naïve mind I thought, oh well, they'll book me then, won't they? It's so dumb really. So I bought the John Barry album, James Bond stuff on, and I learnt the tunes. Keep in mind the fact that about ten years after that, I woke up in a cold sweat one night thinking that, how did I ever assume that the Dansette would be in the right key? It could be a semi tone sharp or flat, and I could have learnt them all in the wrong key, but anyway. You don't, do you, luckily.

So I phoned this number, which was a tenor player called Bob Downes, who was organising it, and I just said: look, I can do all this. He said: come along, we've got an audition at the Aeolian Hall. I arrived there with my guitar and little amp and they couldn't get in, it was locked up. So he actually climbed over the ticket booth and plugged me in. The audition was me, with a guitar and amp, and he put all the music up in front of me and I had no idea what it was; it could have been anything. So, he put it up, and of course I couldn't read it but I did know the title, and I assumed the arrangement was the same. So I played the things and he phoned John Barry while I was there; he made this call again through the booth, we're not talking mobiles here are we, he was basically breaking into the ticket office. He phoned him up and said: John, this guy's good; he can do the songs. I remember he said exactly: Hey, this guy's good. It's always amused me. That was it, I got the gig.

We did mainly one night stands, universities, some theatres. We stayed in these incredible kind of doss house places, I took this all as the norm by the way at the time; I didn't know any different. But I remember turning up at a café on the A1 and it had about eighty camp beds in, and we stayed there and I didn't sleep very well. We used to go round in this van, I remember the roadie's name was Alf, can't remember his second name, nice guy, he got the needle one day, he was in a bad mood, and it was about 7 o'clock in the morning. We'd driven back from a gig and he actually dropped me off with my guitar and amp at Camden Town and said: You'll have to get a train the rest of the way, I don't want to drive to Manor House, which was like three miles down the road and I was the last one to be dropped off. I didn't like that. But then he realised that he'd made a mistake, he got told off. So he took me to see Johnny Kidd and The Pirates rehearsing in a prefab in the Old Kent Road, and I promise you, I'm not on acid or anything, it's true, I can't believe that I saw that, and they were rehearsing at his parents' prefab.

PETER SUMMERFIELD, Booking Agent

I saw an advertisement in the *Sunday Times*, would you believe, for a 'young person to join an agency in London'. I just wrote, and they wanted to see me, it was the Eamonn Andrews Agency. He had a very successful agency where, besides managing his own career, had people like Peter West, Kenneth Wolstenholme, Pete Murray, authors, writers, it was a very successful agency in Golden Square. They also managed Jack Good, who was the TV producer with *Oh Boy!* at that time. Eamonn Andrews Ltd, and Edward H. Summerfield Ltd, which had no family connection with me whatsoever. There was a man called Martin Davis who was the sort of junior before me and he had got promoted, and before this young office junior had been a man called Terry Nelhams, who was Adam Faith. I was put on reception, I was told to make tea, everything. But I was given every contract to read and learn from, which was a great thing to do aged nineteen, amongst these people. I lived in Hertfordshire and came into London every day to Golden Square, Piccadilly. This agency was just unbelievable, the people that came through that front door of that office every day. Their music connection before Jack Good was that they had a PR role with Vernon's Pools, and had formed the Vernon's Girls. They were paid every time the Vernon's Girls were on television; it was purely a PR job. So that was the first music connection for the agency.

The first real one that we thought we liked was a guy called Karl Denver. We found him in Manchester. Jack Good loved the demos and we took Karl Denver to Decca, made some more demos, and it was easy from there. We took I think, Jimmy Grant from *Saturday Club* to lunch, and he booked him, took the demos back to the BBC and we got *Saturday Club*, *Easy Beat*, *Pop Inn*, and all these sort of programmes; and we knew that Karl Denver would have hits, which he did. He had 'Marcheta', 'Mexicali Rose', did the Song for Europe for Great Britain. He did very, very well, for an unusual singer; he wasn't your standard Pop singer.

Karl Denver's house was in Moss Side, Manchester, which we all know in those days was not very desirable, and with his first royalty cheque, the first thing he bought was a Chevrolet Impala. It was about the size of an aircraft carrier; it was huge. There was little Karl, about five-foot five, driving this great big American thing, but he had to have it.

JOHN REED, Musician

With The Qandowns, like so many bands, we wanted to be professional. We were semi-pro, we all had jobs during the day and then 5.30 or 6 o'clock home, quick bite to eat and you'd be out doing a gig five nights a week. It's rather funny because I was earning about £25, £30 a week in 1962 this would be, which was decent money in those days. I still had the old drum kit which wasn't very good and I desperately wanted to upgrade the kit, and I had my eye on a Ludwig classic kit. Everybody else was going out and buying the sparkly Premier kits and I thought, I don't want the Jag, I want the Rolls Royce. I kept on and on at my mum; Mum will you sign the hire purchase forms for this? No. Eventually she said: I'll sign them if you get a proper job. So I applied to be an office boy at Vaux Breweries in Sunderland and I got the job. Out of about 400 or 500 applicants I got the job.

My salary was about £4/7/6d a week. I got a rise to just under £5, but that put me in the tax bracket, and I was taking home less when I got the rise, but my mum finally signed the HP. Well, I've still got the kit in the cupboard and I just couldn't part with it. We'd been all over the world together. I starved for that kit in Germany, I mean I had to buy some new hi-hat cymbals and I used all my week's money and I couldn't buy any food. I was just cadging a slice of toast here or there. But what was important was I had these great hi-hat cymbals.

Then Toby Twirl said: Do you want the gig, and I said: Absolutely. Because they'd just got a contract with Decca. Wow, suddenly I'm not only in quite a good band, but they've got a record contract as well. You know, after all these years and hours of playing and dreaming of this record contract, this wonderful piece of paper. I think on the first gig, they picked me up in Sunderland, put the gear in the van and we're off down Middlesborough somewhere. I'm sitting in the back and I'm all excited and I said: I don't suppose any of you have got the record contract have you, I could have a look at. The roadie put his hand above the sun visor in amongst all the petrol receipts and everything, pulled out this one page, it was A4 paper, printed on both sides, and that was the Decca record contract. There it was, an A4 piece of paper, all mangled around the edges, beer stains on it, and I looked at this piece of paper and I thought, is this what I've been dreaming of all of my musical career.

Our prime motive was the live work and recording was something you had to do. It was quite a nerve-wracking experience because you're so far away from London. If you're a London band and you're in and around the recording scene, maybe a recording studio maybe wasn't such an alien environment. But we would set off from Newcastle at like 6 or 7 o'clock in the morning and we would drive down to London to West Hampstead Decca studios and the session would be booked from two to five-thirty. Our management and agent would have had put a gig in that night somewhere. So we would finish recording an A and a B side in three-and-a-half, four hours maximum, and then we'd load out, back on the road and we'd be off to Birmingham somewhere to do a gig at 10 o'clock that night. There was none of this let's go to a residential studio and hang out man, and see if we can get some inspiration; it was bosh, bosh, bosh, bosh, bosh. Right, that's the drums, that's the backing track, mix that down, because when we started recording at Decca it was only on four-track.

GEOFF DOCHERTY,
Concert Promoter

I got into a few scraps because even though I was only little, I was a good scrapper. Then somebody approached me and said the Bay Hotel, Sunderland wants somebody on the door. You are pretty reasonable, you seem pretty sensible, why don't you go over and see the manager. It's £2 a night and you get a free drink, and some nice girls go over there. I went over, introduced myself to the manager, and before long he's realised my love of music. They had a big ballroom and he said: Will you put some bands on? So I started putting local bands on. Anyway I got started and at that time I started listening to

John Peel and he's playing these bands like Pink Floyd, Tyrannosaurus Rex and West Coast American bands. It all seemed exciting and it was like a new era was opening up, a new vista.

Other people were talking about the music as well and they were saying: Oh did you hear that band on John Peel last week? And I was saying: yeah, or great, we're going down to London to see them and all that. They're going to London, The Roundhouse and places like this. Local bands were good, but if you put a local bands on and they're back three weeks later, then they're back five weeks later, and then they're playing everywhere else around Sunderland and everybody's saying: well, we've seen them about fifteen times, why don't you get somebody else on?

The challenge was getting some of these bands, I said: it would be great if we could just get them here. So I saw the hotel manager and said: Why don't we get Family; Peely was playing them. He said: How much are they? I said: they're £150, I've checked up. He said: £150? You must be joking; I'm not paying that; the local groups were only getting £15, and the odd one £25. I'll go to £50 if you can get anybody for £50. So I got a few bands from Manchester for £50, but they weren't really what we wanted.

By then I'd saved up my £2 a night, kept accumulating it, and when I got enough I said: Why don't you let me hire the hall then? I'll take the chance and if I lose my money, I lose my money, but I'll have a go. He said: If you want to do it, you do it.

I booked Family, and I said: I hope some people turn up, I'll look a right idiot if they don't, in front of the manager and all the people. Plus on top of that I'll lose all my money I've saved; I mean, I could be buying a nice car with this money, I must be crazy. Anyway I said we're going to have Family. I put the posters up and Family came, and Roger Chapman. On the night, I got the biggest shock of my life, the ballroom held about 800 and there was about 800 in. It was choc-a-block. Family played and they were great; they really went down fantastic. Everybody was coming up to me afterwards, in the Bay Hotel and in town afterwards; Geoff, Family were great, who else have you got coming? It was a great night. Family were tremendous, are you getting them back? Suddenly, after I'd paid everybody, I got all my money back; some for the little adverts, and £150 for Family and there was £40 spare, which was a lot of money then when you were working for £2 a night. £40 spare in one go, and all your money back.

JOHN WILLIAMS,
BBC Producer

Stuart Grundy was in charge of BBC sessions, and he would ring me once a week and say, I've got the sessions for the next three months, can you do these dates? I'd say yes; I absolutely loved doing those, I thought this was the most thrilling time of my life, because you'd go in the studio with Simple Minds, or Big Country, whatever.

Then a week before the date, the producer of the show would ring you up and say: Oh I now know who the band is, you've got The Cocteau Twins, or you've got The Waterboys, or you've got Aswad, or whoever it was. So you'd turn up at 2 o'clock at the Maida Vale Studios and have the studio lunch; the BBC lunches were quite good and they were quite cheap, so that was always a big thrill that you could eat properly.

Go and meet the band, and I remember my knack was saying to them: this isn't going to be like any session you've done before; this is going to be fun, we're going to have a really great time. All I want to know is how many overdubs you're going to do, and we'll have a ball. I'd try and instil a sense of fun and occasion about it, and generally the acts would respond by, oh, the guy's interested. Because they'd had a sequence of producers who would be looking at their watches all the time, the pub opens now, we'll take a break, and not be that interested. Which perhaps, if I'd been doing it for ten years I might have got to that state as well but I was kind of intrigued by the whole thing.

As the producer you were given instructions: you weren't allowed to touch the desk, so you could press the talkback button to talk to the band but you weren't allowed to do any knob twiddling, which was the SM, the Studio Manager job, which was either Dave Robinson or Ted de Bono, there was some great, great sound engineers, who would in the very short allotted time be recording four tracks. 2.30 till 6pm, take a break for dinner, and then from 7pm to 8.30 and do your vocals. By 11 o'clock everything had to be finished and mixed. I'd learned so much about records and so much about performances, and realised it's all about the performance and how good a record you've made or how good the session was. If the band put some effort into it and really lived it.

Actually sometimes you were making takes which were better than the record. I remember doing a Simple Minds session where we recorded 'Promised You A Miracle', and they'd done the single the week beforehand, and they said: Hang on, this is better than the record. There was some debate about it and Virgin Records in the end couldn't possibly take the Radio One session but all the sessions were the B sides.

The Peel sessions were odd, generally speaking, because Peel wasn't interested; he'd never turn up. You'd just do them and put them on a reel to reel, one song for each reel, and he would laconically announce it the next week. The DJ never turned up; they never turned up, weren't interested in that kind of stuff, because it was all just about saving needle time.

JOHNNY BEERLING,
Controller BBC Radio One

In the days when Radio One started back in the Sixties there were probably sixty or seventy singles a week, plus thirty or forty albums coming out every week. Every producer working in the main field of popular side of Radio One had to listen to all of these records every week and decided which three or four they were going to add on to their particular programmes. So there was an awful lot of duplication between different producers doing this. The vote for the Radio One playlist came and went at different times but when there was a vote to have a playlist the idea was to rationalise it so that all of the daytime shows had the same records, and not to over-expose one particular record and under-expose others; so there was a logicality about it. Of course you could do it all by computer these days, and they do, don't they? But in those days it was all done with strips of paper called, The Strip System. The Jimmy Young Show would have a sheet of pre-formed A4 with slots on it where various pieces of paper would be put in with the titles of records, or the sessions that had been recorded for that week. It was a rationalisation thing.

'Needletime' goes back to the days of the pirates. Pirate Radio was hugely successful because they could play anything, they didn't pay any copyright fees for the performance. The performance in a record is owned by the music publisher, the writer, and the performer of course, and there are various international agreements whereby the people who do legal broadcasting, namely the BBC and Radio Luxembourg and the commercial stations these days, pay for the rights to broadcast them. Now there was always a great deal of discussion about how much should be paid, because what is the value of air time, and so on? So Needletime was the time spent playing commercial gramophone records, as opposed to non-Needletime, which was film soundtrack, or records in their first week of release which were excepted from Needletime, but that's basically what it was. It was the music that you played off commercial records, and there was a great limitation on it because the Musicians' Union for a start regarded the BBC as a primary employer of British musicians and thought it had a duty to give as much work as possible to their members, so they wanted to keep music live, that was their idea.

The record companies themselves thought that if they had over-exposure it wouldn't help the sales and it could damage the record sales. Then other people in record companies thought the more exposure they could get the better, so it was a nonsense really. It was *the* major constraint, and that was what made Radio One different from the Pirates when it started. What made it more acceptable was the fact that we had jingles, and we had a lot of good sessions and we had a lot of very big-name Disc Jockeys; but we didn't have unlimited Needletime. Why the breakfast show, which I produced, was a success, was because it was the first ever programme on Radio One, with Tony Blackburn and it had 100% Needletime. Tony Blackburn and I had a good idea of what would appeal to the public, which was lots of hits, lots of Tamla Motown oldies, only the best new records that were coming out, and maybe one or two country records, because I was a country fan, but that was always a source of disagreement between Tony and myself. Plus a lot of repetition and a lot of plugs for Tony Blackburn, so that he became as well known as the Radio Station.

I think Noel Edmonds was probably the most successful breakfast show presenter. Everybody remembers Tony Blackburn but Noel was just enormous. He was so inventive and original. Of course, he didn't care about music very much did he! I remember John Peel being terribly upset that Noel didn't even own a record player. I've got a lot of time for John; I knew him, not many people know this but it's in my book so we can talk about it now, I went out to see Pirate Radio when it was operating before Radio One started, and Peel was there on the ship lurking in the background. So I'd known Peel right from the beginning, before he joined the BBC. He was terribly posh when he first started you know, because he went to a public school, but he changed that accent and had lost all that when he came back. His father was a cotton-broker. He made a name for himself with *The Perfumed Garden* on the pirate ship, so my friend Bernie Andrews started this programme called *Top Gear*, and he tried a variety of presenters, which I think were John Peel, Peter Drummond, maybe it was Tommy Vance, I can't remember, there were a couple of others; and the idea was a double-headed presentation of what we called loosely 'Underground' music, left field, not the commercial Pop but more avant-garde music, music worthwhile in its own right. Bernie was a particularly good producer who took a lot of time with his sessions and got good results. He wasn't copying commercial Pop records, he was doing recordings of music that was worthwhile. So Peel was one of the three presenters of this, and he wasn't at all popular with BBC management; they didn't like his druggy voice, which he never was actually. Bernie stuck his neck out and said; well I've signed him for 13 weeks so there's nothing you can do about it. He got his knuckles rapped, but of course Peel was then a big success.

MIKE APPLETON,
TV Producer O.G.W.T.

During the *Old Grey Whistle Test*'s prime days the West Coast sound of America was very strong. There were a lot of singer/songwriters, the sort of Joni Mitchell, Jackson Browne, Jesse Colin Young, that type, and The Eagles and the bigger bands. It was a very dominant era in the album market. Don't forget *Whistle Test* was featured albums, and only albums, although we didn't stop singles that were off albums, but basically everything had to be on albums. So there was a lot of American music that was very strong in the album market.

At the time there was a degree of touring bands coming in, but it was limited because in television terms there had to be Musicians Union exchanges, and exchanges were a pain in the bum. If you didn't have a musical exchange for an English band going to the States then you couldn't have them in the studio at the BBC. So we had to define a way of featuring the music we wanted to feature without the bands. What I did was, I spoke with a guy called Phil Jenkinson who had a fabulous collection of old movies, and we devised a way of featuring music cut to these old films. It was totally Phil because he did the cutting and everything and there were some brilliant ones. There are still people going around quoting 'Trampled Under Foot' by Zeppelin as being a seminal moment in their visual experience on television. It was interesting because it was there simply as a necessity for us to be able to feature the music we wanted.

I had always wanted to do a TV equivalent of *NME* or *Melody Maker* and look at the music more seriously than most TV programmes did at the time. We killed off *Disco 2* and *Whistle Test* was born on this idea, initially with Richard Williams who was then with *Melody Maker*. I planned it as a magazine which people could turn to for information. I did not want it to get too pompous or political, musical and informative. We were tucked away on BBC 2, late at night and we were like a safety valve for the Variety Department. If anybody said what are you doing about contemporary Rock music, they could point at us over there and say they are doing it. We were a different department, Presentation Department, and we got away with all sorts of things as we were very small and had no hierarchical thing to go through. There was no real cut-off time, we were the last programme of the night but there were certain union implications if we went on too long. It was up to us to judge, although I did once put Lynyrd Skynyrd on last playing 'Free Bird' and the titles ran as they played and they just carried on in the studio afterwards.

The programme graphics were by the BBC department, a guy called Roger Ferrin, I asked for something totally different and he gave me what everybody knows, which was much better – that's why he was a graphic artist and I wasn't. I chose Area Code 615 as the theme tune because I wanted a piece of music that was recognisable and whistleable but not so much that you would grow tired of it, something that could run for a long time, I had not expected the programme to run for sixteen years.

I did stop them wiping the programme tapes in the standard BBC way, in conjunction with a guy called Nick Maingay in the tape area. To save money every week, they used to put down a list of tapes to erase and reuse, and every week I went down and countermanded it so that the programme was kept, I think it was my ego probably. I did that off my own bat with Nick, and nowadays BBC Four lives on old *Whistle Tests*. In reality I think of television as a live medium and once it is done it should go but on the other hand if you are doing things that are retrospectively quite momentous you need to have it there. Also for legal reasons, like with Live Aid, you need to have a copy in case anything occurs and you have to have proof of what happened. Practically everything I did in TV was live, but now these days things have commercial value, and you record things for that value. Permits, contracts and the like meant that foreign sales were difficult at the time.

In the early days of *Whistle Test*, Alice Cooper was booked and very few people had a clue that he was a bloke until he arrived with this bloody great snake. We had to work hard to get viewing figures and that was great publicity for us. The first time we knew we were having any effect on the viewing figures was when a virtually unknown Focus were on and then the next day all the albums that were available were sold out within a few hours and Polydor had to turn over their entire pressing plant to Focus albums because the demand was so enormous.

David Bowie came into Studio B with Mick Ronson and band in 1972, did three numbers, took £50 off us and left dressed in a battle dress type outfit. That was the fee everybody got, £50 or you did not come in. The weekly budget for the whole programme was £500 when we started.

STEVE BLACKNELL, TV Presenter

I fancied a career in Telly, and everyone said no, no, no. But I knew that there were auditions coming up. Mike Appleton from the *Whistle Test*, had a new show going. Mike Appleton said to me, you're in the business, we've got a new show coming, but there's no way you're going to be a presenter on it. We can't use anyone in the business. Well at the time I was running a thing called Dial-A-Waiter which was a particularly silly thing; a friend and I went to corporate parties, served people whilst dressed as waiters, and then got completely out of it with them afterwards, and forget to invoice them and all that stuff. So I had assumed this mantle of the waiter; I was plugging records as a waiter. Mike said to me; I tell you what, come down, we'll interview you, because we know you won't shut up. But you're not going to be a presenter, no way; we'll just talk to you. I did the piece and I was offered the job as presenter of *Riverside* about a week later. The phone call was something like: This wasn't meant to happen. I got a phone call from a lady called Jill Sinclair who said: Steve, we're going to give you a couple of shows; don't mess it up, and that was it. We did forty-two of them and my C-list fame started there and then.

The DJ Mike Smith thankfully got very ill one day, so in-between applause I stepped in for him, and I never left the TV sofa after that.

That was phenomenal. By that time I was into the make-up and all the Goth thing. As well as breakfast time TV, I was Peter Stringfellow's PR guy as well. So I was sitting up with Les Dawson, Eddie Kidd and whoever was in town, till four in the morning, going home, having a wash, and then at 6 o'clock being picked up by the limo to go to BBC Breakfast TV. But what they would do, they would take me into make-up and I'd take my make-up *off* to go on the Telly, because I was wearing too much of it. They always said I was a one-off; they said I was the only guy they took make-up off to go on the Telly, but I still looked like Dusty Springfield. How the devil I got away with it I do not know, like a giant panda with all this mascara. Anyway, I'm progressing through kids' TV shows and stuff, and then *Live Aid* comes up. At this time I'm also doing well in America, because of a show on MTV called *London Calling*, which does very well over there. It's shot here, it's an hour-long thing about fashion and stuff, and it airs in America, so I'm pretty well-known over there as opposed to not really known here. But because of that I got selected to do the Phil Collins trip, which was a blessing and a curse, because I never saw *Live Aid*, but I did see the inside of Concorde, and had a pee crouching down on Concorde. That was why I was selected really, because I was known in America.

In Jonathan Ross's first ever press interview he was asked about the future, and he said: whatever it is, I don't want to be another Steve Blacknell. He didn't, because he's got money and I drank mine. The Swine.

ALLAN JAMES, Promotion Man

Alice Cooper on the Road, we did the first ever twenty-four hour flight around the UK when he did promotion for his 'Welcome To My Nightmare' album. We arranged to hire the Bron Learjet and he was staying at the Ritz, so the deal was we were going to fly from London to Manchester to Liverpool to Glasgow to Edinburgh to Newcastle to Luton, do the whole of the UK in twenty-four hours. No-one had ever done that and we'd arranged with every airport, all the local radio stations for everyone to turn up at the airports, to have all their interviews at the airport, have a special room and everything else like that. In those days it took weeks to set up, and we're sitting there and he turns up in the country, twenty-four hours before we're supposed to take off. Now we're supposed to end up back in London at Luton Airport and he phones up and says: Oh, I've just been invited to play on the BBC Pro-Am Golf Tournament from Gleneagles, so can we end up back at Glasgow? So that was alright, we managed to sort that out, we then had to pay for the plane to get from Luton to go back to Glasgow and then had to stay overnight and everything else like that. So we arranged it all and we asked what he would like on the plane.

Of course in those days he was sponsored by Jack Daniels; he would also drink beer but he wouldn't have it out of a can. In those days you could only get Budweiser in a can in the UK, he wanted it out of a little bubble bottle. We found them in an American air force base, so we had to go and buy X amount of crates of this Budweiser; then we had to buy X amount of crates of Jack Daniels, and I had to put it on the plane. The best part of the story was that we got to Luton Airport, we put all the booze on the plane and all the ice on and we were ready to go. There was me, Alice, his girlfriend, a dancer at the time, and two guys from the record company. We got on the plane and the plane was too heavy to take off, so we had to throw off one of the record company execs because Alice was not going to let the booze get thrown off, or the ice. Because that's Rock and Roll.

CHRIS BRIGGS, EMI A&R Manager

I went to an early U2 gig with Paul Conroy and Ben Edmonds of *Cream Magazine*, and I had a terrible stomach, which is very pertinent to this story. We got there, I liked Paul McGuiness straight away, so we end up in The Bailey drinking Guinness. So by now I've had three pints of Guinness and just the sandwich on the plane, I really don't feel great. I'm really hoping the band don't go on at eleven; I'm really hoping they go on at 8.30. We're in the gig and it's heaving and it's hot, and I think: I'm going to throw up and there's nothing I can do about it. I don't think I want to throw up inside. It was about four songs till the end of the set, and I'm sweating, I've obviously got food poisoning, so I said to Ben Edmonds, tell Paul McGuinness I'll be outside.

I go outside, throw up, I'm soaked, spinning, dizzy. But I can't get back into the gig, they won't let me back into the gig; Paddies right, and I say but I've flown from London to see U2. Then I set off to walk, I was so off my head I don't realise it's a half-hour walk. I can't think, I don't wait for Paul and Ben to come out; I think, I'll get a taxi back to the hotel. Paul McGuinness had said he was coming back to the hotel, we're meeting in the Berkeley Court bar and that is in my head. I'll get back there, cold water, sort myself out, be waiting for them.

I get back to the Berkeley Court hotel, get in my room, turn the television on; I think it was The Specials on the *Old Grey Whistle Test*, and I'm sat on the end of the bed, thinking, am I going to throw up again or can I go downstairs? A knock on the door and Paul McGuinness comes in the room raging. I said: didn't Ben tell you that I'd gone outside to chuck up, no obviously not. He just thinks I've fucked off. Well we sit down in my room and he obviously thinks I'm the head of A&R, which I'm not; I'm just the next scout up. I can't sign anything. Well I said: what's the deal? I do the 'what you do when you're at that level of A&R', you talk as if. So I find out what deal he wants for the band, and he wants three albums for him, £90,000 an album, this is 1978, it's a lot of money, and he wants guaranteed tour support.

In my delirium, I say, I really like the band Paul but that's an awful lot of money. I had said it as nicely and as English-ly as possible but that's what I said I guess. I don't know how, but I'm standing up and he's got hold of me by the collar, so I have a swing at him and miss.

I did think it was a shitload of money; it was twice as much money as they got from Island Records. Never mind, should have done it. What anyone with a brain would have done that evening was gone 'uh-huh, uh-huh', you've got a deal. Or left it with 'we're really interested', given him all the old bullshit, but I was completely honest and I have no idea to this day why.

DAVID BOWER,
Polydor Records
Marketing

This was actually in my Polydor days about The Jam in fact. They were sent out to America for their first major tour and the Americans were somewhat, as they were in those days, strong-armed into taking this sort of Punky little band from Woking. They'd come up with this great idea, as they saw it; they were going to put them on a double-decker bus on a support tour with Blue Oyster Cult in the middle of Texas. As you can imagine, it lasted less than a week basically. Not a match made in heaven.

Well I was a young product manager again and was getting way too big for my boots by this stage, and Wham! were on a little label called Innervision. Innervision was run by Mark Dean. Mark and I had formed ourselves into the two young blades around town; you can't touch us. We'd had four hit singles, we knew it all, we could reinvent the record business. Well this had spilled over onto George himself, so George and I basically got together and we said, right, we're going to do something really revolutionary; we're going to create a black and white album sleeve for our first album. Now by this stage Wham! had sold enough records for the Americans to start to get seriously interested that this was something that could really run. So somehow George, I and Mark managed to completely bamboozle all of the signing-off procedures and everything else, and I, along with a tame art director, had done this sleeve, production. We'd got this thing done and we'd printed half-a-million copies of this sleeve.

Anyway, I get this call; it's the MD Maurice Oberstein's secretary: Obie would like to see you. Swaggering up in the lift, I get out on the fourth floor, knock on his door, opened the door. As I open the door, he's got this album sleeve and it comes across the room spinning like a frisbee, boom, and hits me right in the forehead. He looks at me, and goes, Bower, we do not do black and white album sleeves. Get this done in colour! and that's it, end of story. I went back, picked the phone up, rang George, because it was that type of relationship. I went: Well bit of a problem, Obie wants it in colour. Even George went: Oh, then he'd better have it in colour. I said: This is not a discussion we're having, this is what is going to happen. But I can always remember it was no pussyfooting around; it was very direct and it was just landed there.

PAUL KING,
Concert Promoter

The Jam were managed by Paul Weller's father, who was a former boxer, who must have taken a severe blow to the throat at some point in his career because he talked in a low voice, lovely, lovely man, but knew what he wants and he knew when he wanted it. Like Eric Clapton with his mum down the road, The Jam were from Woking, which was less than ten miles from Guildford, so this was their home gig. We ended up doing not just one night at Guildford Civic, but would end up doing two nights at Guildford Civic. We would pay them a fortune because we knew we were going to sell out, so we'd work out the fee even before we started; there was no percentages, John knew how many people were going to be in the hall, and that was the fee. So we built up a kind of trust and nothing was a problem. The week of the gig of the two shows the agent called me and said: John just asked me to give you a quick call, he needs cash out of the gig. I said: but Martin, the contract says cheque. He says: Paul, you know John as well as I know John, doesn't matter what the contract says, if John wants cash, give him cash. I said: I was just checking. If John wants cash he will have cash. It's not a problem, we sold out weeks ago.

So sure enough the two gigs were a Thursday and a Friday, and the Thursday night came and went and John said to me: Can we sort everything out tomorrow in terms of the financial settlement? I said: Yeah, I'll do all that with you. Halfway through the Friday gig he said to me: Paul, can we settle up? So I took him to the Manager's office and shut the door, and opened my briefcase, which was absolutely jammed full with bank notes. In only the way that John could say it, he said: Wotsat! I said: It's the cash that you asked for John. Are you mad? It's Friday! Wot do you think I'm gonna do with that on a Friday night??! I said: But John, Martin your agent, called me and said you wanted cash. No! I don't want cash on a Friday, he said: Put it away! Can't you give me a cheque? I said: With pleasure. So I closed the briefcase and wrote him a cheque and went home that night, and I said to my wife: We've got a real problem. She said: Whatever's up? I replied: You see that briefcase? It's full of money, and it's the weekend. What on earth are we going to do with it? I think we took some floorboards up in the end at the place we were renting and we hid it under the floor.

Drummers are generally some of the biggest pain in the arses on the planet. One drummer's surname was Elias, so there's no prizes for guessing his religion. But he felt part of his job was to drive the Manager mad, and he would phone me about the most trivial things. He would do it every day; a day would not go by without me getting a call from him about something which I could do absolutely nothing about. I was drinking quite heavily in those days so my tolerance level was very low towards the end of the afternoon He rang me late one afternoon and he said: Paul, I'm at the gig, we've just done the sound check, and the showers don't work. Luckily I still had my wits about me, and I thought about where he was, and I said to him: You are in Germany, you are Jewish, you should be pleased the showers don't work. To which he slammed the phone down and didn't speak to me for two weeks.

MALCOLM HILL, EMI Radio & TV Promotions

Pet Shop Boys I always adored working with, and did heaps of stuff with them, and lots of *Top Of The Pops* performances. One in particular I remember: it kind of got into the vein with the Pet Shop Boys that Chris never did anything, so any TV run-throughs it would be Neil, with me standing at the keyboards and trying to do that. One particular *Pops*, Chris was at the show but he wouldn't come down for rehearsals, he was laying on the couch upstairs. He wouldn't even come down for make-up. So I got the make-up girls to go up and do his make-up whilst he lay on the bed. When they'd gone I said: Do you know Chris, I have to say I've worked with a lot of people, and you are the laziest Pop star I've ever worked with. Well to his credit he said: Do you know Malc, coming from you, I take that as a real compliment. I love the Pets. People used to think they were po-faced and boring for quite a long time but they weren't, they were bloody hilarious. I don't know why Neil hasn't written books.

In the late Seventies, I suppose 1976 maybe, Jim Dandy was the lead singer of Black Oak Arkansas and they were playing the Reading Festival and Radio 210 had a radio van on site and they wanted to talk to everybody who was on the bill, and Jim Dandy was on the bill. I really liked Black Oak Arkansas, they were a pretty good band and Jim Dandy was a great entertainer and good singer. We went in there with Black Oak Arkansas who had security, American security as they were a big band at that time, and you didn't know what was going on. So we went in there and Ted Nugent was just being interviewed. Now I was completely unaware that there was bad history between the two bands, between The Amboy Dukes and Black Oak Arkansas, and the guys drew guns! I mean, bloody hell. I'm in the middle of it all and Radio 210 are looking at me and the Black Oak Arkansas guys have got guns, so has one of Ted Nugent's men. It's all: Guys, it's just a radio interview, can we just go off and sort this out? Where the hell they got guns from I don't know, but that was really scary.

£££

DOUG SMITH,
Manager

We had some great times in America touring with Hawkwind. You know they got arrested in America for tax, right. They were there for a 'sold out' gig in Hammond, Indiana. The gig was over and I was backstage, probably the worse for wear. All these guys in suits started walking round us. I mean, they didn't mean very much, they were little guys; there was nothing very particular about them and I just thought, oh, part of the venue. I walked down and there's this guy, I said: what's going on? He pulls this shield out from his jacket and goes: IRS! I thought, oh, why? What's going on? We're seizing all your equipment. Why? Because you owe us $18,000. I went: no we don't, what are you talking about? This time I'm getting angrier and angrier and angrier, and then they go back into the dressing room and they're going through all the band's personal belongings, looking for the stuff there. There must be about twenty five, thirty of them; maybe not as many, maybe only about fifteen of them, I'm probably exaggerating, who knows, but it seemed like lots of them. Lots of police, the police were everywhere. I was letting off to the guy who was in charge, and a big tall copper comes over and grabs my arm and says: If I was you I'd cool down, come here. He walked me to the window of the dressing room and all around the wall at this venue there on the green in Hammond, Indiana, was surrounded by police cars all with their lights pointing in the building. And they were serious. They stuck stickers on the group's equipment that said: 'Do Not Touch, this is now the property of the United States Government of the USA'.

I was watching the roadies peeling the stickers off and rolling them up, and taking them away, not thinking they were serious; I thought they're just taking them as souvenirs. Anyway, it all ended in an affray that night, and they kept the equipment at the venue, and they gave me till Monday morning, this was a Friday night, to raise the $18,000. Our next gig was Monday evening as it happens, which is an unusual night for a gig, but it was, and we had to leave and drive to the next gig.

Over the weekend Richard Ogden made really good press of it; we were in the *Daily Mirror,* all the tabloids, the *Daily Mail* picked up on it. We were all locked in the hotel under house arrest; they had a car parked outside watching so that we wouldn't remove any of our vehicles. Of course we just partied for the weekend; it was just one great laugh for the weekend and everybody went crazy and bought more and more drugs, and found more and more women to bring back to the hotel.

I of course didn't, because I was in my room trying to find $18,000 to get the equipment back. The Monday morning came and the band and the crew had all been down to the local print shop and got these t-shirts 'Do Not Touch, this is now the property of the United States Government of the USA'. The band were taking photographs of them, all these IRS guys with their clipboards hiding their faces: You can't take photographs of us. It was just chaos outside waiting for the venue staff to come and open up so we could go and use their office to do the business and get our equipment back. Eventually the venue opened, they were an hour late, which was good because it really riled these IRS guys. Of course Hawkwind are just stoned out of their heads sitting around laughing. I got into the office and the guy sat down and said: Have you got it? I said: yeah, put down a draft I think. I had a draft for $10,000 and $8,000 in cash, and put that on the table. He said: Fine. He was writing a receipt and he said: Oh, there's another $450. I said: What For? He said: The rental of the venue to store your equipment in. I just let go, I called him everything you can think of under the sun. Then these two guys who were either side of me came across and pulled their jackets open and pointed their guns and said: Cool down, cool down. I'm raggy haired and bearded and God knows what else, and just as they're about to take me to task the door falls in and Andy Duncan falls onto the floor and says, it's alright Doug, I've got $450, don't worry. Off we trotted with our equipment. But a lot of bad vibes for the rest of that tour, and we never got the money back.

ROBBIE WILSON,
Roadie

When I got to Los Angeles, Slade did a show at the Whisky a Go-Go, and I was twenty-one, twenty-two years old and a heavy cigarette smoker. We did a show, got to know the girls who waited on the tables, and got to know the bouncers. We were living in LA at the time making an album at A&M Records. The Carpenters were in the next studio, Herb Alpert was in the next studio, Slade were in the third studio in the old Charlie Chaplin studios in Hollywood. So we were hanging out in the Whisky a Go-Go and we got to know the girls and we're all sitting round, and the girls were saying: Come round and we'll make you bacon and eggs tomorrow, we know you like bacon and eggs, and we'll get HP sauce. One of them said to me: Robbie, what do you really miss living in Los Angeles? and I said: an English fag. She looked at her mate and she went: an English fag? I says: I would give my left bollock for an English fag. You know I've not had one in months. She went: I could probably help you, and I went, fantastic. She says, I'll make a phone call. So I thought, girl on the ground: knows somebody where I can get a packet of twenty Embassy. About half-an-hour later she comes back with this blonde guy with a Union Jack t-shirt who was the English DJ on the biggest Pop station in Los Angeles, and she thought I was looking for a sexual encounter. I was actually looking for an Embassy cigarette.

We were touring Australia with Slade, Status Quo, Lindisfarne and Caravan: the four of us, all record sellers in Australia. We had rented planes to ourselves, 707s, not Lear jets, we had a 707 where we'd load the gear and then we'd all fly to the gig. So we're out in Melbourne, very drunk, I'm driving the minibus, I come back to the hotel. Next morning I wake up in somebody else's room, fire sirens and all sorts of panic. I look out of the thirteenth floor and the place is surrounded by police, fire engines, and I think, fuck, there's been a fire, something's gone on here. I'm still very, very under the influence of Jack Daniels and coke. I open the door and someone said, the problem's on the thirteenth floor and they think the hotel's going to collapse.

As the story unfolded, of course it was my minibus. We had come back from a wild night where we had practically wrecked a nightclub, which was not a problem, we just paid them the next morning and they were quite happy, but we'd been dancing on bars and tables. Seemingly I had come back and driven round the back of the hotel and discovered a goods lift that they used for collecting the towels. The guy would go round all the floors, he would get his trolley, get the towels, put them in the lift, eventually they'd have twelve floors-worth of towels, guy would reverse up, and they'd load them in. So I thought, we'll fit in the lift. But not only did I take the minibus up to the thirteenth floor where we were all living, I drove it outside the lift and left it there. Well had no recollection. I think I got fined $3,000. I think we had to pay the hotel $10,000 damages for all the inconvenience, and they nearly deported me, but we got past that. So I've had some touring adventures. I went to prison in America for doing 120 miles an hour in a 55, that wasn't pleasant. I did seven days in Chowchilla County Jail: long hair, platform boots, frilly shirt, straight to jail, do not stop.

MEL GALE, Musician

A friend of mine somehow joined ELO when they first started and then re-joined years later. Because of him they phoned me up at the beginning of 1975, and said: We're going to do a small UK tour, a one-week Spanish tour, and then six weeks in America. Just hearing the word America pricked my ears up, and that was it. I said: Yeah, okay, I fancy that. I put everything else on hold for a while and went off with the band. But frankly I thought, almost from day one, the first time I went up there, that I'd made a huge mistake because I wasn't used to playing in front of speakers, amps, and all that, it was just so loud, and I just wasn't used to it. My ears took a long time to adjust. It wasn't a problem for them, everyone else was used to it, but for me in a scout hut in Birmingham it was just a bit of a nightmare. I think it was February 1975, might have been March, doing the songs from 'Eldorado' and 'On the Third Day'; and just learning these lines. In fact before I actually got to the scout hut someone from Jet Records had sent me some vinyl copies and put ticks against the track listing on the back by the tracks that they thought I should work out a part for before I went to the rehearsals. They said: There won't be any sheet music there, you've just got to play along.

So I just went through the tracks and listened to them, thought, okay, fair enough, it's in E, or it's in F, or whatever, I'll play along. I could have done with a part being written out to start with to be honest because it would have saved a bit of time, but other than that, once I got in and played the tracks a few times with the guys up in Birmingham, it wasn't so bad. But of course what I hadn't got prepared for was that when we actually went on stage I was supposed to be doing things other than just playing the music. Hugh got up and twirled his cello around. Then they handed me this device, it was a cello that was actually an exploding cello; it had a charge inside and you pretended to play it and then pressed this button on the floor and the whole cello would just explode with a big bang and a cloud of smoke. That was part of the act. I'd never even thought of doing anything like this but this was showbiz I suppose, but it wasn't what I'd been trained to do. So it came as a bit of a shock but after a while it was fun as well and you got into it. Eventually I managed to persuade them to ditch the exploding cello and we sort of carried on from there.

I think we played the Valentine's Day Dance at Newcastle Polytechnic, and there were about five men and a dog in the audience and seven of us on stage; it was pretty dire. We really used it as a bit of a rehearsal; in fact we used the next half-dozen gigs as a bit of a rehearsal really before we went to America. I think during those first few weeks with the band I really thought I'd made a huge mistake and was almost looking there and then for a way out of it, to get back to what I was doing before. But then I thought, no, I've agreed to do America so I'll do America, get that out of the way and then leave. But I actually enjoyed going around America, that was a good trip. I got to see a lot of places I've never ever been to or thought of going to.

I got back to Britain after having already phoned up a few fixers to say I'm coming back in a week or so: Is there any session work going, what have you got? I got off the plane and went: Bye guys, it's been an experience, thanks very much, I'm off. And they said: No you're not, we start rehearsals for Europe next week, I think it was Europe, and then back to The States in a few weeks' time. You're in the band. I honestly had no idea that I was considered to be in the band, I thought I was just booked to do that tour. It was all so loosely organised. No-one had actually come up and said: Look, this is what you'll get on the next tour, this is what we're paying, this is where you're going to be staying, what you're going to be doing, none of that happened. It was just a case of, oh no, you're in the band; whatever we do now, you're doing. And that was it. So from then on I was in the band for the next five years.

JACKIE LYNTON, Singer

Do you want to come for an audition? No, not really. I was living in Weybridge at the time. This bloke phoned me up, Harry Simmonds, obviously Kim Simmonds' brother. I've got a band, we need a singer; he'd been and seen me with the band, you know, Jackie Lynton, the HD Band or whatever it was called. No I can't be bothered. I'd had so many let downs in my time, you know like you do, you're going to do it. Jacko, you've got the voice and all that. I thought, fuck it; in the end you can't be bothered. So I kept putting the phone down, I put it down about three times. Then I spoke to a mate of mine called Roger Wedder. I said: I have had a call from a bloke called Harry Simmonds, he keeps phoning. I was on a building site out in High Wycombe doing the old labouring, whatever. In fact I was painting and decorating, that's what I do, I'm a painter and decorator really, cum Rock and Roller; but I'm a painter and decorator really, I can paint and decorate your place. That's what I really do, in reality, but fuck about with Rock and Roll, Elvis fan, or whatever. He said: Who is it? I said: a bloke called Harry Simmonds. He said: Don't you know who that is? I said: No. He said: He's the brother of a bloke called Kim Simmonds who's a guitarist for a band called Savoy Brown. I said: I've heard of them. He said: Fucking hell, they're massive in America, which they were.

I said: You're joking; what does he want with me? He said: Obviously he wants a vocalist; he's seen you and you can carry a tune, which I can. I said: Fucking hell, I hope he phones back. Which he did, about a week later. Jack, he said: I've asked you time and time again, do you just want to come for a run for rehearsal? I said: I'll be there tomorrow. I was there like a flash at Twickenham Rugby Grounds. I went along, sung a couple of Chuck Berry songs like everybody does, even McCartney does that. I went, I passed the 'audition', the so-called audition for Savoy Brown and off I went. We got on the plane and I'm from a building site, imagine me on a building site paid £40 a week. We ended up in Denver, and I thought, fucking hell, everyone looks like Lee Marvin, you know, the coppers; they all had the helmet straps hanging down, didn't do them up, and I thought, fucking hell! We were on tour with Deep Purple because I know him very well. Ritchie Blackmore's a great mate, and off we went. So I had a year with them, and then it all got a bit political really. It all got a bit naughty; Harry got upset with Kim, and phoned me up one day, and that was it really. He phoned up and said it's over.

Bidwell was the drummer, who died now unfortunately with an overdose. He used to like his thing. But he died with his boots on, he died with his fucking boots on. I used to share a room with him and he always said to me in America, he said: When I die Jackie, I want to die with me boots on. He had these cowboy boots on. He died with them on, Dave Bidwell. It's a wicked thing to say really but he died with them on. He never used to take them off at night. He never took them off because he thought he was going to fucking pass away one night in his sleep, which he did, and he still had them on.

RUPERT PERRY, MD Capitol Records

Touring in America, for all of us going to America, going to the United States for the first time from the wonderful, small, beautiful, green country that we have here, it's the size and the magnitude of the United States that gets you, and just how many different places you have to go to. I remember one of my first jobs at Capitol Records was going on the road with Heads, Hands and Feet in 1972, and immediately I was staggered that we seemed to be on the road for about ten days and going to all these different places, Albuquerque, Phoenix, Tucson, Salt Lake City; and I thought, we've barely been anywhere but it seems to have taken a huge amount of time. I quickly realised that from an artist's point of view this took a lot of stamina because if you turned up in Salt Lake you were expected to go to local radio stations, you were expected to go to a retail store, you were then expected to do a sound check, you were then expected to go on stage and give the performance of your life, and then you were expected to go back to your hotel room, get up the next day, catch the flight, catch the bus to wherever the next place was. Doing that every day, now that took a lot of doing.

I was pleased I'd had that initial experience because it always helped me to understand just the amount of commitment as an artist that you would have to put into trying to succeed in the United States. For some it was okay, for others it proved too difficult, and for others it was their downfall. We had Status Quo signed to Capitol Records at one time. Quo were always considered to be one of those English bands that had already been on a couple of labels in the United States but had never really broken through. Everybody couldn't quite understand: they haven't broken through, why haven't they broken through? Their sort of Blues/Rock/go for it, was perfect for America. I remember, they'd come over, and they were huge in the UK and Europe: Huge, so they'd come over and the first gig was the Whisky in Los Angeles. They'd say: Bit of alright, it's a little rinky-dink club, alright, fine.

I remember the manager was a man called Colin Johnson who was a wonderful character, but then after they'd been on the road for about three weeks he calls me up and he says: We've had enough, we've had enough. I said: Well where are you? He says, I'm not sure, I think we're in Nashville or Memphis but the band have had enough, they're going home Rupert. I said: What do you mean, no, no, no, you can't go home. No, we can't do this any longer, he says: They're sick to death of playing the opening slot on somebody's tour and having to play some small club. He said: We're used to playing these big arenas, we play all these big stadiums. We're losing money, while we're here in America, trying to break America, we're not making any money. Thank you for supporting us, you're trying to help us, he said: I appreciate all of that but no, we're done, we're going home! And that was it and it's interesting that they never ever broke America.

CHARLIE GILLETT, MD Oval Records

Since I came to London, I've always lived in South London. Somebody who was a neighbour at the time was Gordon Nelki, and Gordon said something like: If you weren't doing what you're doing now, what else would you do in music? I said: what else? I mean, it didn't seem a reasonable question. I said: I suppose you'd start a record label. When I play these Cajun records from Louisiana on the radio people really like them and it's impossible to get them over here. So how would you get hold of them? You'd have to go to Louisiana. Well why don't we do it? and it was pretty much like this, as quickly as this, this conversation just happened. So we went down there, had a wonderful adventure in Louisiana, and what encouraged Gordon was that the people running these little labels down there were, you could only say, amateurs. One of them ran a TV repair shop; another guy was the Sheriff of Crowley, Louisiana, and his office was at the back of a hairdressing salon. So if these guys could call themselves record labels, anybody apparently could do it. We made our contacts and found some material we really liked, especially a guy called Floyd Soileau in Ville Platte, Louisiana. He ran a label called Swallow and another one called Jin.

On our trip, the first night we were in New Orleans playing pool in a bar. We both of us were pretty hopeless but we loved just to go and play pool, to hear what's on the jukebox. What could be better! Neither of us were drinkers at all. Then I heard 'Promised Land' start up, it was a tune I knew very well by Chuck Berry but there was no guitar; instead of guitar there was accordion. I went over and checked out A47, 'Promised Land' by Johnnie Allan, and I could see that it was actually the B side of some other song, and it was on Jin Records, and we had Jin as one of our targets.

We get to the address in Ville Platte and as we were walking in the door there's this guy, very nice guy, Floyd Soileau, shakes your hands, and I'd barely touched his hand I said: have you got 'Promised Land' by Johnnie Allan? And he said: Calm down, calm down, have a cup of tea. Everybody would say have a cup of tea. I don't drink tea. What, you're English and you don't drink tea!! This was like a constant dialogue. Of all the places we went to, this was the only one you could say was a proper record company, the whole thing, it was a record shop and it sold not only its own records but every local label and every national record as well, it was a bone fide record shop, but in the back, he was a semi distributor. All his own records in boxes and other neighbouring labels, he supplied them too. But Floyd was totally reasonable, the royalty he wanted was affordable. He just said: Take everything away, work out what you like, let me know, I'll send you the tapes. And it all did come to pass like that, and we put together the compilation on Oval.

MARTIN MILLS,
MD Beggars Banquet Records

I got a job in Record and Tape Exchange. Previously I'd written to every record company asking if I could get a job doing anything and no-one replied. I think Trojan replied actually but said, No. I don't think anyone else replied. Music was what I loved and what I wanted to do but the possibility of actually doing it as a career was pretty remote really. But the Record and Tape Exchange job turned into us opening our first record shop and then that first record shop turned into a rehearsal room, into concert promotion, into band management, and then finally into a record label.

The record labels that I considered to be great arbiters of taste in my youth were probably Island and Elektra; those were the labels I grew up idolising really. But when we started a label it wasn't anywhere near as grandiose as that; it was just because we were managing a band, we couldn't get them a record deal – it was that simple. Of course in those days starting a label was quite a big deal, there wasn't any instruction manual, whereas now it's something that some kid does in some garage every day of every week. But it was really pretty unusual when we did it.

That was The Lurkers first single: 'Shadow / Freak Show'. In those Punk days you could sell whatever you put out because there was so few Punk singles so many people wanted them. The same ten or twenty thousand kids wanted every Punk single that came out, so we sold ten or twenty thousand. I used to take them in the boot of my very old £50 Jaguar round to Lightning Wholesalers and Small Wonder, and eventually Rough Trade, but that was a year or two later; we just sold them through the network, and then also through President. It went pretty well. We sold out, it was a success, and so we thought, well, we could do another record by The Lurkers, so we did. Then we put out a compilation album of independent Punk singles, from all the Punk labels that were springing up at the time, The Nose Bleeds, and that kind of stuff. I think that may have been the first Punk album;

200

it might have even come out before the Sex Pistols album, the Clash album, but it sold, twenty or thirty thousand, which these days would be totally impossible.

I think we survived because, number one, we had Gary Numan and The Tubeway Army, which was obviously an enormous series of records. At one time we had three albums in the Top 20 at the same time, which is pretty insane. Gary's now dead bass player, Paul Gardiner, brought a tape in, and we played it over the speakers, as we always did. I remember going down to the studio, Gary was in Portobello Road at that point, and then hearing 'Are Friends Electric' for the first time, and thinking, that's got to be a single. Doesn't sound like a single but it's got to be a single, I thought it was amazing. So we had that much luck to get floated in the first place.

But between Gary's first and second album we were seriously going bust; we were bouncing salary cheques, we stretched the cash flow of the shops as far as it could be stretched to fund the record label, and it was pretty much the end. We got an introduction to Warner Bros and they did a licence deal with us. We had a band called The Doll who had a hit with a song called 'Desire Me' who Warners thought were going to be huge. They didn't see Gary Numan at the time. They gave us £100,000 advance, which was absolutely insane as far as we were concerned. How on earth are we ever going to make that back? It was completely nuts. £100,000 is a lot of money now; imagine what it was like then. But of course a few months after we did the deal Gary Numan happened and they made it back within the first year I think.

But you actually asked me why we survived and others haven't. I think, number one, it was the luck of having Gary Numan early on, and number two, just being prudent really: just kind of being the right combination of being prudent but ambitious.

TED CARROLL,
Rock On Records

When we went back to Ireland in December of 1970, I was played a test pressing of the Decca Thin Lizzy album by a friend of mine who was managing them, a guy called Brian Tuite, so I went into partnership with him to manage Thin Lizzy. I hadn't intended to, as soon as I finished with Skid Row I was going to go back on the buses but in London. I was going to go on London Transport for a while driving one-man buses, and find a little back street shop somewhere right off the beaten track that you rent for a tenner a week or something, and open an oldies' store. That was the idea, but then I got Skid Row kind of diverting me off that track for a while.

I opened the first Rock On store in Golborne Road in August '71, so within seven or eight months I'd got my first store going, and that was it. It's like location, location, location; the location was great, because everyone came to Portobello Road then and up Golborne Road. There was nobody else doing that kind of thing in London because Saturday was fantastic business, and time was right for it. I had been collecting records; in fact I'd already started doing some mail order, but I'd been collecting 45s assiduously. How I discovered this place in Golborne Road was because every Friday and Saturday I would go down to Golborne and Portobello and the other street markets and scrape around and buy as many 45s as I could afford to. Plus I had stuff I'd bought in America when I was there with Skid Row. Then I suddenly discovered this flea market which was about to open, took the stall there. I went to Ireland for a quick tour with Thin Lizzy, and while I was there, because they were obviously on Decca and I was in Solomon and Peres, which was the Decca distributor there, I discovered that upstairs they had a whole roomful of deleted London Records 45s going back about 20 years. So I bought 1800 of those, cherry picked 1800 of those at three-and-a-half pence a throw, came back and combined that with what I had, I mean, it was fantastic. I'd actually go down to open the store on a Saturday morning and there'd be a dozen, fifteen people waiting for it to open, and hands would be coming in, I want a copy of that, snatch, it was just fantastic.

BRYAN MORRISON, Manager

The first American I met rang me up really early in the Pretty Things career, when they were hot, and he said: Son, I want to meet you. I said okay, great. He said: I'm staying in the Mayfair Hotel, want to have breakfast? So I said, yeah, alright, great. A morning breakfast, and I walked in the Mayfair Hotel, I asked for him, go up, this suite, the size of a palace. I had never seen anything like it in my life. Sat down, he said: What do you want? I said: eggs? He said: You want a steak for breakfast with your eggs? I said: a steak? for breakfast? That's dinner if I'm lucky. Well actually I didn't say that because I don't think I'd ever had a steak at that point. The waiters came in with the steak; I couldn't believe it, I was a pig in shit.

So he said to me, I've just taken The Dave Clarke Five to America and I want another support; I want your band The Pretty Things. I said: great, love to, what's the deal? He said: I want 20% agency commission, and I said: No, I can't do that. 10%. He said: No, 20% and I said: No.

That was the singular biggest mistake I ever made in the music business. I think the only one I ever made, well, not the only one, but I said: No. So The Pretty Things didn't go to America.

DEREK LAWRENCE,
Record Producer

I knew Rex Oldfield from EMI, who was by now running MGM Records. I produced four singles for MGM, and an album with an act called Sun Dragon, which was Deep Purple playing on the backing tracks. Because of the Joe Meek thing and knowing Ritchie and Chas, Ritchie phoned me up and said: Look, I've got these two mugs, they've got a lot of money and want to finance a band. There's Chris Curtis and Bobby Woodman, come down and see what you think. So I said: Okay. This is like a Wednesday, but by the time I went down on the Friday, Chris Curtis and Bobby Woodman had gone and Ian Paice and Rod Evans were in.

I lived at Cockfosters, which is four miles away from South Mimms, and John and Tony had put them in this farmhouse type place in South Mimms. I went: Great, really good, I like them. Then they introduced me to John and Tony. One had come from advertising and the other was running his mum's baby clothes business thing. There was a third one, who by this time had been arrested for selling forged paintings, so he got blown out. They came to me and I sat down and said: Okay, I'll do the deals for you, which I did.

Twice there's been lawsuits by various members of Deep Purple saying they were ripped off in the early days but everybody has subsequently agreed: No, this is as good a deal that you're ever going to get in those days. The fact that they got an EMI contract, that I negotiated, which was that EMI had them for the world outside the USA, Canada and Japan, was the first I believe. The publishing deal was like a 60/40 deal and in 1967 that was a great deal.

Through Feldman Music and Ronny Beck I was asked: Would you record this band called The John Evans Smash? I went: All right, if you like. So we went into CBS studios in Bond Street, as it was in those days, and I did three tracks, or four tracks with The John Evans Smash, who were basically a show band with brass and whatever. I went to him and I said: Well you should really become a Rock band and lose the brass. The singer said: We're losing the brass but we're not going to become a Rock band, per se, and that was Ian Anderson. Meantime I'd taken them to Abbey Road and done four tracks with them and called them Candy Coloured Rain, because flower power was 'in' at the time and that seemed like a good name. Ian Anderson phoned me and said: We're changing the name to Jethro Tull. I misheard it and thought he said Jethro Toe, because I'd never heard of this seedpod drill or inventor or whatever. I phoned up MGM with the label copy details and said they are called Jethro Toe.

BRIAN WILLOUGHBY,
Musician

I went to Belfast, I'm originally from Northern Ireland, and my elder cousin took me to see Them in a club in Belfast. I was only fourteen, probably, and she was sixteen or seventeen. I started playing guitar when I was fourteen and I was in a band in no time at all. My first guitar, which is still unplayable, was a small sized acoustic, and a friend of mine at school was selling an electric one, so I bought that shortly after I got the acoustic. I was in a band, I could always do the twiddly bits, I didn't know any chords but I could always play the twiddly bits. I was playing with guys who were much older than me, and we used to do youth clubs around Isleworth and Heston and so forth, playing Chuck Berry stuff and sort of Stones-y things really, that kind of material. There was a guy, John Vanstone his name was, who had shared a flat with Brian Jones of The Stones in Richmond, and he was a drug user. My mum and dad forbade me but I used to see him because he was a great guitarist and I used to go round after school and pick up bits of guitar from him. I used to go to the Ricky Tick in Hounslow, opposite the bus garage, and I saw The Yardbirds with Jimmy Page playing bass, and Jeff Beck playing guitar. I saw all sorts of people there, Geno Washington, Steampacket, you know,

The British Birds. Wonderful, fantastic club. I saw Hendrix there. I'm ashamed to admit, I was such a Clapton fan at the time that I was one of the faction of would-be guitar players who kind of shunned Hendrix. I've since become a fan but at the time I was too much of a Clapton nut, or Jeff Beck; Jeff Beck has always been my numero uno.

I missed Eel Pie Island, I was just too young. I went to the Windsor Ricky Tick, I went to the Richmond Athletic Ground. When I was eighteen my mum and dad bought me a tape recorder, a Grundig TK144 tape recorder, and I used to write songs and tunes and put them on the tape recorder. Dave Cousins from The Strawbs was a friend of mine; he ran a Folk club in Hounslow called the White Bear, I used to go every single week, so I've known Dave since I was sixteen-ish. I gave Dave a copy of my tape of some songs I'd written, and about three years later Dave played on a Mary Hopkin album; he and Ralph McTell played guitar on this Mary Hopkin thing. She was looking for somebody to go out and play guitar live with her as Ralph and Dave had played on the album. Dave very kindly passed my tape on to her and Tony Visconti, her husband, and I got a job with her on my twenty-second birthday.

When The Strawbs were going, the four of us, drummer, bass player, keyboard player and myself, we called ourselves Turkey Leg Johnson, and we went out and did the London pubs and clubs. When we weren't on the road with The Strawbs, we had a sort of residency at a pub in Mortlake, the Jolly Gardeners it's called, and one night Lonnie Donegan turned up, and we all nearly died. He came up and said: Can I play with you? He got up and we did 'Cumberland Gap', 'Rock Island Line'. Fantastic, marvellous, marvellous stuff. He actually took my number and to this day, it's up in the loft here, I've got a cassette tape from my answer machine with him ringing me up and saying: Do you want to be in my band? Unfortunately I had too many commitments at the time, but there you go, I met my hero.

PATRICK HUMPHRIES, Journalist

One day in '76 there was a famous Hip Young Gunslingers advert in the *New Musical Express*, and I'd done sort of writing, but never had anything published, and I did, from memory, an *NME*-style interview with some rock sort of Jon Anderson-type figure, very pretentious thing. I found it years later, it was actually quite funny, I had got that rather cool, *NME*-style of interviewing, and I got that very pretentious Rock star response. I have to say it was quite amusing. I was on holiday in Ireland when my mum rang and said: Nothing wrong dear but the *New Musical Express* would like you to go and see them. So when I got back I went to see dear old Tony Stewart, who did the initial interview and said basically: Would you like to do some freelance work for us? I said: I'd be absolutely delighted. I later learn, I don't know how true this is but it's nice to know, that Nick Hornby, Sebastian Faulks and Neil Tennant applied to be Hip Young Gunslingers, and weren't.

I think all writers are fairly egotistical. If you're not worried about being published, you just write it in your room and it never comes off your computer. I think you want an audience for what you write, whether it's a novel or a review of ELP. I mean certainly, who wouldn't want to be in a Rock and Roll band surrounded by screaming fans and adoring groupies.

One of the first things I did when I joined *NME* in the Seventies, was to go back and look at the reviews of the classic albums to see what the journalists thought of it. The classic one is Nick Logan I think, and Van Morrison's 'Astral Weeks', which is regularly voted one of the greatest records ever made, quite rightly so. But the actual original review is about a paragraph, and it's along the lines of: Intriguing solo debut from ex-Them singer, but frankly could learn a few tricks from Jose Feliciano. The Beatles 'Sergeant Pepper' for example got a page, but complete bafflement: Maybe The Beatles are running out of inspiration, they repeat the title track.

I think the one point is, you had to make snap judgments when writing reviews. 'Sandinista' is the other one; because when 'London Calling' came out, wonderful record, and the reviewer said: What could be better than a double Clash album, a triple Clash album? Well of course you've been given 'Sandinista', and so you had six sides of vinyl to review. You got it, I don't know, on something like the Friday, and you had to get 750 or 1,000 words written by the following Monday; so that's the weekend gone and, oh, there was one track in the middle of side four that was quite good, and is that a bit of 'Stagger Lee' there? So physically it was actually difficult. When the CDs came in it was wonderful for reviewers because of course, oh track three was that and now let's skip 'Revolution Number 9'. So CD's were great but the old vinyl review thing was quite a challenge, and it was always a snap judgment.

MUFF WINWOOD,
CBS Director of A&R

I was taking the Clash down to see Glyn Johns, the famous record producer who did The Eagles and all this kind of thing, you know, really taking The Clash to a different level, right. This was like making Clash Americana this was. I took them all down to Glyn Johns' house, and he lived in this beautiful mansion down in Surrey somewhere, with a long gated drive, and we got to the gate and we got out of our car to open the gate and he rode down on a horse. He rode down on horseback. You can imagine what they thought. He's very, very tough, Glyn Johns, he's a real boss. He kind of looked down at them from the horse and you're thinking, what, are they sussing out about this guy? He was saying things like: I'm not going to stand any nonsense from you guys, if you're going to start playing around doing this, you listen to me, I know what I'm doing. Well I'm still edging back, you know, thinking, Oh My God! But the interesting thing was of course, he was so strong and so pointed that they actually liked him in the end. I can't remember if we ever went in the house in the end. I think the whole meeting took place at the gate, and he was on the horse. I can't remember going into the house at all, because I can remember the frontage but I can't remember the house, so I don't think we went in. The whole meeting was done at the bloody gate, and we went home again.

As it happened, we couldn't work with him. They were prepared to have a go with him in the end. As we were driving back I was still kind of going: Go on, give it a try, but they did like him. I thought they were going to lynch him, but they actually really liked him. He would have been ideal for them. But this was all about, you know, they were massive in the UK, and the Americans couldn't get them going properly. They did in the end but then they couldn't get them going properly and they were saying to me: You've got to find another way, their stuff would sound like classic Rock and Roll if it had proper production values. So that was the idea, to cut an album that was really more American, and as it happened it didn't work out. But, you know, all that was, was a bloody painful day where you drove all the way down there with this bunch of moaning bastards. Then all the way back trying to convince them to improve their career, and you're dragging them through mud. You get home and all you think is, bloody awful day that was, and you want to forget it. You've got somebody really nice to deal with tomorrow, like Barbara Dickson; oh at least I can speak to Barbara and have a nice cup of tea.

TOM NOLAN, EMI Records Press Officer

Malcolm McLaren had come out with this fantastic poster, it was genuine art, I still think so. It summed up that whole thing with The Sex Pistols. We then took them for a photo session, me and Peter Vernon, who was the EMI house photographer. Pete and I had always hit it off great, and he was a very clever photographer, a witty guy, people liked him. The Pistols liked him straight away, all four of them. We had a real laugh that day, and Pete took the iconic photograph of The Sex Pistols, which is them coming through the doorway. We went to the basement and we got these little cans of beer and stuff, and they were just fooling about, they were just four young guys in a Rock group. Actually they were three young guys in a Rock group, and Johnny Rotten, who was different to the others.

Eric Hall was our TV promotion guy, and really didn't like The Sex Pistols, I mean, he just thought they were absolute junk, but Queen had pulled out or something. Anyway the Pistols were suddenly appearing on TV at 6 o'clock on the Bill Grundy programme. Eric was crowing about it all: I've got the boys on television, fantastic, amazing promotion. It's the sort of thing I do for my artists. Come and have a look, everybody in my office. We're all sitting there boozing away, and on it came, you know, Bill Grundy. It slowly developed into this ludicrous thing where it was always going to be Steve Jones, wasn't it? Bill Grundy said: Well say something outrageous. He said: You Fucker; you Dirty Fucker. It was nothing really. I knew straight away, well, this is just going to be absolute murder. Eric rushed out, I always remember that, Oh my God, they'll never work for me again, I'll never work with The Sex Pistols, they are finished with the music industry. That was the end of that. But there was a lot of laughter, and I thought there was a lot of humour in the incident.

The next day, bloody hell, off it came. We got phone calls, well I got them because they got put through to me, and there it was. A few members of the public, not many, mainly journalists wanting a bit of this and a bit of that, funnily enough, they were okay, the press were fine. The most annoying call I had was from an actress, I've never liked the woman since, we got this phone call, and one of the switchboard people said: This women is being really heavy on the phone. I said: Okay, put her through. Quite abruptly, and said: I've rung up to complain about The Sex Pistols. These disgusting young people are absolutely horrible. How can anybody sign something like that, it's an absolute disgrace; it's not even as if they're clever. I found that annoying that she said 'it's not even as if they're clever'. I said: why should they be? Actually if you listen to those lyrics they are quite clever, and it's artistic. She said: No it's not! They're not in Equity. I'm in Equity and I'm going to get all my members. I said: Well, they're probably not even in the Musicians' Union but it doesn't matter. We had quite an argument about it, and it ended up with me saying: Look I've had enough of this, you want to speak to our Managing Director, and I put her through to the fifth floor. I've never liked her since, I just couldn't see it. I think she was wrong.

JONATHAN MORRISH, CBS Records Press Officer

We did a launch of the Abba album 'Arrival', which on the cover had them inside a helicopter. November, I would say November 1977, if my memory serves me right. I wasn't their press officer, their press officer was Julia Barnes, and it had been decided that the best way to launch the album was to get the band to helicopter in to the Battersea Heliport. But it is November, and November in London can be foggy.

More to the point, they weren't in London the night before. They were flying in from Stockholm. We got all the UK media onto this boat that leaves one of those moorings at 8.30 in the morning. We go up the Thames, and then we go back down. But now it's quite clear that they haven't even left Stockholm yet; so we go up and down the Thames and everybody is beginning to get quite twitchy, because all that we wanted to do was set up the helicopter landing at Battersea Heliport for the photographers. In those days, when there was very little media, and whoever was producing *Top of the Pops*, they were on the boat, it could have been Michael Hurll himself and Terry Wogan. These were very, very powerful people saying: Enough is enough, you've got to get this boat back to land. But of course we had to make sure that there was a big crowd there when Abba landed, which eventually they did.

I think the boat had been drunk dry, and I can remember having this very odd conversation with the guy who operated Basil Brush, who obviously let his alter ego come out, and I just remember his anger and venom at having been kept on this boat for four or five hours. Probably, and I have no recollection of this, or maybe not: probably, like me, he had had an awful lot to drink. Anyway, we delivered it. I remember Julia Barnes their press officer literally being in tears because all of Fleet Street was there and everyone was just desperate to get off this boat.

DAVID MUNNS,
EMI Marketing
Manager

The Queen stuff was probably the most exciting stuff because it worked so well. 'Bohemian Rhapsody' was a record that nobody thought was do-able. I remember getting the bill for that video. That was when I almost lost my job, because the bill came in and it was £9,000 or something. L.G. Wood the chairman found out about it, Ron White and Roy Featherstone were always the guys who claimed to know nothing about it. How the hell did that happen? Bob Mercer was going: I think this is great. I got the royal rollicking of my life, because they'd never spent more than £1,000 on a video before. I think it was just under £10,000, £9,000 and change. Stupid bloody record, it's too long. We set that record up just perfectly, and one play on the radio, bang, that was it.

Kate Bush, I drove her to a sales meeting in Manchester, she'd never stayed in a hotel before, she was seventeen. I made her play to the sales force in the Posthouse Hotel in Manchester; she's in there with a piano in the sales meeting playing 'Wuthering Heights'. Four weeks later they were beaten away from the front door, a household name. A month, you think about it. Amazing. They were the things that I really liked.

We were supposed to release thousands of butterflies at Queen's Hyde Park show, and we ended up ordering all these butterflies but they were designed to hatch on that Friday or Saturday. They were all in a fridge on the first floor at EMI and when I got to the fridge, they were all dead, all dead. So we never did have the butterflies, so we got doves in the end, that afternoon, a few doves. Freddie Mercury used to ring me up and he'd say, I've got the new single ready dear, I think I've got the album, you should come and hear it. I'd go up to Newcastle and sit with him for two hours before the gig. He'd open the fridge, there was half a bottle of Stolly in there and he'd drink the whole lot, and do a few other things, and then go out and play for three hours. He was astonishing. I never knew anybody could do that. I did so much stuff with him over the years I can't even remember now. He was great fun really, Freddie, and he knew the business exactly right.

I guess as you got into the Eighties it got more about budgets. I spent all the marketing budget of the EMI label once on Queen, on 'A Night At The Opera'. When that album came out it was the first year we had an EMI label budget, that I remember anyway. I spent the whole lot on that one record, I think it was £400,000, the entire marketing budget for the EMI label. No-one said anything until the end of the year, and then Bob Mercer called me and said: You spent it all on this record. I said: well it sold a million records, what's the problem? He said: Yeah, right. Now, you wouldn't get past the first week without some accountant showing up in your face, you wouldn't be able to spend it would you? You couldn't just spend it, there'd be too many people signing off on something. It has turned into a business, inevitable really. Big money at stake. So it was inevitable really.

ERIC HALL, EMI Records Head of Radio & TV

People who knew Freddie Mercury in those days, if you were a man it was always 'she'; he never referred to somebody as 'him', it was always, ooh what's she up to, blah, blah, what's she doing? All men were she's, and women were she's too. If there was a lesbian, He. I mean, he used to call Dusty Springfield 'he', oh, is he coming again tonight?

I'm sitting in my office at EMI Records in Manchester Square, second floor, I'm sitting there and in walks Freddie Mercury. Eric, we've come to play you our new record. He'd come with Roger Taylor, the drummer of Queen. Great, I want to hear it. We've come off some monster hit record at the time. So he puts the tape on the old tape machine, Heuer schmooer or whatever it was, sticks the tape on the thing, reel to reel, pressed the button to start it, and he starts whatever the intro was, and Moet Chandon in his fancy cabinet, hair like Marie Antoinette, dada, she's a killer queen. 'She, She, She', I love it, love it. Freddie, it's going to be a monster. What do you think of the lyric?

Well yeah, I love it, but I love the whole thing, the record's going to be a monster. My dear, you're not listening to it. Roger, tell her she must listen to it, she's got to listen to it. So I listen to it again, he said: Eric, that's about you. I said: what about me? You're a killer queen, he said: Because I'm the queen. I don't want to sound big headed, he fancied me like mad. He said: I'm the queen and I can't have you. Whatever I was, I wasn't really into that shtick, and he said: You're killing me; you're a killer queen.

As you hear it now it is me; I had permed hair in those days, with a Marie Antoinette cut. Somebody said to me recently, hey I've heard this Killer Queen record and since you told me that story I listen to it more than ever. But it's all 'she', and 'she' this and 'she' that. I said yes but he called me 'she'; he called you a big butch... you know, Mick McManus was a 'she' too.

BRIAN SOUTHALL, EMI Records Head Of Press

Freddie was always amusing. At EMI I was having lunch with him and Ian Groves, sadly departed, in the French restaurant on the corner of Duke Street and Manchester Square, downstairs, run by the former French brothel keeper, very expensive, very nice French restaurant, which we took special people to. I remember going there with Freddie and Ian Groves, and having lunch down there. The man had a 26-inch waist and didn't eat but preened a lot, there was a lot of shaking of hair, and it was, stop it, just eat your bloody food! Well we had had lunch and he has his driver and his limousine with him, and the restaurant was just there on the opposite of Manchester Square from EMI, and it was quite a nice day. Freddie boldly decided: I think I'll walk darlings, shall we walk? So we walked the 100 yards round two sides of this square, one-and-a-half sides to be fair, back to EMI, with the limousine going at the same pace with the door open, just in case Freddie had a moment, or got recognised or got all tired and had to slip into the limo. A whole bunch of people were going, what the hell is that, limousine with the door open going at two miles an hour across Manchester Square with us. It was very funny.

He was a generous man, you always liked being with Freddie. I remember very cruelly that there was a certain editor of *Billboard* from America, who I got to know quite well, very tall 6ft 2in blond, very good looking, wholesome American footballing player. We were on a boat on Lake Montreux, on a boat at the Queen reception to do with the BBC Rock and Roll Montreux Pop Festival or something. Freddie said to me: Ooh, he's nice, do you know who he is? and I said: yes, I do know who he is, he's a friend of mine from America and he's gay. Of course, he wasn't, but Freddie would not let up. This man never forgave me because Freddie followed him round that boat going, ooh. I shouldn't do it because it's terribly cruel, but it was so funny. He didn't forgive me for weeks. I did have to buy him several bottles of champagne; but it was funny.

NICKY HORNE,
Capital Radio
Disc Jockey

I went to New York to interview John Lennon. In fact how it happened was, Kenny Everett, when we were together at Capital Radio, Everett came to me one day and said: Hello love, would you like to go to New York and interview Mr. Lennon? So I said: Yeah, that would be brilliant, fantastic. But why me? Well, he said: John's been in touch and he wants to talk about heavy things, the silly sausage just wants to talk sort of politics, and that's not my sort of thing. So I suggested you go, love. Thanks Ken. So I went off to New York and I was absolutely terrified. Lennon was always my hero, out of all of them, he was the one that I kind of idolised.

I got to the door of the Dakota in New York, went upstairs and as I was standing outside this huge oak door, my hand is shaking, and just as I'm about to knock when the door opens and there's Lennon, in the trade mark glasses and the white t-shirt; and he goes: How! Which kind of broke the ice. I go in, and I'm just shitting myself, there I am in the Dakota. He said: I've just baked some cookies: would you like some cookies? I squeaked: Yeah, that'd be great. He said: This isn't a mix, I made these myself. So we sat in the living room with the white carpet, the white piano, and I remember a brass telescope overlooking the East River, and I was terrified. I was holding the coffee cup and it was shaking, and he could see how nervous I was. Normally what would happen in these circumstances is that I would be warming him up to do the interview, so we'd talk crap for five minutes and when he was ready, I'd start the interview. But this time he turned the tables, because he realised that there was this young bit of jelly in front of him, and so he warmed me up for at least an hour, talking about London, talking about Everett, talking about tons of stuff.

Then when he knew that I was relaxed, and when I obviously was relaxed, he said: Right, let's record. We recorded an interview that's become quite important because he talked about for the first time about how the FBI had been tapping his phone and following him, and how he was under surveillance. He had never talked publicly about this before. When the interview went out people poo-poo'd it, but a few years after his death the FBI opened up their files under the Freedom of Information Act, and in fact everything he said at the time was true. I was due to interview him again, go out and interview him again, four days after he got shot. Andy Peebles who was my mate, did the last interview with him and he was flying back when Lennon was killed, and I had been booked to go out there to do another interview.

JON WEBSTER,
Virgin Records
General Manager

We were this jumped up label, still operating out of Vernon Yard and in 1982 we were the top singles label in the country. That year we had Phil Collins, the Heaven 17 hits, we had Culture Club, we had Fat Larry's Band 'Zoom' at Number Two. Larry couldn't get through the door of the building he was so fat, it was unbelievable. Then of course we had 'Penthouse and Pavement', we had Japan, 'Tin Drum'? Yeah, because the one before was 'Gentlemen Take Polaroids'. I think it was 'Tin Drum'. We had OMD on DinDisc, and then in September we had consecutive Number One albums in three weeks with the Culture Club follow up, 'Colour By Numbers'; UB40, 'Red Red Wine' and 'Labour of Love' and Genesis; we had three singles in the Top Five and we went Number One album, Number One album, Number One album over three weeks. We could do no wrong. Then just before Christmas we had Simple Minds, oh, and Simple Minds, 'Waterfront' came out, that was the first single from their next album.

That was the point where I sat down with Stephen Navin, who was our lawyer, called me in one day, because by that time I'd been made General Manager; that's right, Steve Lewis moved to the publishing company so I became General Manager. Stephen said: who are we going to license all these hits to? I'm getting faxes every day from all the compilation companies, K-Tel, Arcade etc. Arcade have come out and they've offered £30,000 for this, and K-Tel have come out and they've offered £45,000. I said: Why don't we do it ourselves? and he went: What do you mean? I said: We've got enough hits, can we put our own album out? Well he said: Oh, that's not a bad idea. So we literally got out an envelope and wrote down the costs. I'd spend quarter of a million on TV marketing, and we need to press this many. We sat down and went, good God, you could make a bloody fortune out of this. So we went and talked to Simon Draper, and then I think it was me who said: Hang on, the TV advertised albums are all double albums, we haven't got enough to make a double album but what about our friends at EMI? They've had loads of hits. So that's when we went to EMI Records. Peter Jamieson was running it at the time and said: Why don't we do this together? Why don't we form a joint venture? Which we did, and we had a meeting in Simon Draper's office, which is where the Danish Bacon poster from 1930 was on his wall, which was the pig and the chicken saying 'Now That's What I Call Music', and that's where the title came from.

We all sat there and said: Well we can't get it out in time, and why not? Well, gatefold sleeves, gatefold sleeves take two weeks. Oh, do they? Oh God. The production department is going: Nah, we won't get sleeves then. We won't have it out until the week before Christmas. Oh, we can't do that, can't do that. Richard Branson's going: Why do they take two weeks? Well they do, it takes two weeks to make gatefold sleeves. And Richard says: Who makes our sleeves? Tinsley Robor. Who's he? Lee Newbon, you've played golf with him. Oh yeah. Get him on the phone. Lee? I've got a bit of a problem: bang, twenty-four hours. We later asked Lee Newbon, why does it always take two weeks to make gatefold sleeves? He said: We just didn't want to make them any quicker. It sold a million in three weeks.

CAROL WILSON,
Virgin Music
Publishing

I dropped out of music college and went off to live in Majorca and lie on the beach, and there was quite an interesting ex-pat community there at the time, and one of the people there was a woman called Eve, who was dabbling in property there. Her name was Eve Branson. I came back to England, we used to just chat, and she told me all about her son and he'd started this record label and everything, so when I came back to England, I mugged up on the music business a bit and got a job as a secretary to Nat Joseph at Transatlantic Records. Then I saw in *Music Week* that Virgin were advertising for a Marketing Manager. So I applied for the job and got down to the shortlist of three out of fifty applicants.

Richard always went by the face and whether he got on with people rather than what they knew, and finally he said: Well, I can't give you this job because actually you don't know anything at all about marketing, do you? I said, No. He said: We'd like to give you a job, what would you like to do?, and I said: well anything but a secretary, because in those days all of the women were secretaries, there was nothing else. He rang me up a few days later and said: How would you like to run our music publishing company? So instead of just saying yes, I'd already got the bluffing sorted out which is why I fitted in so well at Virgin I suppose, and I said: well, it sounds like a very interesting idea, but I'll only take it on if you give me my own head in running it and let me run it the way I want to run it. I didn't know what a music publishing company was. He was delighted at that, because Richard delegated everything; he never got involved in detail, he didn't know anything about music, and he just relied on getting a team around him who would work it all out and achieve everything for him. So that was music to his ears when I said that's how I wanted to do it.

I signed Sting in that period before he was a Punk, before he became The Police. I signed him because someone tipped me off: You must go and see this guy who's singing in a pub in Newcastle. He just had that star quality, and I always looked for the songs plus the star quality, and he had both. Sting met Stuart Copeland and Stuart became part of the band, and Stuart's brother, manager Miles Copeland was signing Squeeze to A&M. This is three years after I'd signed Sting, and he said to A&M, if you want to sign the Squeeze deal you will also have to pay £3,000 for The Police, because Miles, was out of pocket. He had paid for them to go into the studio and they recorded the first Police album for £3,000. He said I want that £3,000 back, you have to sign The Police if you want to sign Squeeze. This is not a great entry into a record company roster. Of course the records came out and they bombed, no-one was interested and they were an embarrassment because they'd been in an advert, and they were Punks. I forget who it was, but there was a producer in A&M, in America, who got all the new releases from England, and he put this album on, and he just said: Wow, this is going to go gold. Everywhere the record was released they did a tour and as they toured the record went to Number One, and eventually of course England had to get in and it was a hit in England as well.

JOHN SCHROEDER, EMI Records A&R

Norrie Paramor got a phone call at EMI from Norris Burman who ran a School of Music, I think it was in Baker Street; somewhere down there. He said that he had some pupils that he was teaching at the school and could someone come round and audition them, because he thought he had some students who were worth hearing. Norrie said: Well, I don't do that anymore, I'll put you over to John Schroeder, he's the one that goes out and listens to new talent and so on. Of course I went and in walked Helen Shapiro, and she sings 'Birth of the Blues'. I'm absolutely blown away. I'm a person that never shows any emotion when I listen to anybody, so no-one knows what I'm thinking, and afterwards, when I'd heard everybody, Norris said: Well? I said: Helen Shapiro. He said: Absolutely right. She was the one.

I got an acetate, we called them acetates, they were discs of this audition, and I had a few qualms I'd actually made a mistake, maybe it wasn't as good as I thought it was. But when I heard the acetate, I knew it was. I thought, I've got to get the right moment with Norrie, so I caught him one night when he'd finished and was going to go home, and just as he was going to leave I said: Norrie, give me five minutes of your time. I've got an audition I did with a young girl, would you please listen to it? Would you sit down and listen to it. He said: Yeah, sure, sat down at his desk and I put this acetate on. It went through and I was looking at his reaction and it was like completely bland, there was nothing. I thought, oh God. After the audition there was an awful pause you see. He looked at me and said: He *is* good

220

isn't he? I said Norrie, that He is a She. He said: No! I explained: She's thirteen and a half years old. He said: I don't believe it. I said: Yeah, she is. He said: Get her parents in, get her in.

For six months we couldn't find a song for her. Remember she was thirteen-and-a-half or fourteen years old, people didn't write songs for that age group. You can't give her an adult type lyric or anything like that, she's only thirteen or fourteen years old. We had all the publishers looking for songs; I listened to songs, he listened to songs, and we were desperate. After six months Norrie said to me: Listen, we're going to be in trouble with Helen Shapiro because we're getting near the termination of her first year's contract and we haven't recorded her yet. I said: Well, we can't find the material. So Norrie said: Why don't you try and write something for her. I said: Well I've never written anything. He said: Well, you don't know unless you try, have a think about it. I knew Helen's voice absolutely, every detail, her phrasing. I thought what do teenagers like: well they don't like being treated like children. Then one day my lodger, a writer Mike Hawker, caught me playing around with a tune on the piano and asked what I was doing so I explained that we needed a song. He said, do you mind if I embellish it or change it? So we wrote 'Don't Treat Me Like A Child' and all her subsequent hits too. Then Jack Good put it on his TV show and it all accelerated, it was slow to start with but it got to Number Three in the end.

Our job was to make hit records, it was all about hits. If you didn't get a hit record there was no point in continuing. If an artist failed to make the charts after three singles they were dropped. That was the rules of EMI Records. We couldn't retain an artist for longer than three singles, if it didn't happen, they were immediately dropped.

MIKE HURST,
Musician

The Springfields 'Silver Threads' turned out to be a Country record, and that's why of course it was a hit in The States. They thought we were American, and they were totally upset when we got to Nashville and realised that The Springfields were not American. Really. You could see it in their faces, shock. The record was a hit and we were booked to go onto *Grand Ole Opry*, and so we waited next door, in the bar. Do you know, they didn't want us on there because we weren't American? They didn't want us on. We were in Tootsie's next door, we even signed the wall alongside the Webb Pearce's, the Hank Williams's, everybody, we signed the wall, and they still didn't want us on that show.

We went to Nashville before anybody else from this country. On our sessions we had Jerry Reed, Jerry Reed! Bill Black! I looked at this guy, the other two, Tom and Dusty, couldn't understand it because I kept saying: That's Bill Black, and they'd say: Who? I said: He's Elvis's bass player! I mean, please! We had these guys and I was just blown away at the playing I mean, they did it by numbers, because even then it was a machine. They did it by numbers but it was still good. Those were the recording sessions, we were there for three weeks making The Springfields record. I met Johnny Cash, his brother Tommy, I met lots of faces. It was, you're nineteen, you just take all this in. Afterwards people would say to me: God you must have been petrified and I'd go: No; it's fine.

It was all extraordinary, which made it even more extraordinary when we came back from the States and we made 'Island of Dreams' which was Top Five here, but did nothing in America, nothing. Which did always strike me as strange really because 'Island of Dreams' written by Tom, it's got a lot of Country influences in it. It should have been a great Country song, I think it's one of those that escaped. So that was that. Big in England again, but we stopped being big in America within about three or four months. Yet it was right around the corner with The Beatles. It was all going to happen. This is now end of '62, and of course end of '62 we're back here in England

and win the NME Poll Winners Award. Top British group you see, Top British group! That year at Wembley when we performed, the Best Newcomers were: The Beatles. We'd already met them, we met them in Liverpool at the Cavern, and in fact John Lennon made us honorary members of The Beatles Fan Club. So we knew how good they were, there was no argument, we knew it. So that was all just around the corner.

LES REED O.B.E., Songwriter

Gordon Mills as you know was with The Viscounts. We became incredibly good friends and we started writing together. We wrote a song for Dodie West called 'In the Deep of Night', which has become a Northern Soul hit, as well as other songs. He called me up one day and said: Les, I've seen this young Welsh man, I think he's going to be good, we ought to write a song for him to demo. I'd like to get him in the recording studio, do a few demos of our songs and then we can go from there. I said fine. I went to his flat, which was in Notting Hill Gate, and we started this song. Gordon already had a couple of bars of it, which was lovely, 'It's Not Unusual'. It took three or four days to complete the song; he wanted it in certain rhythms and I said: No, we've got to do it in a baión rhythm. We put a new middle eight to it, put all kinds of things on it, reworked the lyric, and it took us five days overall to finish the song.

When it was finished Gordon said: That's good for Frankie Vaughan. I said: No, no, it's got to be for Sandie Shaw, because it was in a baión rhythm and it was just like 'Always Someone There To Remind Me', that lovely song she did. I said: so let's do it for Sandie Shaw. He said: Alright, but I wanted Frankie Vaughan. I said: He's not as big as Sandie is, so we'll go for Sandie Shaw. Now I'd already seen Tom Jones perform, I'd gone to the Top Rank cinema in Slough and I'd seen him and he'd come on all dressed out with a rabbit's foot, medallion, shirt open here, black skin-tight trousers, and I didn't like him, but I liked his voice. I thought, he's got some voice. He loved Otis Redding, Jerry Lee Lewis and all that. Anyway we taught him the song and took him into Regent Sound in Denmark Street to do the demo, and I got hold of Mitch Mitchell who was playing for Jimi Hendrix on drums at the time. Vic Flick was on guitar, Eric Ford on bass, myself on piano, and Gordon Mills played tambourine. We did the demo of 'It's Not Unusual', which was lovely, and Tom sang it beautifully, and Gordon and I then put some backing vocals on it.

Three days later I said: Let's take it to Sandie. Eve Taylor, who was Sandie's manager, was also our manager for the John Barry Seven so I knew her well. Gordon, Tom and I went by tube to Evie's place, and we sat there for about half-an-hour. Gordon said: Who is this woman? I said: she's an agent, don't worry, she's got somebody important in there' he'll come out. Well we didn't have a lot of time there so I knocked on the door and said: Evie, it's Les. She said: What do you want? I said: we've got this singer and we've got this song we'd like to play you. I'm very busy with Des was the reply. I thought she meant Des O'Connor, but it was Des Lane, the penny whistle man, who I knew because he'd been on tour with us, and I knew he was a fine whistle player. I said: Well okay. So we waited until she'd finished with him, and she said: Okay, you can come in now, but I've still got business to do with Des. We went in, I played her the demo, and she hated it. She said: That'll never be a hit. We said: It IS a hit. She said: It's NOT a hit, now please, will you go? I've got Des Lane, the Penny Whistle Man here.

We strolled out of her office and Gordon said: Who's Des Lane? I said: he does tours, he plays this penny whistle. Oh.

Anyway, on reflection, for Des Lane she turned down about a billion dollars that day. She could have had Tom as an artist. She could have had Gordon and I as writers, we were stoney broke at the time. She could have cleaned up with the Jones, Mills, Reed partnership. She could have cleaned up, but unfortunately she turned us down for Des Lane the Penny Whistle Man. So on the way home Tom said: If I don't do that song I'm going to kill myself and he meant it, he really did.

VIC FLICK, Musician

My father was a music teacher and a general studies teacher who finished up as a headmaster and my mother was a very fine singer. They insisted I learn the piano so I started at the age of five on the piano and when I got to fourteen this was when my father and a neighbour formed a band. My father played piano, the neighbour played violin, his son played saxophone, my brother played bass and of course there was nothing for me, so I learnt the guitar very quickly. The neighbour who played violin worked at Shell-Mex and he got the hint that I wanted to play another instrument and he saw this advert on the notice board in his office for a Gibson Kalamazoo for £5. So he bought that and brought it home and gave it to me as a present which was wonderful. I played it till my fingers bled and all that, just to learn to catch up with everybody as it were. I had to make it loud somehow, you cannot just sit there with a little acoustic guitar, so I bought this tank commanders throat mic, and I clamped that on the machine head and played it through my father's big radio which we had to hump to the gig. We only did about two little gigs a month but that started me off learning the guitar.

Then I met a good bass player called George Jennings who worked for the Bob Cort Skiffle Group. Ken Sykora was the guitarist and he got a job within the BBC in the West Country to be a production whizz-kid or something. So they were looking for a guitarist and George suggested me to Bob Cort. We were doing a gig and he turned up with about fourteen big records and said, listen to those. So I took them home and learnt them and did the audition and Bob said: Fine, you start Saturday. Then being with Bob Cort we did this tour with Paul Anka. Paul Anka's first tour, where judging from the stories I heard and the look of him on occasions, he went from boy to man, suddenly. The John Barry Seven were on the bill and I got kind of friendly with John Barry and Les Reed. John and I used to go out looking for Chinese restaurants which were few and far between then. That tour finished and about three or four months later, I got a phone call from John Barry because he knew that I could read music and he had already lost one TV show because the guitar players could not read music. So he asked me to join.

The big thing which broke me into sessions was that most of the fixers or contractors were violin players and I did this album called 'Stringbeat', which if you listen to it is me playing with a background of strings. I think there are fourteen numbers on it and we did it all in one day. I was sat in a chair with the rhythm section slightly behind me and to one side. John Barry on his podium and we had EMI Studio Two full of violins, cellos, violas and basses. Of course the front row was all these stony faced violin players looking at me, but by the end of the day they kind of warmed to me. Most of it was sight reading. So it was *the* audition of all time, you know, all day long. That was quite an important time and John Barry was the avenue into sessions. We were both grateful, because there were some shows he would not have got if it wasn't for me, but he certainly was an integral part of my career.

Later on I remember Jimmy Page when he first started doing sessions, because I worked a lot with him. We used to get paid in little brown packets with the money folded up. No details, no tax or anything and one day Jimmy said to me: What do with your money Vic? I said: Well I put it in the bank, I've got a house to keep going and kids. Jimmy replied: Well I haven't got any expenses, I live with my mum and dad in Epsom. So I said: Well what do you do with your money then? And he actually said: Well I'm putting it under the mattress!

I'd never met anyone who put their money there, of course now he would need a rather large mattress.

DAVID HOWELLS, PWL Records

We were making several of these masters, mostly dance tracks, and we were distributed in different territories by different companies, and in Australia we had a deal with Mushroom Records, a guy called Gary Ashley at the time, this is 1985 or '86. Gary sent me a tape one day and said: I've just found this girl Kylie Minogue, she was singing in a football stadium at an event. She's a soap star down here and they'd invited her to sing, and this girl in my office said you really need to come and see this artist. Well I think she's terrific but I have no idea what to do with her. You guys know what to do with this kind of artist, because it's now, it's Pop. I played the tape and I just loved the voice, just ordinary demos, but I just like this voice and I thought this is really good. So we signed her up on the basis of this cassette.

Pete and I owned the company and Stock Aitken Waterman if you like, worked for us. I didn't have any direct creative contact with Stock and Aitken, although they were in the next room and we talked all the time, but on creative matters this was their business. They wrote the songs, they produced the records, they did the arrangements and they hired the musicians. We then took the master and went off and did our stuff with it. So now we've signed Kylie. She's in this soap called *Neighbours*; she works five days a week, she gets half a day off, and on the Sunday she's learning the script for the next Monday, Tuesday, Wednesday. I mean, it was a really punishing schedule for this girl. She gets two weeks holiday a year. The show is obviously, in its territory, a big success story.

We set a time to bring her over to record, and we work out calendar dates and we say, yeah, we can fit it in there. She's only got two weeks off a year, she's given us a week to come in to the studios and do some recording. I liaised everything with Gary. Anyway, come the date Kylie arrives with Terry Blamey, her manager, and the studio was in a cul de sac, so there's Council Estate down one side, rundown buildings all around it, place is falling down, and we were in this nondescript cul de sac. Because it's an old power station it looks like Fort Knox with tiny windows but when you came through these steel doors in reception there was a Ferrari racing car sitting facing you. There was the reception desk with Sherry the receptionist, who was wonderful, and then around the walls, gold, silver, platinum discs, and the signs off the sides of steam engines. Pete was a steam fan, so he had scale model trains, plus the name plates off the trains, big things. So this was like a toy shop, you walked into a toy shop. When you got upstairs to the first floor, studios were both downstairs and upstairs, the reception room, we called it the missile room because hanging on the ceiling we had an English electric guided missile, de-armed of course. It was just a toy shop and everywhere there are these train signs, and so people were mesmerised when they came into this place. It was fun, and this is what Pete created, this fun factory.

Anyway, we do the tour and I introduce them to everybody and take them into the studio; the studio's busy but we look through the window and I go, these are the guys, this is what they're doing. Of course they loved the hits that had come out of this place. I said, look, you've just arrived, take a few days, it will take us a couple of days, and Terry's going, we have to leave 3 o'clock Friday because she has to be back. I said: yeah, we'll be fine, we'll probably start work on the Wednesday morning. The next day I see Pete and I say, okay, how's this going to work? Well, we're finishing this project and that project; we don't have the time, just see what you can do for a day or so. So I call Terry up and say, Terry, here's my suggestion: why don't you take the Harrods' bus, go to Stratford, great day trip; give Kylie a chance to acclimatise and adjust to the time zone, and we'll start on Wednesday, or Thursday, whatever it was. He goes off and does that and the next day I go to Pete and he says, well we still haven't finished this project. Alarm bells have not rung yet; I must have been very slow on the uptake. I said: well they've got two days, or whatever it is, left. Terry's getting really irate and Kylie's not happy. My wife and I have taken them out to dinner, we've taken them to lunch, shopping, we've run out of things to do or suggest. Terry is now really getting very angry, and he's saying, Dave, tomorrow we leave. They're completely disillusioned and I've got Gary on the line from Australia and everybody's going, what? And I said: this is the way these guys work, but they're geniuses; they turn things around, don't be surprised.

So comes to the Friday, and the guys used to start about 9.30, 10 o'clock. So this morning I'm standing at the studio door waiting for them to come in. I can't find Pete anywhere, no sign. I'm the only one who knows every number that Pete has, I know every place he's going to be, because over the years we got used to all this stuff. Can't find him, nobody knows where he is, completely disappeared. So I break the rule, I have to stand at the door, wait for the guys to arrive. They arrive at 10 o'clock, something like that, and I say: Hi, bit of a situation here, I've got this Australian artist over you're making a record with. Mike says: Oh yeah, I heard you had an Australian girl in town, how's that going? I said: it isn't going anywhere Mike, she's done Harrods, she's done Madame Tussauds, she's done Stratford. She's supposed to be in the studio. Really? Why's that then? I said: because we've signed her and she's making a record. He's going, Oh, I haven't heard about that. Pete has not discussed this with him, and all the off-putting has been because he hasn't discussed this with him. I said: look, here's the story, and I give him the background. They've been here five days, she has this break. Any minute now Terry is going to be on the phone and threatening my life. I think it would be nice if we could actually make a record with this girl, because she's come all this way out, she deserves a shot in the studio. I played them the tape; I said: this girl can sing, we can do this. Mike said: Yeah. By now it's about quarter past ten, he said: get her in at eleven, we'll do something.

So I go to the phone and Terry's ringing me, but before he can launch in I say, Terry, great news, get in a cab now and be here in the next thirty minutes, the session is ready; they've finally cleared the desk, they're ready to go, where are you? Terry's like, oh, okay. So they arrive on time, really pissed off. He's angry, she's not happy, and you can understand why, and I'm trying to tap dance like crazy. I introduce them, they go into the studio. They finish about three hours later and they're going to the airport about five, or whatever it is, and Kylie comes up, as it happens I'm walking by the exit as she comes out the door, looking really mad. I said: oh, everything all right? She said: I've no idea. I said: what do you mean? Is it a good song? She said: I've no idea, they gave me a line at a time. Mike and Matt had written the song in forty-five minutes, they were still writing it when she arrived and they were literally feeding her a line at a time.

She said: I've sung a whole bunch of lines, I've never heard the song played through once. I've no idea whether it's good, bad or indifferent and went away very unhappy.

The guys delivered, and about five days later they said come in the studio Dave, have a listen to this. They played 'I Should Be So Lucky'. It stemmed from the point at which when I walked into the room, I think it was Matt, I can't remember exactly, I think Matt was reading a copy of Viz, which is usually what he was doing, and at the point I was going through all this talking to them, Mike was listening, Matt was reading, and I said: she needs to make a record. He looked up and went: she should be so lucky.

Then we took that record, there was Pete Waterman, Tilly Rutherford and myself and we divided the record industry between the three of us, and we knocked on doors. We must have seen thirty more labels, thirty plus, everyone said No. Everyone said: It's not a very good record and you can't have a hit with a soap star!

PAUL CONROY, Chairman Warner Brothers Records

I went to work with Rob Dickins and at the point of moving over from Stiff I was just about to sign Howard Jones, who was managed by the lovely David Stopps, who I'd known for years as an agent and various other things and running Friars Club, Aylesbury which I used to go to all the time with Genesis and one thing or another. So I persuaded Howard not to sign to Stiff but come with me to Warner Brother Records, and so we signed him to Warner / Elektra. We had some very big hits, and he sold a good few million albums in America as well, so that was quite a nice little signing really. But when I started at Warners they had Modern Romance and a few other acts, but we didn't really have much of a UK roster. Rob brought in Echo and The Bunnymen, we signed the

Sisters of Mercy, and we had Matt Bianco. Slowly but surely we built a few things within Warner's family.

Max Hole was there and it was his job to sign the UK acts, while I really ran the American division, which was to make sure we made sense of ZZ Top, Paul Simon, all those sort of acts, and also the Atlantic acts. We had some massive hits during that time, and obviously Madonna, which we nearly didn't have because Phil Straight, who was running the International side at that time, had been bombarded with Madonna tracks and records. At one point Rob Dickins had got a note or a telex from Seymour Stein saying that, if we did not sign her, then Roger Ames wanted to sign her to the London label. So we had to go and find a copy of 'Holiday' in the International Department and Phil Straight had left a lot of his American vinyl against the radiator. We were playing it and this thing was jumping up and down because it had got warped, but we said: Bollocks we are not going to let Roger Ames have her and so we kept Madonna and the rest is history.

ROB HALLETT,
Booking Agent

I remember once we were in Nice in the South of France and Duran Duran were recording 'Seven And The Ragged Tiger', just outside of Nice in a country house. The Cannes Film Festival was on, I'd flown out there to talk to them about the world tour that was going to go with this next album, but that was an excuse really to have some fun and party. So we went into town and we went to one of these ridiculous clubs in Nice where it's £10 for a can of coke. We were buying bottles of Dom Perignon because it was cheaper, in our minds and trying to pick up chicks. Everyone had sort of had enough, and John and Simon, I can't remember exactly who was with us now, but Roger definitely, and myself. They said: We're going back up to the house, we've had enough. Roger and I are going: Well actually, that girl over there that's quite nice, we'll see you later, we'll catch you up. So they go off on their merry way but two minutes later, if not five minutes at the most, the club closes and everyone starts leaving. Roger and I left there, and neither of us speak particularly good French, or any French, and we think, fuck, where was this house? We couldn't remember where the house was, we couldn't remember anything. This is before mobile phones.

So here we are stuck in Cannes, okay, there's no point in worrying about it now, let's find a hotel room. This is Cannes Film Festival, so we're walking around all these hotels: Avez-vous un chambre deux? People were looking at us strangely: Non, non, avec les deux bed. We couldn't think of the word for beds. Anyway eventually we found somewhere who let us in with twin beds and Roger and I went up and fell asleep.

We woke up in the morning, had showers, and went out and tried to find the boys. We had no idea; we didn't know where the house was, we had no phone number, no nothing. So we start thinking, okay, they're going to get worried about us, they're going to come and look for us. If we go and sit out on the Croisette in the nearest open-air cafe and just sit there and just wait till they come past, it's going to happen. Sure enough a couple of hours later this convertible Gold GTR, I think it was, came spinning round. John was going out with Miss World or Miss England at the time. So there's John, her, and I think Nick in the back, all standing up and shouting out Roger, Rob! We saw them coming down the road and jumped up. It really was funny at the time.

WILLIE WILLIAMS, Sound Engineer

Bruce Springsteen was used to using a radio microphone and in those days there were two or three bad radio mics but the best one was made by Sony. They had brought these two Sony radio microphones over with them to play in the UK, and then they weren't allowed to use them because they were on the wrong frequency. I don't know if there was interference or not. Anyway, for the Birmingham gig they went over to a cable mic, and in those days, when you had a cable mic, you had a really long mic cable and you had people called cable pagers, who would feed the cable out and bring it back in. Well Bruce had the screamers, so he had in front of the stage a runway about a metre below, and this runway ran right across in front of the speaker stacks, up some ramps, right up to the edge of the football ground. So effectively it was round from side to side of a football pitch. It had little runway lights on it for the mic cable to get caught in, and there were two of us roadies, one on stage right, one on stage left, and our job was to keep the mic from catching on these things. It was relatively straight forward until the song where Bruce ran from far stage left, right across the front, right across in front of the audience, and then up to the far wing. I think it must be 'Dancing In The Dark' because then he comes back again, and then he would jump off the front of the stage, at which point the cable is definitely going to get caught on the runway lights.

So I have to come out from underneath where I'm hiding, and now I'm walking on the catwalk, holding the mic cable. So everybody in Birmingham Football Ground, or Aston Villa Football Ground, all they can see is me, because Bruce has now disappeared off the front of the stage. I'm just walking along holding the cable in two hands, guiding it over the lights. It's all very well and Bruce does the bit where he goes down the front centre, goes out the crash barrier, chooses a girl, gets the security men to bring her over the barrier and then takes her up on stage to dance with him at the end of the song.

All the rest of the tour Bruce has had a radio mic, and when it came to the bit where he had to leap manfully on stage he'd just tuck it in the front of his jeans and come up. Well I'm standing there with 100ft of mic cable in my hands, standing on the front of the stage waiting to pull the cable up, make sure it misses the runway lights, when Bruce approaches the front of the stage and realises he's got a cable mic, which he's not going to put down the front of his trousers. I'm standing there as I see him look up at me, and throw the microphone to me, as I stand there with 100ft of mic cable lopped around my hands, and a look of sheer terror passed across my face. He just tossed the microphone up at me, I just had to drop the cable and just grab it to my chest. At which point all the cable turned into a heap of spaghetti, and then I'm desperately sorting through it to get the mic in a hand, and the cables free, so I could give it back to Bruce so he could go up and finish his song. That was my moment of greatness, nothing that good ever happened to me ever again! Although I did get to do half the Amnesty Tour when Springsteen and Gabriel and Sting went all round the world, and I did the European leg and then I flew down to Africa and did the Ivory Coast, and then flew on the freight plane to South America to do São Paulo and Buenos Aires.

I also had the privilege of being the monitor engineer and doing the last two original Sex Pistols concerts. I did Plymouth, I can't think what the place is called in Plymouth, and I did Penzance; I did the something-or-other Ballroom in Penzance, and they were the last two shows The Sex Pistols ever played in the UK. I set everything up working for the sound company that had been doing all The Pistols shows, and I was to be the monitor engineer and I'd never done them before. The first night I set up on the same side as Sid Vicious in this club in Plymouth. It was very strange because the Pistols were banned, and the posters were going up 'Top International Mystery Group'. We got to the venue and there were all these Punks there going: Are The Sex Pistols playing, are The Sex Pistols playing, and we were going: No, no, no. Then we opened up the truck and of course there were the flight cases with Sex Pistols written all over them. So we got all these little Punks to carry all the gear up two flights of stairs and we set it up, and then The Pistols' people showed up and immediately threw them out of the building.

But it was probably the most exciting show I've ever done. The atmosphere was unbelievable. This was forbidden. Even Springsteen playing to 80,000, which is pretty impressive, was not as much fun really as The Sex Pistols. Although the clouds of spit and snot was coming in, I hadn't realised what it was going to be like, and I'm suddenly grabbing towels. It's just coming all over the monitor desk, I've got towels, coats, whatever I can to protect the desk and I'm physically moving it further and further and further and further away from Vicious, because he was the target at which most of it seemed to be aimed. The following night I set it up on the other side of the stage.

BOB MERCER, MD EMI Records

We were shooting the cover for Pink Floyd's 'Animals', with the pink pig over the Battersea Power Station, and their manager, Steve O'Rourke, had asked me to go down to the shoot. I wouldn't normally go to a shoot but it was Pink Floyd, and I'd kind of gotten to know the guys in Pink Floyd, which no-one else at EMI had done to that point, they were always very remote from EMI. So I told Steve O'Rourke, yeah, I'll come down and have lunch with you. I never turned up, as I was handling this hotel room Sex Pistols debacle, and at about 6 or 7 o'clock I get a call from O'Rourke, where were you? Oh man, I can't tell you what a fucking day I've had, and I started to tell him about the Pistols. Then I said: how did the photo shoot go? He said: Oh, bloody mess, the pig escaped. I said: but it was on cables. Yeah, but it got a bit windy and the cables broke. I said: but I thought you had an army marksman who was going to shoot a hole the size of a dinner plate in the side of it, then it would just fart its way down the Thames. He said: No, he had flu.

I'm just about to leave the office and our press officer, Brian Southall, comes in to see me and says I've got the head of BAA,

British Airports Authority, on the phone, wants to talk to you. I had spoken to this guy once before because of an incident at Heathrow Airport with the Pistols, which again never happened, I always had to go to the top of the company, find out, then go to the top of my own company. So he calls me up and goes: how are you doing? I go, not a good day: and he goes: well, the strangest call, I thought of you instantly, he said: We've had to divert three planes coming in from Paris to Gatwick at about 10,000 feet, because each of the pilots reported a pink pig in the sky. One pilot, you figure he just had a few before he left the airport, but three in a row, I'm thinking to myself that sounds like Rock and Roll. Do you know anything about this? And I said: it's funny you should say so....

Then I had to call the guy in Paris who ran the French company because that seemed to be where the pink pig was heading. So they had it out on radio in Brittany and all the places around the coast: look out for a pink pig. Pink Floyd were huge in France so this was a good piece of radio for them.

The pig came down in a farm in Sussex, and that farmer spent the next ten years suing Pink Floyd because he said that the pig scared his dairy herd into being milk-less; he couldn't get any milk out of his dairy herd and he spent ten years suing Pink Floyd. I think it was ten years later when I was managing Roger Waters that the suit was finally abandoned. The guy had broken himself either through too much money on lawyers, or not paying enough attention to getting milk out of his cows after they'd seen this pink pig. But that was a great Tuesday, I remember that very well.

JIM CREGAN, Musician

On tour with Rod Stewart, in order to stop the incredible boredom of touring which we all know exists, we invented this organisation called the Sex Police. The job of the Sex Police was to stamp out illicit sex on the road. That meant that anybody who was having sex, other than you really, would have to be punished. Essentially they broke into their room while they were having sex, anything you wanted to do was all right, except if it was the wife or girlfriend. Even then that occasionally got a bit hairy. So one day we're sitting around, Rod says to the new bass player: How are you getting on? Everything all right? He said: Yeah, I'm fine thanks Rod, a bit tired. Why are you tired? He said: Well, the Sex Police keep breaking into my room and stealing all my furniture and my bed and everything and I go to my room and I haven't got anywhere to sleep. Oh, he said: That's sad. Tell you what, I'm flying back to London tonight right after the Irish gig; you guys I know are staying on here, why don't you have my suite. So duly this lad slept in Rod's suite.

Well of course the Sex Police were absolutely pissed at this. We told Rod, we said: You're completely out of order for doing this, I mean, the Sex Police were busy on a mission, destroying this young man and you've come along and given him a bed. I said: There'll have to be punishments. No, No, do your worst. So we had several meetings about what we were going to do to punish Rod. The next time we could get ourselves together we broke into Rod's suite by the usual method of kicking the door in. Of course that was the other thing, if the Sex Police knocked on your door and you didn't answer quick enough they'd kick the door in, and you had to pay for it because you didn't answer the door quickly; there's no way of doing it.

Rod wasn't there in his room; it was after the gig and we got the bass player and we stripped him except for a pair of paisley Y-fronts and gaffer taped him spread-eagled, face down on Rod's bed, just his little paisley underpants and this great pale body. Rod, good as gold, came back with some young lovely, went into his bedroom with the young lovely thing that he'd met, determined to have his wicked way with, walked into the room, saw the bass player spread-eagled on his bed, said: Ooh, Sex Police have been here. I see, fine. Moved into another room in the suite where he carried on with his business and just left the bass player there. What the girl must have thought when she saw the sight. It was very good of Rod, he never let on, whatever terrible thing you did to him he never acknowledged it. I remember filling his boots once. He took his cowboy boots off on some flight and I filled them up with mustard and peanuts and it must have really hurt. He just put them on and walked out to the airport, didn't go: You bastards, or anything like that, not a word, just put them on and walked out. We went: How does he do that?

Well there you are dear reader, you have had a brief glimpse into the changing British music scene as it evolved over a lifetime for the lucky participants, from above, from under and from sideways on. Stories as the guys recounted them in their RockHistory interviews. We hope you have enjoyed the show. Still not enough memories from the ladies though – come on ladies join in, you know were there too, so contact the website, and chip in please.

Anyway we have taken the liberty of editing out the obvious errors, when someone has said something that is generally accepted to be utter cobblers. The memory plays tricks after all these years plus sometimes words come out of the mouth upside down, the first single released by a band may actually have been their third, that sort of thing. So treat everything you have read here as deeply unreliable, part-fiction and uncorroborated truth, dependent on their particular views of the musical events at the time and the sharpness of their memory now, god bless 'em.

RockHistory is about collecting the British music stories and the anecdotes while we are still able, while we can still remember and in case we all die before we get old. But all in all, it is not a bad legacy for the 'My Generation' who spawned some of the greatest music the world has ever heard. Play that riff Keith.

Mark Rye

Also available from RockHistory.co.uk

(978-0-9576881-0-0)

For the first time ever, we now have sales charts of the WWII favourites as sold in Britain on 78s records through to the start of the NME Chart in 1952. Compiled from the record company sales sheets by music historian Colin Brown, this book has been talked about by those in the know for years.

A hardback edition with 300 pages covering this important 12 year period, this book lists the week by week top 30 best-selling singles, it lists the songs with the most recorded chart versions, itemizes all the Number Ones, featured artist profiles, highlights the hits artist by artist with original catalogue numbers and is published with the support of the Official Charts Company.

Ironically, sales of UK 78s were known to have been highly significant in the late '40s and early '50s, as Britain staged an economic recovery after WWII, so it has always seemed mildly incongruous that there was previously no statistical information available to tell us exactly what the big hit records had been.

This book shows the music that a restless British generation grew up with on record and on the radio, leading them on to Rock'n'Roll, Skiffle, Beat and beyond, around the world. These were their roots of their music.

Double CD sets of British music that are an essential part of the story.

VARIOUS ARTISTS - **HANK, BRUCE, BERT, JOE, BIG JIM & MORE....**
The UK Instro-scene 1956 - 1961
RHUK21 The "Golden Age" of the UK R'n'R/Beat Instrumental occurred between the late 50s and the very early 60s, peaking in 1961 on the back of The Shadows' monumental breakthrough the previous year with the chart-topping 'Apache'. Indeed, more than half the sides featured on this compilation were recorded in '61, many of them in fairly straightforward attempts to copy The Shads' irresistibly twangy sound and style.

VARIOUS ARTISTS - **MR PARNES SHILLINGS & PENCE**
Presents His Stable Of Stars
RHUK22 Generally speaking, success owes everything to good luck and good timing, and Laurence Maurice Parnes was perhaps the classic case of a man being in precisely the right place at the right time. Rock'n'Roll was very much in its infancy in the UK and he had no real competition, therefore there were no 'rules' for him to break. He subsequently became the most powerful man in UK Pop, active as a manager, agent, impresario and music publisher; just about the only area he didn't bother with was records, presumably because artists' royalties in that era were so poor!

VARIOUS ARTISTS - **FREIGHT TRAINS, LAST TRAINS AND ROCK ISLAND LINE**
The History Of Skiffle
RHUK23 When Lonnie Donegan's frantic 'Rock Island Line' burst into the Top 20 in January 1956, "The Establishment" recoiled in collective horror. The UK music industry was appalled to its very core - "Skiffle Is Piffle" squeaked one Melody Maker headline - whilst the nation's parents/guardians/MPs/clergymen/ schoolteachers/ scoutmasters/etc clasped their foreheads in dismay, convinced that the world was about to be overrun by knife-wielding Teddy Boys. Conversely, the UK's teenagers embraced Skiffle with almost indecent enthusiasm. So much so that within just weeks, virtually every club, hall and coffee bar in the country was presenting Skiffle groups, and sales of scrubbing boards were soaring! An almost exclusively British phenomenon, Skiffle had its roots in three distinct strands of Americana - Delta Blues, Folk and New Orleans Jazz.

VARIOUS ARTISTS - **JOHN, PAUL, GEORGE, DAVE, BRIAN, TONY & MORE**
The Birth Of The British Beat Boom
RHGB24 Received wisdom would have us believe that The 60s began in Liverpool in 1963, commensurate with the arrival of The Beatles and the ensuing British Beat/R&B Boom. Well, that's certainly the romantic view, but the seeds of the British Beat Boom had been sewn a few years earlier - in an altogether different grimy, down-at-heel European port, viz: Hamburg. And whilst The Beatles would, of course, subsequently

242

go on to grab all the credit and glory, a great many other groups and singers had been paying their not inconsiderable dues in the years immediately preceding 1963. This compilation presents 65 tracks which anticipated and/or helped shape the Beat Boom, and includes a number of the names who would go on to achieve enormous mid-60s successes.

VARIOUS ARTISTS - **BOUFFANTS, BEEHIVES & BACKCOMBING**
Early Brit Girls Vol.1

RHGB25   Although the arrival of the archetypical 60s 'dolly bird' was still a couple of years away, by the turn of the decade a whole 'new look' Brit Girl was emerging; a slim, wan, wide-eyed young gazelle, the polar opposite of the overtly glam, well-upholstered, tightly-corseted, over made-up filly of the 50s. This fine compilation traces the rise of UK ladies from the R&R era to the early 60s, and heralds the newly emergent Brit Girl sound.

VARIOUS ARTISTS - **TRUMPETS, BANJOS, CLARINETS & STRIPED WAISTCOATS**
The Very Best Of British Trad

RHGB26   Coming along, as it did, almost directly on the heels of Skiffle and Rock & Roll, Trad was perhaps the least likely Pop Music phenomenon of the era. Yet for a brief spell at the end of the 50s and the very early 60s, it was massively popular - and not just in the UK. Many Trad hits sold well internationally, several even making significant inroads into America and Japan, the two biggest record-buying markets at that time. This unique compilation includes virtually every major Trad hit record, collected together for the first time.

VARIOUS ARTISTS - **TAB COLLARS, SLIM JIM TIES, DRAINPIPES & WINKLEPICKERS**
The Very Best Of British Rock'n'Roll

RHGB27   Rock & Roll got off to a fairly slow, low-key start in the UK, and it peaked late; indeed, it would take a couple of years before we got the collective bit between our teeth, the first genuine classic British R&R record (Cliff's 'Move It', of course) not being recorded until the Summer of 1958. This compilation attempts the (near-impossible) task of presenting the Very Best of early UK R&R, and includes the handful of benchmark sides which stack up comfortably against their American counterparts.

VARIOUS ARTISTS - **SAMWELL, GODDARD, WORTH, LENNON, McCARTNEY & MORE**
Great British Songwriters

RHGB28   British songwriters only really started to come into their own during the latter half of the 1950s, commensurate with the arrival of Rock & Roll and the gradual development of a genuine home-grown scene (i.e. as opposed to the 'manufactured' version which the music/record industry had earlier tried to foist upon us). Prior to that, British songwriting had been an almost entirely Tin Pan Alley-driven affair and very few of the genre's established writers would overlap into the R&R/Teen Idol/Pop era with any noticeable - or sustained - commercial success.

VARIOUS ARTISTS - **CALYPSOS, BOOGIES, ROCKERS, BALLADS & BLUEBEAT**
The Rise Of Black Music In Britain
RHGB29   In 1948, the Empire Windrush famously docked at Tilbury, carrying 493 passengers from Jamaica and Trinidad (plus, by all accounts, one stowaway!). Pathe News were among the media gathered there to meet them, and a remarkable piece of newsreel footage survives in which the freshly disembarked King Of Calypso, Lord Kitchener, serenades everyone with impromptu version of 'London Belongs To Me'. And although this by no means marked the birth of black music in the UK (it wasn't even the first boat-load of migrants from the West Indies - a smaller vessel, the Almazora, had delivered some 200 Jamaican passengers to Southampton six months earlier), the symbolic landing of the Windrush is very much seen as a rallying point for much of what would follow, socially, artistically and musically.

VARIOUS ARTISTS - **TELSTARS, MEXICANS, MANHUNTS & WONDERFUL LANDS**
The UK Instro Scene 2 1956-1962
RHGB30   This second set of predominantly twangy and/or keyboards-driven toons concentrates largely on 1962, with just a couple of hands full of goodies left over from 1960/61 which were omitted from Vol.1 due to lack of space. Ultimately, there are far too many artists included here to discuss them all. The Dave Clark Five, Tony Hatch and Barry Gray would go on to become major players in the 60s, while conversely, groups like The Barons, The Phantoms, The Echoes, The Jesters and The Dukes were sadly all destined to languish in obscurity, their legacies restricted to just one or two great tracks.

VARIOUS ARTISTS - **HELEN, DUSTY, SUSAN, CAROL & MORE - Early Brit Girls Vol. 2**
RHGB31 Like its predecessor, (RHGB 25), this compilation traces the rise of UK ladies from the R&R era to the early 60s, and heralds the newly emergent Brit Girl sound that was evolving at the dawn of the Beat era. As we have learned, although the arrival of the archetypical 60s 'dolly bird' was still a couple of years away, by the turn of that decade a whole 'new look' Brit Girl was emerging; a slim, wan, wide-eyed young gazelle, the polar opposite of the fiercely glam, tightly-corseted, frilly-petticoated, carefully-coiffed, severely made-up filly of the 1950s, who'd ruled the roost. During the 60s, even the 'old guard' underwent serious makeovers, with the result that establishment figures like Alma Cogan, The Beverley Sisters, Petula Clark, Marion Ryan and Shirley Bassey began to look younger than their mothers for the first time in their lives.

Available from RockHistory.co.uk and every knowledgeable record shop

CPSIA information can be obtained at www.ICGtesting.com
Printed in the USA
BVOW05s1007200514

354052BV00001B/169/P